Retracing Steps

by Robert Mazibuko

RoseDog 🐾 Books

PITTSBURGH, PENNSYLVANIA 15238

RoseDog Books
585 Alpha Drive
Suite 103
Pittsburgh, PA 15238
Visit our website at *www.rosedogbookstore.com*

ISBN: 978-1-6376-4709-7
eISBN: 978-1-6376-4749-3

Retracing Steps

To my two sisters, Thobeka and Noxolo, whose progress has been a profound inspiration and also to the generality of African women who have advanced educationally and socially so much over the years.

Contents

Childhood, Those who mattered in author's upbringing
A Note to remember, Rules of the family, The Township Environment, My
Mother, Chores, Early Morning in the Home, Church Going and Change,
Early Schooling Challenges, Nokhaya, Nokhaya to the Rescue, Nokhaya and
the Green Coat, Nokhaya and the Stole, Education, Nokhaya and the Elec-
tricity Account
School Friends, Activities with "Shortie', Friendship at Junior High, Trials
of Weekends and Holidays, Street Manners, Getting Lost, Buying Clothing,
I learn Music,
Movies and Books of the Day,
My Latin Master "VC", Firing Interest and Enthusiasm, The Scope of Study,
Study at JT's, The Last Task Performed

Preface

When the first book the author attempted became known in the country of his birth, some persons with whom he grew up complained that the book did not mention many events of childhood. The author then had to admit that the book, " This Side Up" was the bare bones of his story, and he still asserts that no book can exhaust all one goes through in life. However, to further satisfy such persons and still the voice of protest, he has undertaken to write the present book, which reflects on his life prior to his moving to the United States. It is good fortune that the author has to write the book in that it also points to assistance from many other grownup persons who he now attempts to mention, as their assistance in his growth and maturing mattered in ways he could not explain in a short story. Even so, the attempt does not at all exhaust all he has experienced. Short of writing a confession, which is an undertaking he would not attempt as, in his faith such issues as the intimate life of any soul are to be determined in a more religious way and in another life. With that said, some real names will have to be mentioned, but in some cases, to protect others and their involvement , names may have to be changed but not the true events. This then is his story.

Illustrations

Nokhaya Norah Weziwe (Sidinana) Mazibuko
Reverend Samuel and Alice Nondlwana
Cowan Secondary School in 1959
Robert Mazibuko as a server in the Anglican Church
Picture of Andrews Sisters
Picture from serial: "The Mysterious Dr Satan"
Picture from serial : "Drums of Fu Manchu"
Picture from serial: "Nyoka, the Jungle Girl"
Scanned cover to to the book "George Washington Carver"
Picture of Mr. V.C. Qunta Principal of Cowan secondary School in 1959
Picture of Mr. J.T. Galo the Science teacher at Cowan High late 50s
Julia Galo with a friend at a university graduation ceremony
Picture of book ' The Essays" by Francis bacon
Inside Cover of book :"Naught for Your Comfort" by Trevor Huddleston
Cover of the book " A Romance of Two Worlds" by M. Corelli
Scanned VDR Cover of Movie:"The Devil Rides Out"(D. Wheatley)
Cover of book :"The Confessions of J.J. Rousseau"
Cover of book :"The Merchant of Venice" (Shakespeare)
Picture Matron Eucinia Thobeka Melane, sister to author
Picture Dr. Eileen Noxolo Mazibukp Phd. Sister to author
Library Helpers with Rosemary Sala at Cowan High late 50s
R. Mazibuko at Dr. Jiya's home in Alice South Africa

Luthando Mazibuko at Convention in Umgababa, South Africa
Onke Mazibuko, son of Dr D. Mazibuko
Picture of a hearse at Donald's funeral
Card sent from Sweden by Dr. D. Mazibuko to author
Card sent from Sweden by Dr. D. Mazibuko to author
Picture of remaining Mazibuko family members
Picture of traditional wedding of Donald Mazibuko
Inside cover of book:"Bahá'í Answers " by Olivia Kelsey , a gift to author from
Professor B .Brown
Group of American Pioneers and Africans in Africa
Letter from Professor B. Brown
Letter from Professor B. Brown
Wandile Mazibuko as Supervisor at the Ford Engine Plant
Wandile Mazibuko receiving an award at Ford Engine Plant
Michael Moorshead past Head of Department in authors employment, with
his wife Marge
Note from Michael Moorshead to author
Michael Moorshead with grandchild
Michael Moorshead fishing in USA
Group of graduates from a course in Pharmaceutical Production
Peter Persicaner visiting with Daya Moodley in Port Elizabeth, South Africa
Email from Peter Persicaner to the author
Peter and Phoebe Persicaner
Robert Cheong , a Pharmacist in Canada
Bahá'í youth of Cape Town at a conference pictured with author
Robert Mazibuko on Mnandi Beach during a break at Bahá'í summer school
in Cape Town
A Mosque on Gray Street in Durban
Grace Fudu of Port Elizabeth, South Africa
Ivy Gcume of Port Elizabeth, South Africa
Mr. Ian Semple of the Universal House of Justice
Patrick and Christine Beer with their children, David and Simon
Rose gates and Robert Mazibuko on Mt Carmel in Haifa , Israel, during the
International Convention of 1978
Hand of the Cause William Sears delivering a talk in Ciskei with the author
translating

Bahá'í National Assembly of Ciskei
Mr. Glenford Mitchell of the House of Justice
A Prescription form Dr. C. Manga
Bahá'í Temple in Kampala
Hand of the Cause Enoch OLinga
Mona Mahmudizad
Cover of book:" The Meaning of Anxiety" by Rollo May
Poinciana Tree
Dog Cameron
Gretchen Misselt in Swaziland
Clive Stanton
Invitation to author to a farewell party
Picture of Robert Mazibuko by Dr. Robert Clarkson
Portuguese Grammar book from May Seepe
Portuguese speech manual from May Seepe
May Seepe
Yoshie Ragland
Note from Yoshie Ragland
The Piggotts
Robert and Reginald Vimbi in Ciskei
Mother Teresa
Rose gates in Mdantsane with African believers
Excerpt from Bahá'í News Rose Gates Knight of Bahá'u'lláh
Letter from Don Fouche to author
Don Fouche , Rosemary Sala, Lowell Johnson, on Pilgrimage
Krish Naidoo at the African regional Conference
Mxolisi C. Gawe ex Mayor of Uitenhage, Cape, with friends
Mxolisi C. Gawe picture while visiting author in Port Elizabeth
Mxolisi Gawe at Nelson Mandela University in Port Elizabeth South Africa
Note to Nozidima Sishi's funeral
Prof . E.N. Mazibuko
Gretchen Misselt and Robert Mazibuko with grandson in Evanston , IL.
Thank you note from H. Prussoff
Gretchen Misselt at the weaving loom
A room in Gretchen Misselt's apartment in Evanston, IL.
Gretchen Misselt in front of the House of Worship in Wilmette,IL.

Psychiatrists note of advice to author and clinic
Hand of the Cause Collis Featherstone
Robert Reedy
Deborah Dadgar
Chocolate Cake
Eghbal and Sarah Ma'áni with a child
Cover of book:"The Covenant" by Lowell Johnson
Lowell Johnson at his apartment in Hillbrow, Johannesburg
Sue Greer
First Bahá'í National Assembly of the Transkei when Sue Greer was secretary
Picture of DVD cover of:" Anne of a Thousand days"

An Initial Observation

There has got to come a time when one pauses to think in terms of the worth of one's life. Life on the planet as measured from birth to death. Having that in mind one has to come to the thinking of just how much one has done with the time has had and to what gain it had been. It is obvious that none of us are His image at death, for we go with all our imperfections. So it may seem that the trip to perfection has not been reached at death. So at that point we are not at all His image. Considering that He is portrayed to be the End that has no End and the Beginning that has no Beginning, we stand in awe of what that may mean with regards to who we are as portrayed by the text of the Holy Books.

Writing , therefore, about one's life cannot at all be considered to be an entertainment. Rather it should be a warning to those who read that this is not the end, and that there is much to be gained and updated from one life to the other. This would certainly be applicable to the young who still have a long trip to the grave. It may even come sooner than the predecessors they may have. One can learn from the lowliest to the highest and still find the lessons that life teaches so earnestly. Let no man feel pride at achievement or derision at any other's failures, for none stands perfect on this plane. Otherwise we would not need the messages from life and would be His perfect image forthwith.

This book and the tales told are fragmented because the telling of life can be fragmented, as the sequence of events may escape one at the time of the telling. The mystery of life is that one is expected to negotiate life at an age when one is young and unaware, and when one reaches maturity and old age ,one wonders at all the stupidity they indulged in earlier. At that point there may be nothing to do but to meditate on life, without justifying wrongs but by facing up to the reality, guilty if so, and proud if proven right by life and the Books.

Because of this tricky relationship of time and circumstance, one cannot at all reveal the entirety of one's life to anyone, for all stand imperfect and at fault, in one way or another.

Behold us then as fragments of dust crawling on a rock, and finding fault one with the other, and seeking aggrandizement and preference one above the other, when all the while we have not reached the perfection expected from us beyond time! We should all be falling on our knees to beg Him to point us not to judgment but to mercy…Our teacher, the earth, we, the learners, and yet the earth stays impervious to our plight.. Time itself continues uninterrupted.

> **They should conduct themselves in such a manner that the earth upon which they tread may never be allowed to address to them such words as these: "I am to be preferred above you. For witness, how patient I am in bearing the burden which the husbandman layeth upon me. I am the instrument that continually imparteth unto all beings the blessings with which He Who is the Source of all grace hath entrusted me. Notwithstanding the honor conferred upon me, and the unnumbered evidences of my wealth — a wealth that supplieth the needs of all creation — behold the measure of my humility, witness with what absolute submissiveness I allow myself to be trodden beneath the feet of men...."**
>
> **(Baha'u'llah, Gleanings from the Writings of Baha'u'llah, p. 7)**

Introduction

The author has been employed in hospitals , factories and sundry work-places,. In his time he has worked as a hospital receptionist, a telephone operator, a construction worker and time keeper, a library hand, a hospital kitchen worker, pharmaceutical quality controller, quality control clerk in a glass manufacturing factory, and part time computer teacher. He started work as a hospital clerk and retired as a nurses' assistant. He then is acutely aware of the workplace involving women and men functioning side by side . His mother taught him to be manly without being bossy, and to always respect the work of women he encounters. He was brought up however, by both a mother and a father in strict religious observance, and strict adherence to the nature of chores in the home without distinguishing those chores as either male or female duties. He has then learned to recognize that men and women are equal but have differing chores that they may prefer or are better equipped for than those of each sex.

For a proper understanding of the African social setting one would have to study some Sociology. Since this is not such a study , only those particular experiences which relate to the actual life of the author will be mentioned, this done in the full knowledge that the author is himself an African in origin and has been brought up to adulthood in that culture. This being the case, it has also to be recognized that the author was brought up in the township surrounding, in African terms and not in the rural Africa but has resided for periods in the rural areas. At the time of the writing of the book the author was living in the United States, having transferred residence there because of marital arrangements with an American lady with whom he now lives in that country.

Upbringing and Youth

A Generation Sacrificed

On the onset one could see how in South Africa a generation was sacrificed in order for the country to attain freedom. My generation of young boys and girls sacrificed being educated and answered the call to strike and not attend school. This had to be acknowledged so that all may find peace and recognition. It is in a way , no kind of joy that I was one of those who stayed in school through those very difficult days, but considering the issue that this was a transition from living village life to living the overcrowded life of a township life, it helps to recognize the struggle of those who saw the need that their children should gain some education in order to survive township life. One has to consider the following aspects of involvement to actually visualize to what straits living in a township had come to:

Streets and Safety

As a boy growing up in the township, fighting in the streets was no rare thing. One had to brace one's self up and act as if nothing was directed at one's person, and continue to do the best under the circumstances. Among the children, a fight might develop because one gave one a dirty look; or bumped into one, or said something someone does not agree with, or even to prove whose stronger than the other. Most of the time among children fights would be fist fights but as they grew older it would develop into knife fights. The popular brands of knives were the "Best"; the 'Scotch"; the "Tree Star", the "Okapi" which each kept in the back pocket of the pants. This was popular among those who had left school even before the strikes. Such fighting did not include fights between the streets. At some point a fight would involve all those of a group of a street, who would attack any intruders from another set of streets.

What then was a mother to do but attempt to keep her children on some honorable task in the home? Granted , our education was not much as the teachers knew, but it kept one at some safe task from roaming the streets finding whatever…

Newspapers and Magazines

There were not that many newspapers being circulated in the townships in the late forties and early fifties. One local newspaper which seemed to be bought by my family and others, especially my father, was the "Advertiser". My father in late years used it to view horses that would run in Fairview or in Durban. Later in years we had the "Herald" and the "Evening Post", all in English.

Still later on my father would purchase African magazines called the "Drum" , "Bona" and "Zonk". In time there was also the "Hi Note" which one could purchase at the bus square. There was one African newspaper called "Imvo Zabantsundu" which was called simply the "Imvo". Comic books and other books were in English. The only two books that were in Xhosa which I could read as a boy were the "Holy Bible" and "The Pilgrims Progress" which had a translation called "Uhambo lomhambi". Hence my time as a grew was spent in making wire carts and kites to play with because even in playing with marbles with other boys, cheating and fights could occur. Such activities bring to mind the playing of dice in the streets. That very activity made it hard to have any money one one's person while walking the streets. This was also not easy, bearing in mind that shopping for tea , sugar etc was done at the local store by any child sent by parents. To some boys it meant devising pockets on clothing that were not there during the sale of such clothing in order to hide pennies..

Apart from motorcycles with soldiers , there were very few cars in the township and just about one police van called "Sotewu".

It was only after the coming of serious apartheid and the appearance of the reports of underground movements that the "Special Branch" and the "Security Police" also sprung up. Then we began to see many policemen in the township. A knife found on ones' person was measured by the police and if it exceeded the length of a hand's fingers held up and outside of the thumb, one was due for prison. The clash of that was observed with newly circumcised men, for after circumcision they were to carry a knife for meat anywhere any time, and a box of matches. This had its adverse results, for then a knife became a weapon of choice.

Very little or any at all of arrests featured in the news but we had two journalists living in the township in later years, one for the "Invo" and the other for the newspaper office in the city. Events such as marriages would go into the paper, but one could languish in jail for days if one's parents did not search the police station. In later years there was a police station in New Brighton and another in Kwazakhele, but during the riots the streets were patrolled by soldiers with machine guns and armored cars. Outside of that, the greater number of arrests were for not having documents on one's person when in the street, or being in the city after 6:00 PM., without proper papers For both of which yours truly was jailed twice in youth.

Fights among Adults
When I was a child fights among adults were common in the crowded townships we were not used to. Jealousies, sexual partner clashes, mutual hatreds, hidden grudges, were all cause for a fight. Most of the time it was with sticks. This did not include beatings of wives by husbands. As people got educated and many women took up professions, this ceased to occur and the idiom that: " A stick does not build a home" was taken up by many. This latter is a separate issue dealt with elsewhere. Here one has to note that children could be seen to watch parents fight.

Under such circumstances, I do not blame my parents for requiring that all their children be educated. Besides all that, my mother was a proud and progressive lady of her generation and wanted her children to attain some worth in their lives. With the limited prospects of living n a township of that time, the only avenue, outside getting rich some day, for making any progress at all was through education.; of that she was aware. My father hoped to some-day win a huge amount at horse racing, and accumulate revenue by curing with herbs. However that did not seem to hold any hope for extended survival at all at that moment and in those years..

Childhood

Those who mattered in the Author's upbringing
A Note To Remember

While one reads this story one has to keep in mind the following, for it is undeniably the course the author had to take and in which he found defining moments in his life: It is amazing that men and women are all born onto this earth through a woman, and yet it is that same woman who gave birth to both sexes who is relegated to be merely ' my rib'! I have to testify that from the time I entered school until I reached the age of thirteen, all my teachers were women, and I am proud of that. Besides this, in my schooling I came across the theories of Evolution and Heredity, and subsequently found out that the same features that are in men are present in women. Therefore the interpretation of Biblical stories, as it stands in many minds to today has to be in error because all assert men were created first. This would have to alter Science and Zoology as we know them in this day.

After my second year at school I was taught by a lady who was challenged in many ways, but , as attested by my own mother, who knew her from a young age, that even so, she was a good teacher, and I owe much to her first teaching as in the first five years of my schooling I was taught by her.

The second teacher of much note in my upbringing was a teacher I met at secondary school. She was religious and belonged to the group called Jehovah's Witnesses. I learned my appreciation of the English language from her.

My final teacher in English was a lady who was Canadian , who not only taught me to appreciate education, but respect for women, and devotion to the religion I now adhere to, the Bahá'í Religion.

I salute all the women who gave me the chance to be educated and gave me the courage to carry on. When any issue is raised in my life , I often ask the question:"Why?", and this question has served me well in defining a path through life. One man once said that if you see pigeons bobbing their heads as they walk, do not call it an optical illusion , because they do. Find out why. Another pointed out that an occurrence may happen once , and you may legitimately call it happenstance , a second time, and you may call it coincidence, but a third time, do find out what goes on!

Importance of Prayer in My family

My uncle and his prayer

My uncle Sam Nondlwana was a minister in the Methodist Church. When he and Alice, my father's only sister visited my home he would each night say the same prayer which had the words as translated into English:

> *Tonight we shall be the image of those who are dead*
> *You should not forget us*
> *We are the work of Your Hands.*
> *Should You forget us who then shall pick us up*
> *Be Thou jealous because of your servants...*

The prayer went on but that part I could never forget.

We would, each night of my uncle's visit, line up as children against the door and say the "Our Father" and the Catechism. Following that, beginning with the eldest of us as a group of cousins, we would each say "Good Night" , chronologically to each person present, starting with my uncle who was older than my father and go through all those parents, ending with the youngest child. This would be before we could sleep , just after dinner.

They, the Nondlwanas' were important as relatives in my family and their picture was always on our dining room wall for years as we grew up. We rejoiced each time my cousins and their parents visited us in New Brighton, for they were from out of town in Queenstown or East London, depending on where Sam, the minister, was assigned to work.

Rev. Sam Natu Nondlwana with his wife Alice Nontombi Nondlwana

When we were together as family without any visitors, my father would undertake leading in prayer and saying the final prayer in the evening. If he were not there then my mother would take this position. I remember the two of them having different styles in praying. My mother would pray for all kinds of people: Orphans; widows; people in jails; poor people; people in difficulty.

While praying my father would end each request of God with the words: *'"O Sovereign of nations and tribes!"*

An Alteration of an old arrangement

This long standing situation of visits with my uncle and aunt was altered by my mother sometime in the late 60s. It was New Year's Day and the whole of New Brighton was at the beach for the day. I was the only one home when my aunt and uncle arrived without notice. When they were informed that my mother was out at the beach they set out by car to find her. I was present when they did find her. My mother refused to go home until the setting of the sun. They had to wait in the car for her to make up her mind. After that day they ceased to visit and would let us know when they were in town with other relatives

Nokhaya Weziwe Norah Mazibuko (Sidinana) : my mother

The Rules in my family

The rules of the family with my father were far simpler than my mother's. My father found it easier to emphasize the Ten Commandments and to promise reward from "Father Christmas" for those who obey rules. In the main he wanted obedience in chores like watering the garden and never messing around with what 'belongs to the father'. The last rule applied mostly to yours truly, for I was known as an investigator of all items in his area. This particular rule applied to his Bible which he wanted left alone. My mother's rules were far more complex but practical. Because of this complexity they need enumeration and perhaps elucidation. They appear here not in any order but as they were, for, they were meant to be observed in total or a beating followed to keep you on track. Some had to be altered as we grew up to be school-going especially pertaining to going to church each morning to being present during Holy Communion, or during midnight services in church, as yours truly had to attend all:

- All children had to be in doors by 6:00 P.M.
- Learn to hold out both hands out and say " Thank you" when given a present by an adult.

- When making a noise like for example belching aloud remember to say :" Excuse me".
- When you fail in anything try again.
- Do not chew food with your mouth open, close and chew.
- Respect all adults and remember to use titles for them and never call any by first name.
- If your mother leaves special candy of fruit on the table when she goes to work, remember not to touch it until she says so.
- Always remember that there are two angels over your shoulder, the good and the bad and always obey the good angel.
- Know that in the home there are no male and female functions. All have to be performed by you.
- Wash and be clean and dress neatly. Roll up your sleeves.
- Eat what your parents give you and never go to ask neighbors for food.
- Remember there is no art known whereby people can see what you had for your meals at home.
- Never trivialize women.
- Act manly if you are a boy, but to remember to do any work you are asked to do by your mother or your wife when you grow up. Know when manliness applies.
- Put your hand in front of your mouth when you yawn.
- Wherever you go, learn to touch home now and then.
- Learn to do your laundry of school clothing and iron those yourself.
- Do not chew gum while talking to a parent or an adult.
- If you buy new clothes or have new clothes, do not wear that immediately you get it, give it a day.
- Know that your mother will not allow any man to give you rules she does not know about, but listen to advice of women on the street.
- Learn to walk properly and not to slouch.
- After each chore you perform away from home, head straight for home and report
- If you are out playing, learn to respond immediately when your mother calls you home.
- In the streets learn to fight back when attacked and not to simply run home.
- Never be home when you are supposed to be at school.
- Observe religious ruling.

- Work for the good of the home , your family and parents.
- If there is work to be done, you should not be found playing instead of working.
- You are never to be punished by your mother on your birthday, for any wrong, but will be cautioned about the next day.
- When a neighbor gives you a gift, you are to reply in kind some time or other.
- Obey your teachers and work hard on your homework. Regard your teachers as parents.
- If your mother passed you in a group of school children she will always recognize you with a penny or something, so others know you are cared for.
- When you pass a class, your mother will send a gift to your class teacher, afterwards only.
- When you find a stroke of luck on the road, before spending bring the luck home.
- All have to be able to do simple sewing and tasks, mother would perform the major tasks..
- Foul language and swearing were a taboo. Use etiquette and clean language.
- Children need time to play otherwise they play when they are adults and supposed to be responsible.
- "Our Father" and the catechism have to be said each night by all children lined up along the wall..
- After prayer at night greet each person in the room, with :" Good Night" before going to bed and remember the sequence of greeting from father to the youngest child.
- Other instructions were as needed, but those were basic. One of those instructions is to wake up each morning and make tea for parents.

The Township Environment

One would wonder why the many rules for children if one did not know New Brighton in the forties and the fifties. To me it was wilder than the Wild West. Death by knifing in knife fights was common. Dice playing and dice stakes were danger zones for young and old. Rape was the order of the day for all girls, as we settled in the crowded townships. Robbery was a public and a common occurrence, and sometimes one had to reserve money for any impending robbery to pay one's way out of danger. Worse of all, there were the wild kids from the golf links who came into town after months of living in the wilds as caddies. When they came in all hell broke loose. One had to keep in doors. My only salvation on Sunday morning was to be seen carrying a red and white cassock and surplice. That bought my way through to church. One had to be careful not to offend anybody on the street by look or action because one could be marked not as a "Wanted' but as a "Reward"(a notion taken from movies), which sometimes meant one would be sentenced to the "Endless Penny" in which case, one had to pay the kid a penny every time one meets him, anywhere. It would probably puzzle one why a penny was so important as payment. Most kids would have a penny. It was large and larger than a "tickey", which could easily get lost. With a penny also one would be able to buy four "squares", two "bulls eyes" or even three "Bacas", the candy of the day. It is surprising how insulting some names for simple things were when one considers that there was candy which went by the name of "nigger balls". However, in those days the word "Negro" had a different meaning and as kids we had no idea what any English word might mean in the township surrounding. It was when I had learned Geography that I learned of the Negroes and Negrillos of Africa as against the Bantu who had shorter hair. In Latin at junior high the word turned out to mean "black"(niger), and since I am black, and the sky is black, I begin to realize that the Lord bathed His Universe in a cloak of blackness from which we the creation, should emerge after learning from the Suns of Truth that there is light of the soul in creation. There is nothing political about calling me black except if one has a connotation of their own, a thing I can do just about any word, English or not. We never knew who originated the word as kids, but if you did not use it at the store you never got what you wanted!

If you saw blood on the road, you did not stop to look or wonder. Put a child in that surrounding and you will know he requires conduct and good conduct charged with wisdom at a young age. That was New Brighton at a glimpse. That is where we grew up and schooled.

Beatings of mothers and women were observed all the time as structures of African society collapsed in the townships. This was accepted as a sight, just as the beating of children was.

A side note

It does fill me with wonder as a grownup, how the word "Kaffir' had such a negative connotation that is not related to its meaning. Kaffir means one who is not a believer and is an Arabic term(He who did not keep the covenant promised by God). Among the Muslims it is related to one who never accepted Muhammad as a Prophet. If one peruses the Bahá'í Writings in Arabic one would find that where the word "infidel" occurs the equivalent in Arabic is "Kaffiir'. Tell, me then, how many of us are Kaffirs according to text of the Books? In the Bahá'í context "infidel' is one who is a non-believer or has not accepted belief in a prophet when He manifests Himself. This is the reality and not a fantasy. The origin of the word in Latin is related to ""fidelis" i.e. faith as in one who has kept faith with somebody else, in this case, God. For all prophets are promised to man in the Books of God, but man remains the denier when they come and executes each one of Them.

My Mother

In all the rules that my mother enforced for all children in the family she emphasized obedience with the words from the Bible. The following might have been her source for she said she heard in one dream the words: *Be patient unto the end and I will give thee the crown of life.* I was supposed to endeavor to be an example in the home in all things, as an eldest son.:

> **2:10 Fear none of those things which thou shalt suffer: behold, the devil shall cast some of you into prison, that ye may be tried; and ye shall have tribulation ten days: be thou faithful unto death, and I will give thee a crown of life.**
> (King James Bible, Revelation)

The first woman I met in my life was my mother, which is why I have to begin with some of the events I can recall about her. These were my beginnings and they are a greater part of the reason for my choices in life. It is to be remembered that the first lessons and experiences define one's initial perceptions of life, and sometimes these cannot be reversed in old age, but can be the cause one sees the foolishnesses of youth, yet finds that there is nothing to be done about that to reverse them. We learn while young and very naive, and view life with some wisdom as older men and women.

One teacher at a college level brought home the reason she was teaching, because she mentioned that she was not teaching us so that we receive certificates , but so that we all do something about the conditions women live under in our era. I stand identified with that wish today.

I have to thank Nokhaya, my mother, for all I am today. Yes, she called me all kinds of things as a teenager, but to me that was her way of telling me that, if I wish for solutions I need to be on my own and keep being strong. Her assistance is not lost, for in times of need I call out and say " What now Nokhaya?" The Laundry Woman knew her business about bringing up kids! I salute her with pride and gratitude for she said:" You are the eldest. You fail, many fail!" That gives me the impression that the world quietly watches success to see how far success will go. If success fails, all hearts of many trying the achievement will fail. In that sense we do not struggle for ourselves but for many like unto us! To argue sex with her was a very ridiculous notion, for she proved that what any man did for family, she could do alone and smile. My other believed in working for God in silence, for He rewards much publicly. So when she knelt in prayer to say : "Lord, I am a girl with no forwards and no backwards; I need You", she meant every word...

Chores

In order to begin one has to start with what children did in my family. There were chores which were shared by both girls and boys , involving cleaning the house, cooking, including washing dishes, and clothes laundering ; then there were chores for boys which were seldom shared with girls but were at certain occasions . Examples of the latter are working with hedge clippers in the garden, cutting the lawn, watering the garden, painting. As a young boy I was supposed to do my own laundry by hand, and learn to iron my own school uniform. As we grew up and had some younger siblings, it became a necessity that the boy and the girl should know how to change a baby and how to feed a baby. However, the washing of nappies was the mother's chore and left to her. This chore was decided by my mother as being hers. These chores were assigned as awareness begins to dawn on the young person. Naturally, before then these chores were undertaken by the mother and the father easily. These may seem to some to be a disadvantage for the boy, but as he grows up to adulthood and to have a home and children of his own, these strategies, learned in childhood, become a necessity and an advantage for both young parents, as they undertook to bring up their own children. For this, I have assurance in my own life. As we grew up, any discrimination of duties was not only frowned upon by the mother but was a cause of a stern remonstration with the child. Any outstanding performance in these duties resulted in much appreciated praise from the mother. This method of upbringing was not really typical in the African family in my area but many parents adopted it, because all parents had to work in the city all day, and therefore the children had to learn to survive in the absence of parents from the home.

My mother always insisted that when one works , one has to look back on the progress achieved to see how much has been accomplished, and in that way, have courage to proceed to what has to be done. I have found this a good encouraging strategy in my adult life.

Early Morning in the Home

There was a chore to be performed by my sister or myself each morning and that was to make tea for both parents before they even got out of bed. So, when the clock in the dining room which was set every night, rang, it meant that my sister and I should be up, and lighting up the fire in the stove and preparing to make tea.

Tea for my mother had to be just right or she would wake someone else up to make her tea; and one did not want that to happen. You did not ask my mother if she wanted a second cup, you poured it out and brought to her. My father was a little different in that he accepted tea anyhow it was made without any complaint, depending on whether it was tea or not, for he could, as an herbalist, detect herbs from ordinary tea .The only time he complained about food was if you did not cook his stamped "mealies" properly. These were idiosyncrasies one had to observe.

This chore of tea-making became almost mine entirely when my little sister was born, for then my big sister had to assist my mother with her baby. The thing is that the boys shared a room with my father while both girls shared a room with my mother. The situation of the making of tea changed slightly later.

When I was a youngster, I was a small guy, while my younger brother, Donald, was larger and more robust. He was said to be like unto my uncle to my father, for my uncle Brucebain was more robust than my father. I look more like my father. Donald loved the fields and outdoors while I loved books and music. No wonder I had the name "Mousie" all my schooling years! With my grandfather called "Abel" one can see the "Esau and Jacob-Abel and Cain" dynamics there. It grew so bad that when I started to work in gardening outside the home, my brother found a job at the docks each weekend. My embarrassment was in trying to find the same kind of job and being told I was too small for it! Somehow this manifested itself in my being an avid reader admired much even by my brother. In fact the reason he started reading anything was because he mentioned he had completed reading a book as I used to. It is a wonder that Donald became a Medical Doctor eventually. He was not even expected to go far with schooling, for as the third child he found allowances of stepping off the rules more often than we did.. All the time of my young age, my job was telling stories to my two brothers , Donald and Enthen, both from books and comic books. This task was sometimes forced upon me by my mother in search of quiet moments with the children, for the two boys clamored for a story incessantly each night..

Cleaning, gardening, cooking, reading and looking after my little sister became my major tasks for years. I was observed working in the garden by a neighbor who soon became a minister of religion, and who found me my first job for Saturdays and holidays, a job I held for about four years, before abandoning it for studies each weekend and movies, latter endeavors which were hard to pay for, especially the movies.. But copper , other metal and glass collecting assisted there, for sales of copper were highly paying at the time at the local Savage and Sons Company downtown. My little brother, Donald and I had joined other boys in this endeavor of collecting and selling metal materials and bones, to factories.

The reading helped so much that I became a dear to our Librarian at secondary school, and it proved to be a great source for general knowledge at high school. I will admit that at high school I began to lag behind in school work, because my interests were outside the school syllabus always. I could not stand some things that were taught, without finding out outside the school syllabus, for myself. However, in high school, instead of coming first and second in exams as I used to in lower classes, I was in the first ten then. How were my teachers to account for my learning French, Italian and Spanish from other books not supplied by the school? For that I blame all the books I got from the library and Rosemary Sala! For a more detailed account of this, and more of the above, one would have to go to the book:"This Side Up", by the same author.

Church Going and Change

When we changed churches in early fifties from Presbyterian Church to the Anglican,, it did not escape the notice of my mother that I liked going to church. I was therefore from that time, honed to become a minister of religion like my grandfather. Each morning, Sunday to Thursday, I was in church at 6:30. I did not attend on Friday because the service on that day was conducted in English, and then I did not know the language at the time, so was not expected to turn up. Saturday was again a day for practicing service for all choir boys, because I had become a server in the church. All servers were supposed to attend practice and a team would be announced for the Holy Communion Service on the Sunday. I was always on that team as a server, which meant I would be with the Priest serving communion to the public.

I remember that sometimes in winter my father would be persuaded by my mother to go with me to morning service. Most of the times, however, I was on my own, walking in the dark of the morning. My fear sometimes was that someday as I passed some hedges in the township a snake would bite me, to which my father replied: " No snake can come out of a bush just to bite you!". That gave me some confidence in the hope that snakes conform to that pattern

I got to know the text of the communion recital very well, as the priest and I ascended to the altar to prepare. It went like this straight from the Bible, but in Xhosa, below is the English version:

> **43:1 Judge me, O God, and plead my cause against an ungodly nation: O deliver me from the deceitful and unjust man.**
>
> **43:2 For thou art the God of my strength: why dost thou cast me off? why go I mourning because of the oppression of the enemy?**
>
> **43:3 O send out thy light and thy truth: let them lead me; let them bring me unto thy holy hill, and to thy tabernacles.**

43:4 Then will I go unto the altar of God, unto God my exceeding joy: yea, upon the harp will I praise thee, O God my God

(Psalms of David)

As told in the one book , and that is :" This Side Up", I gave up the career of becoming a priest on reaching junior high at fifteen through learning more science and a bit of logic.

Early Schooling Challenges

The time I started schooling was after WW II and the taking over of government by the Nationalist Party, and no one was happy in New Brighton. Because the schools no longer were under British rule, it meant the end of even what was termed then " The Feeding Scheme" whereby children could get milk and bread served free in the schools and would have occasional delivery of fruit in the school for all children. That part mattered to children But soon all that changed ,because ideologies of freedom took over. As time went on, these ideologies matured in all students and so the strikes began , where many children left school. This in my view was the disastrous side effect of strikes, for many of my age missed out on getting educated when they left school to strike.

To my mother, concentration on schooling was of the essence, and not ideologies. She wanted all her children in the classroom everyday while she was away at her job. Supervision of children to her, was very necessary and that they should not run around doing whatever they liked without consent of parents. Those were days when many children, to their later regret, dropped out of school because of the demands of rioters that they should be involved. Worthy as this cause was it caused a lagging behind of many a child and led to a dangerous social situation to all. Theft , hooliganism , were the order of the day then. Besides that, my mother who observed a moral code for her children based on the Bible, deplored the decadency caused in the changes and chances that overtook marriages in the day, and herself opted not to join any organization. My father , on the other hand, who had had to deal with adjusting to the Xhosa culture after being brought up in the Sotho culture, wanted friends for the family and so secretly joined an organization. My feeling is that this action was a protection for the family. Besides joining an organization, my father , as an Herbalist, had to cure many a sickness in the town, where there was just one doctor, such that even bullet wounds had to be attended to .In a sense this was a protection from any harm. Indeed, all the hooligans on Msimka Street and the surrounds knew my father, as some of them could not attend any doctor without being arrested for their criminal involvements. For a long time, my father was the person to consult for any problems in health in my area.

It can be noticed then how a boy of my age would school with a boy of my younger brother's age, at college because of the late return to school at some stage in life .For, between high school and college I had to work for a year.

The only thing that held men in line in Port Elizabeth , at least , was the custom of circumcision whereby a man could realize recognition in the town. To girls, it was the desirability of marriage and attending cultural activities that assisted that held life in a balance that was more or less acceptable.

Nokhaya

My mother's marriage name, by naming tradition among Xhosas, for all new-lyweds, was Nokhaya or "Mother of a Home". She was called that because her main chore was to build a home and status for the family who had just arrived in the Cape Province from Lesotho, where the spouse's parents lived for years until the death of my grandfather. This story is told elsewhere. Most of the time we all referred to her by the marriage name.

Nokhaya kept the rhythm of her life with music. Not only did she sing songs of joy but very religious songs, for she was religious in attitude. This resulted in music being important in her family. Songs were not only a teaching but a kind of admonition, and she always sang as she worked.

Such an activity one could not avoid, as both parents loved music and would oft sing to themselves as they worked in the house. As this was her mode, the following stories do have music partly intertwined with them. However, one sees also just how serious some conditions were and how my mother handled them in order to give us the green light we needed in life so that we would never yield because of paucity of abilities and succumb to abandoning aims in life.The following stories demonstrate that aptly.

Nokhaya to the Rescue

When I was a young boy, my mother named through marriage 'Nokhaya', was approached by a lady whose husband was physically abusing her badly, to find answers for her. Nokhaya asked her in conversation just what standard of education she had. She replied that she had completed junior high school. The lady was willing to find an option of divorce but did not know how she would survive in the community without a husband. My mother advised her to secretly apply for a nursing training post out of town , using our address as a base. When accepted she was to use the same address to save clothing for a trip, and plan to go on training.

The lady applied secretly and obtained a training post. She could now plan her trip to leave home and go on training. My mother advised her to purchase a travelling bag and keep it at our home; to buy and pack her clothes and required articles , one at a time , in the travelling bag until she felt she had enough.

When the lady had enough clothing, she then purchased a train ticket and moved secretly out of town to her post. She had to make sure she departed from home in her work clothes and nothing special. Having done this and arrived at her post, she would then engage a lawyer and file for a divorce.

The lady came once or twice during her nursing leave to visit, never forgetting to write often to Nokhaya. Nokhaya planned this even though the husband to the lady was her relative by marriage. This was not because she encouraged divorce, but saw an injustice in the treatment and was never in favor of abuse by husbands. She herself , remained married to one man until she passed on.

Nokhaya and the Green Coat

My mother worked a few miles from the city center in a suburb. On her way to work she had to pass the shopping center downtown. Once she saw an all-weather coat that she liked. On inquiring of the price, she was told by a saleslady that the price of the coat was far above her means because she was not even professional . That was the wrong thing to say to Nokhaya. She now wanted the coat. On asking if she could buy it in terms, she was given a deposit price and permitted to pay in installments until the purchase was complete while the shop held the goods. Out of her meager wages Nokhaya paid for the coat in very small installments until, after months, she completed payment. This coat was kept for special occasions and she owned it until her death. This is one reason she never felt her children should be satisfied with a minor situation if they can work themselves up to better status; a good reason for educating her children.

Nokhaya and the Stole

Nokhaya loved dressing up for church and for the temperance meetings . She was a member of the Independent Order of the True Templers(the I. O. T T)which was derided by many to mean: "I Only Take Tea) . Each year she would attend bigger meetings of the Temperance Organization out of town as a delegate for her group. So, on these occasions the ladies dressed well to present reports and take part in discussions and addressing meetings.

Passing through the city center again Nokhaya saw a stole she liked. Before I proceed , let me mention that we all know that as we travel in our cars we kill a lot of little animals, and that our bodies are full of bacteria which, when we step out line will multiply to a great extent causing us much misery. Let the no man or woman contend that they do not at all set anything from an animal on their body. The stole my mother saw was made of a skin of some animal and she liked it. In fact she called it the 'jackal'. She had no hope of buying the stole but wished for it dearly. So she also bought it in installments and would rarely wear it except on certain occasions when she would call for her 'jackal'.

She made these optional choices to show that as a black woman, she could still buy what she wanted without being limited by shopkeepers. It was usual for a saleslady to determine what a Black person could or could not buy, and Nokhaya never liked to be limited to a section in a shop in areas where she had to have a choice.

Education

Even without Nokhaya attaining any educational certificates, she was able to encourage and produce children who all but one attained degrees in education. The fifth who did not attain a degree worked in the motor manufacturing industry for thirty five years, rising there to become a foreman. This , Nokhaya did by disobeying her husband and vowing to get all her children educated. In the times of the fifties and the seventies , this was phenomenal even for women who had enough education to wish it for her family. In her family she produced a medical doctor, a qualified hospital matron with a Bachelor's degree, a computer expert and a doctor in Economics. This tells me that her other behaviors were no more than an adjustment to her environment and a defense for her family. Granted she never joined any political organization as my father did , yet she had a great concern for the modern progress of her family and others in her circle of friends, and encouraged all to learn some Western strategies in their lives and conduct as that learning would be an advantage in life.

Nokhaya and the electricity account

In the late fifties, electricity was introduced to the houses in the township where candles and kerosene lamps had been the norm for lighting. Each house was equipped with one light centrally situated to light up all the rooms. This was hardly enough to do ironing and other house duties. Nokhaya got my father to find a way of installing metered electricity in the house. She went and engaged the company with the assistance of her husband, to install metered current on the house. For many years our house was the only house in the neighborhood to be visited by an inspector who came to read metered current each month. Of course she was very touchy about the use of the current as she wished to employ it in her work. Nokhaya worked for several Jewish families and would tell us their sad stories of the war that had just passed, on some days.

Teenage Life

School Friends

Between the years 1948 when I turned six years and entered school and the year 1959 when I left junior high, I made a number of school friends which I wish to mention now. My friends at primary school were Thozamile and Lungile. Thozamile's family was of the Jehovah Witnesses sect and his father, an electrician was a good source and assistance with all electrical problems in the years that New Brighton had electricity installed. His mother was a good but younger friend of my mother's. There is not much I can say about Thozamile except that he introduced me to concepts in other religious sects in the town. Later I was to have an English teacher who was also of that sect. Perhaps this induced me to look into the question of why we have religion among us, but that is another matter.

The other friend I had , that is , Lungile was a good fellow who befriended me in class. I soon learned that his older sister schooled with my elder sister at some stage. Lungile was quiet in his friendship and at intervals at school, we spent time at his home which was nearer to the school than mine.

Perhaps the best friend I had at primary school was my eldest sister, who was not just a friend but an advisor and protector as she entered school before me and therefore knew much more about the involvement with school. This has been mentioned elsewhere so I shall not go into it.

Schooling in those days was structured such that , one had to do Sub A and B before going into standard one to six. At six one obtained a certificate to enter junior high if one so wished. During those riotous years of the fifties, many stopped at standard six of before and entered the work-force. This was because of the 'stay-away' strikes that occurred frequently then. Thus many a youth never got the education they needed to start a healthy life. Usually one did standard four to six at a higher primary school and not just at the primary school.

At the end of my days at primary school I then entered higher primary. This is when life got very interesting. The school I was supposed to attend at was Molefe Higher Primary, but by the time I passed primary school, there was no room at the main building of the school to take in more children. So three classes from that school were housed at the Baptist Church, while another group was housed at the Moravian Church. We were to be there for the year we studied standard four and would be transferred hopefully to the main building at standard five.

Occasionally there would be times we had to be summoned to the main building which was at Connacher Street, and that is where I met some good friends from the Moravian Church with whom I would be associated until , some of them , until the last year at junior high. One of these friends was Jeremiah, of "Shortie" or "Shortman" as he was called by friends.

I had noticed Shortie at primary school. He was a good runner in athletics but never followed that line at junior high. There were , of course two other boys I was associated with , who were Mongameli and Victor. Victor stopped school after standard six, while Mongameli , Shortie and I continued to junior high ,parting company when I attended high school.

Shortie and I lived on neighboring streets and used to enjoy buying "honey cake" at one store on the way home each day when we had any money. Shortie was from a more affluent family for his father was a headman in the township. For reasons I learned as a young man , my mother never quite agreed with the friendship with Shortie and I found it had to do with our parents. However, Shortie and I never acknowledged the difference even after we left school.

Activities with "Shortie"

At this stage in schooling we had learned reading in English. Shortie and I spent time at his home reading and enjoying copies of the "Stage and Cinema" magazine, which were in those days floating around among the pupils at our school. Also , at this time, Rock 'n Roll music was the norm. So we spent time listening to that music on an old radio in Shortie's house's living room. I should mention that Shortie's family had a six roomed house while mine had a three roomed house. At Shortie's it was the possible to have a room to ourselves to listen in. Besides the magazine, these were days when trading in comic books was the main occupation. Both of us knew many characters from comic books and would share many stories. The days we spent together from 1954 to 1956 were pleasant days .By 1957 we entered junior high and there was a brief change.

Friendship at junior high

At junior high I met another friend who was to mean quite a lot in my life. Today he functions as a priest in the Anglican Church and is therefore a respected member of the community. It is amazing to think that our friendship started with a fight which was aborted. At Form 1, we had had a quarrel in class and had decided to meet and settle the score after school. I learned he was more skilled in boxing and I in wrestling.

On that day we met for the fight surrounded by many of the boys in the school. The fight was in a classroom. As we started I found the fight was to my disadvantage. In order to fight in wrestling one has to have grip of the opponent, but at the fight they wanted a hands-off fight. In those days it was my duty at home to return in time to open the house for my younger siblings, before returning to school for afternoon studies. As we continued the tussle, I found there was no point in the fight because neither one was winning. It may sound silly, but I declared to the boys that I had work at home and could not stay for the whole afternoon fighting. The fellow I was fighting agreed that we were wasting time and we stopped the fight. From that day we became close friends going through much in life together. His name was Ezra Vuyisile . I soon found out that Ezra loved music and had stacks of the music of the Andrew Sisters at his home. I had a few records of Elvis Presley and Little Richard. He found out that I loved singing and could sing. The reason he found out was that Ezra was also server at the Anglican Church at St. Stephens, where I attended church and was also server there. At school therefore we started a group of rock 'n roll singers, with Shortie and two other boys joining in We would entertain the class and other students with Rock 'n Roll music. I had, of a force, to be the rock star , with accompaniment from the fellows. However our music was not strictly rock, for we had music from the "Crew Cuts" and the "Mills Brothers" in our repertoire.

Those raucous days ended when I left for high school, and took on a stance of being quiet and sober for two years. Those two years never stopped friendship between me and Ezra.

A year after high school, Ezra attended a boarding school at Lovedale near Alice, Cape,, while I attended a nearby university. We still visited but later would not. Ezra was soon arrested for political activity and spent some time in prison, being pardoned later after about six months. After that he went on into a quiet profession as a minister of religion, having studied for his Master's in Theology, I believe in the UK.

As for myself. After those years at high school, I had a difficult time adjusting to being a person in a society I did not agree with and subsequently became a Bahá'í, serving as travelling teacher, a translator and an administrator in that religion..

Cowan Secondary School in 1959;
Robert Mazibuko on extreme right with a few classmate

Trials of Weekends and Holidays

When I turned twelve years in age, it became necessary to introduce me to employment and work outside of home. For some years I then was broken into a workman by my father. Later when I turned fifteen . I was approached by a neighbor who used to see me work in our garden , trimming hedges etc. He asked if I could work for his employer who was some kind of supervisor at a place called " Tatlow and Pledger". I was to help him build a wall around his house and later work in his garden. I agreed to the deal and went in search of his home in Adcockvale, a nearby suburb. My employer was an ex-pilot in the Royal Air Force and went by the name of James Brown. I , at first found the name strange. It sounded so easy. Soon found that "Jimmy" as his wife, Peggy, called him was actually Scottish in origin. He was to pay me 50 cents for a Saturday's work. I accepted but soon had to go on strike for higher wages, as I understood that other workers in the area were earning more. Jimmy Brown upgraded my daily wage to 60 cents. The work was not bad and I had had much training earlier with my father who worked in parks and homes as a gardener. My father, even though he had a standard six certificate twice, in Lesotho and repeated it in South Africa, found that doing the same class twice cured him of school. So he refused to work in any office or factory. It is curious to note that I later learned that when I took up the Bahá'í Religion I could only become a Bahá'í at fifteen and be allowed to vote in administrative elections in that Faith, at fifteen, actually after twenty one years in age. So the time I started work was related to my faith.

Jimmy brown had lots of books in his garage and bundles of the "Daily Mirror". On rainy Saturdays I could turn up for work and spend the day reading and still get paid . By looking through the stacks of books I learned more about a publisher called "Horder and Straughton" which published books about "Bulldog Drummond" and 'The Black Hawk". There was also a fair sprinkling of books by Leslie Charteries , all about the "Saint', which I learned to adore.

Jimmy Brown was good at handing out Christmas presents. At one stage I found a watch on a rainy day, on the road. Jimmy Brown who, was also a watchmaker repaired the watch for me for nothing. I had the pleasure of handing the watch to my sister on her twenty first birthday as it happened to be a lady's model. Jimmy Brown's house was the first house outside of my home, in which my mother allowed me to spend a night in. I was invited by

Jimmy's family, to an evening on Christmas Eve to help during a party they had, and my mother felt I should spend the evening there. In fact my mother on the occasion, had no option at choosing hours of absence , for the party was to be at night.

On one of these Christmas Eves , Jimmy bought me a khaki pair of pants, the kind used by men after circumcision in South Africa. I enjoyed the pants but they got me into a lot of trouble with circumcised men who wanted to know where I had undergone the manhood process.

I stopped working for Jimmy Brown when I got to high school when I was asked to join the school soccer team. This was because matches were on Saturdays. Jimmy Brown who appreciated soccer himself let me go to matches, but I soon saw that it was not going to work because I wished to attend movies on Saturday afternoons, and studies each morning at the local high school, Newell High. James Brown reluctantly let me go and I suspect it was because he had once told me:"You look to success and you will succeed; you look to failure and you will fail". He could not go back on his word, but that did not stop him later pleading with my mother that I go back to work. However that arrangement ended.

The sixty cents from Jimmy Brown, though a small amount helped a lot with school feeding in those days and my mother appreciated it. So, when I stopped working , matters got very hard financially , but somehow with tips from my father I was able to keep going.

Street Manners

At fifteen I was learning to smoke. At that same age I was learning to survive in the tough streets of New Brighton. I learned that one had to have three things in one's pocket:: a packet of cigarettes, a box of matches and a knife sitting in the back pocket of the pants. Later, to this at sixteen was added also the "Reference Book". The coins could be loose in the pocket if there were no chances of being searched in the street. Bullies were plenty and 'chance takers " flourished.

In the old days, at school one could buy two "fatcakes" and a piece of fish per day, as there were ladies selling same every school interval. One did not carry food to school, one found cheap ways of eating. During the days of the Union of South Africa, there was a school-feeding scheme where each pupil got a cup of milk and a slice of bread each day. This all disappeared at the beginning of the Bantu Education System, to the anger of both children and parents. For parents now had to be involved in paying for food for all children at primary schools.

While living in the township, going to the movies was a must for every kid. In my family this was not permitted until we grew up to be young teenagers. My mother felt that no good children would learn much from behavior shown by children attending the bioscope, as it was called then, however mothers could attend movies sometimes, as was the case of watching one called " The Sentimental Journey". We heard of this movie from my mother at what could be called "ad nauseum". and heard from school kids all about "Roy Rogers" and "Gene Autry" without ever being allowed to see any of this. At about thirteen we were allowed through an announcement from my mother , to attend a movie on a Saturday, a day I will remember. We saw Robert Mitchum acting in " The White Witchdoctor" at the Rio Cinema in New Brighton.. We had , per force, to wash and dress up for this occasion.

After that initial day we were allowed to attend movies, but had to find our own money for that .So began the collection of copper, iron, glass and bones for sale for movie money! Every Saturday became a movie-day, and all week , collection-of-metal became compulsory. We would be stooped at the junk yard separating materials,: copper from cast iron and rejecting any alloys as they were not acceptable. I got to know that copper and cast iron sold for much ,and that alloys do not sell so well! Bottles and bones, always made a good sale. One had to tell copper caps for bottles from metal ones.

Of course going to the movie brought some behaviors we did not have before. I soon found out I could wear my father's old waist coat like a cowboy! Of course it has to be understood that we had to dodge being robbed on the way to selling our items at "Savage and Sons" in North End, for the path was manned by all sorts of "types" waiting to rob us of our gains. It was no easy run to go selling , but it had to be done if we wanted to see the next chapter in the serial at the theater.

Soon selling metals became more important than the hunting of birds that we used to indulge in earlier and the sun of Saturday ceased to shine the same way it used to; it grew brighter with anticipation!. The trick of avoiding issues with my sister and my mother, was for us boys to leave some of the gains in the house and "offer" financial help before disappearing for the afternoon. My sister probably guessed what was happening but held her peace.

Robert Mazibuko as a server at the St Stephen's Church.
Picture cropped from picture taken after Sunday communion in the 50s.

Getting lost

In the early days in New Brighton, it was easy for one to get lost but if one could remember the street name and the name of the family one could be found. I got lost once and know the feeling. In the days when we first transferred from the Presbyterian Church to the Anglican Church, I had joined both the boy scouts and become a choirboy or a server as one was called n those days. Our church the St. Stephen's was closely associated with another Anglican church called St. Cyprian's. St. Cyprians was across town in Korsten where most Africans used to reside before being moved to New Brighton. Because of this association between the two churches we had constant visits of one to the other . There were joint projects and rallies undertaken by the two communities.

We sometimes could visit St. Mary's Church which was for Whites in the city or enter the city to buy implements for the boy scout movement. Once, when we visited the city I barely made my way to the bus home, and still do not remember how, for somehow I lost the company of boys I was with and had to find my way back on my own. This kind of separation from the group happened once with disastrous results.

We had gone to St. Cyprian's across town for reasons I cannot recall. We were a group of boys from St. Stephen's but somehow on reaching St Cyprians we separated because I chose to remain in one spot while the other boys decided to roam. After a while that they had gone, I realized that it was coming to sundown and I did not really know my way back to New Brighton and depended on the older boys. I was then about ten years in age.

I decided to walk home somehow . I knew the direction very vaguely and continued to walk, until I realized I was totally lost. I knew that the road home passed through some woods, but which woods? There seemed to be lots of similar places in the woods. I was almost in tears with fear that I would never find my way home and there was no person to ask. I was surrounded by walls of factories and woods.

While blundering around, I came upon an older person, possibly coming back from work. When he saw me he asked where I was heading and I told him: "Msimka Street, New Brighton". I added shakily that I was not sure of the way there.

The old man turned to me and said :"Walk with me". It was already sundown by the time we reached the outskirts of what looked like an occupied area. I kept close to the old man as we entered. I soon recognized the kind of houses that looked like those of New Brighton, for all were of the same style.

The old man turned to me again and asked if I recognized the place. I told him I did. Whereupon he asked if I could find my way from there. When he was sure he let me go saying "Good night!" He had asked me my name and clan name, but never asked to meet my parents for any gratitude on their part, but simply bade me good night.

When I got home I kept this story to myself, for the first thing my mother would have asked would have been:" What were you doing in Korsten without permission?" I avoided that question for it carried with it punishment and stern remonstration.

Buying Clothing

My mother could find used clothing for family but there were times she would buy clothing new. She knew a number of Jewish stores in the city where one could have a deal, and would sometimes take me along to a store and choose clothing for school and for estimated fitting. Some of these times, I would have to be measured for clothing instead of fitting it on, because in those days,

Blacks did not fit clothing in stores as there were no separate facilities for them there. This did not bother mother because if your pants were too long she could get the sewing machine and shorten them herself. However, she shopped at Jewish stores and they were alright.

My mother made most of the dresses my sister wore, and was handy with the sewing needle for patching up shirts and pants.

I learn music
From the time we started living in New Brighton in the early forties , until around the late fifties, we did not have a radio in the house. My father and an uncle who lived out of town owned some gramophones, however, ours was kept in a shed with a number of tools, and was not used much as it did not work so well. I never could understand why that gramophone was in the shed. So, for music we depended on visits from my uncle and his family whose gramophone was functionary . There were some musical records also kept in the outside shed, which we were not allowed to touch. In secretly playing the gramophone I found one of the songs on one of the records had the words:

> *"anywhere you are*
> *It is always right*
> *If you are doing well."*

This was a thrill to me as a child as I began to figure out the meanings of the words and I would spend secret moments playing the one song. In the late fifties we purchased a used radio which had a turntable, and my father bought some records which ran only at 78 rpm. As we grew up, larger records running at 33 1/3 became available, and in my ignorance I ripped them up by trying them on a 78 rpm stylus! This of course improved as I began to be expert at choosing speeds between 78 rpm , 33 1/3 rpm and 45 rpm. Change of speed had to be initially done manually as the turntable was not built for that! Changing the stylus became a challenge!

When I started junior high school , there was a nurse living in our lane, who would hear some of the music we played, as sometimes I increased the volume. One day she stopped me in the street and asked if I would like to borrow some of her music. She has some good music by Glen Miller and Patti page. These were my first recollections of 'big time' music. The lady let me know that she appreciated obedience to parents and encouraged me to keep up that standard. She also admitted having some respect for both my parents. When I got into a fight at high school she was the one to patch me up with a bandage , and look after my other medical needs at no price, as in those days there was no medical doctor living nearby in New Brighton .It was a great advantage to have her in the neighborhood, and it helped to hear speak so highly of my mother. I felt appreciated and encouraged. The musical records she loaned me opened a large vista of what was music in those days. Thus my first musical shows that I ardently enjoyed were not only "King Kong" and African show, but "The Glenn Miller Story" and " The Benny Goodman Story", which told me a great deal about the world outside New Brighton, and even, as I learned later, outside South Africa.

There was also on one street another friend of my family who soon found out after visits to my home that I loved music. I remember her loaning me her records too, for example the music of the "Fontaine Sisters", and like mothers in those days used to encourage me to help work in my house and in helping my parents. Perhaps this lady observed me passing her house as a boy, each day, carrying a surplice and a cassock over my arm , on the way to church, for her home was on the road to church.. Love of music and attending church were activities that were available to young and old in those days, as they filled the weekend and kept children involved.

So the very first people who were interested in obedience to parents and who attended to my need for good music were the women of my township who knew my family.

When I got to junior high school, one lady asked me if I had a girlfriend or a friend who was a girl, when I replied in the negative, she introduced me her little sister, but I lacked interest in her and she never pushed for an extended friendship. I not only felt appreciated, I also felt the trust of some of the ladies in the neighborhood. This showed the care one got from the ladies when one took the right steps in life, and how they propelled one to greater achievements later.

I learned during the rock 'n roll era, when they played some of the Andrew Sisters music that my mother knew of them and appreciated their music. Hence I place this picture at this point which I found in later life when I resided in Illinois.

Andrews Sisters.
Photographed by author from a poster purchased at a used goods store in Illinois

Among certain nations of the East, music was considered reprehensible, but in this new age the Manifest Light hath, in His holy Tablets, specifically proclaimed that music, sung or played, is spiritual food for soul and heart. (Abdu'l-Baha, Selections from the Writings of Abdu'l-Baha, p. 112)

Growing up in the Township

Some ladies in the township made sure they knew where you stood with education and work in your home. Whenever they saw you in a compromising situations they would remind you that your mother would not like that situation at all. In that way, it was easy for them to report your activities to your parents. As I grew up I would regard them as my mother's espionage system. I would find my mother making a statement like :"You were standing at the bus terminus with a girl for twenty minutes, why?". I knew that she was at work at the time and was never near!

In my day mothers took care of one another's children, and it was no offense but was much appreciated by all. In those days , it was possible for a mother whose child had done wrong, to pass the punishment to the school teacher by writing a note to be delivered by the child to the teacher with the words:"Kindly punish that child!". .. No word of why.

Movies and Books of the Day

While I liked reading on my own, movies were attended by myself accompanied by my brother, Donald, later nicknamed "Tumana". The nickname came from my mother who would sometimes call him "Tumie" in the same way she would call me "Kholie" after my name , Kholekile. Best movie times were on Saturday and perhaps Monday or Wednesday, if one found a way of not being in school on those afternoons, as we grew up. What played on Monday would play on Wednesday, and what played on Thursday would be feature on Saturday.

A picture of the "Copper Head", an investigator in the serial, being tackled by the "robot" belonging and operated by Dr. Satan. (from the serial :"The Mysterious Dr. Satan" (Retrieved from the Internet, prior to 2007)

These were the serious serials of the times, and my two brothers and I would find time to sneak off and see while my big sister stayed behind. This was during the time allocated to us as little boys to go and play in the fields around my home, or to hunt in the woods. As a girl my sister had her dolls and tea sets and would entertain friends. The money of course was always the problem. For that we collected copper, steel and bones for sale for reprocessing. at some company then called "Savage and Sons", located in the North End . These were pleasant times, but hard for little boys, because even getting into the movies theater, subterfuge had to be utilized. It was very easy to have all that cash taken off one if one was not careful in how they entered the theater or how they stored the money on the person. It was more like what one would term now "eat and avoid being eaten". However, part of the game, if a game it was, was in the risk one had to take and win. Life in New Brighton, especially near Ward 9, where we lived, and the surrounds of the theater, was tough. One gets a very funny feeling when one talks of danger in the cities while having lots of other protection from some kind of authority. There was no protection in New Brighton. The one time, as grown up, one saw a policeman was when one got arrested for possessing a knife that was too long , or when being taken in , later in life, for not possessing relevant documents on one's person. The other time one saw policemen was when they came to destroy stocks of homemade liquor in some old lady's home. That was the old days. Today the story is slightly or drastically different, because in my later day, policemen armed with stern guns were a usual sight in the township, for rioting was by then a commonality…not to mention armed helicopters above…

Picture from the movie serial "Drums of Fu Manchu" another serial featuring a popular actor called Allan Parker. (Retrieved from the Internet in prior to 2007)

Picture of "Nyoka the Jungle Girl" in a serial of the name "Perils of Nyoka", which was supposed to be based in Africa. (Retrieved from the Internet prior to 2007)

It is funny that the word "Nyoka" in Xhosa means "Snake" and does not have a good connotation when applied to one. Usually it is derogatory and relates to being untrustworthy.

Besides the movies, reading was a great pastime in those days, because with reading one could travel and see many sights while one was home. This became a pastime of my choice, after trying sports for some years. The problem with sports was that one could attend training for months and yet never get picked for any matches and that was discouraging. Perhaps the fact was that, outside of out running with some of my school mates in house athletic sports , and refusing to run in the general inter-house sports, I was left with the indoor reading. This did not really mean that I was not supposed to attend to outside work, in general at home., No... I was , at that time employed as a gardener. This was however unofficial government-wise, as I did, not at the time own a Reference Book as a school-attending child. That came when I turned nineteen. Later I would have to have certificate on that book that stated that I was exempt from taxation as student and did not need to have a paid tax certificate on the book..

Working as gardener for an ex Royal Air Force pilot of WW II was a help, because , besides having the "Daily Mirror " to read each Saturday, I had the advantage of a man who loved reading books on the "Saint", ", the "Black Hawk"; the "Black Gang" and a lot about Peter Cheyney, Agatha Christie, Craig Rice etc . I had come to know some of these authors through exchange with my fellow readers in the township. One could refer to an earlier book called " This Side Up" for a more detailed treatment of that boyhood subject.

This habit extended from the days of reading about "Robinson Crusoe" in the early days proved to be a great asset, even in writing essays at school. One example of this help was when we were asked to write an essay on "The Drum". I found I could write extensively on that subject, so much so that the essay was read in class by my English school teacher.

I have mentioned in one book I wrote that I did win some awards for library work and in the English class. The books I remember to have won at that time were as follows:" Biggles in the Interpol"; "Kidnapped"; and "Man in the Iron Mask". I treasured these and found time later in life to view some of them as movies. Of course reading "Man in the Iron Mask" could also be the reason I found reading and watching the work" Les Miserables" both as a book and a movie, thrilling! At university I found these initial readings following me even though I did no studies on them in any college course. One example was finding a book called "Muhammad and Charlemagne" so interesting.

There are many books I remember receiving from Rosemary Sala while I was a young high school child. Some of them have meant so much in my adult life. Such books would be in the caliber of "Treasure Island" by R.L. Stevenson; " Memories, Dreams , Reflections" by Carl Yung ; "The Devil Rides Out" by Dennis Wheatley; "Dracula" by Bram Stoker and many others. Mentioned here are those that has have had a lasting impact that led to the kind of person I perceive myself to be, though it is hard to be objective about oneself in entirety, I still recognize the roots of these in my life, as the causes of my present disposition as a grown person..

There are however, several books I received from Rosemary Sala, which I appreciated very much but never mattered in my youth until I reached adulthood and began to see their import and the reason she felt they did demanded perusal. One of these is displayed below:

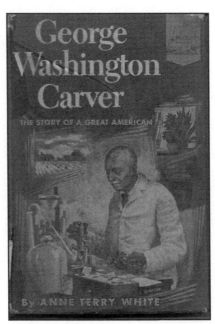

A book recommended for reading by Rosemary Sala when I was seventeen attending junior high school in 1959, which was never returned to library by self. (Scan of original cover by author)

On the inside of the cover are these words in Rosemary Sala's handwriting:" Presented by Mrs. J. B. de Mille, Little Rock Arkansas, USA".

Rosemary collected many volumes of books from libraries in the United States and Canada, for the school libraries of the New Brighton, Kwazakhele and Zwide areas of Port Elizabeth, South Africa..

Youngman Searches

My Latin Master "VC"

Principal of Cowan Secondary School in 1959

Mr. Qunta was not only the principal of Cowan but was also the Latin Teacher. He went by several names among the students. Some called him "Princepts" the closest to the Latin equivalent for "principal". Others referred to him as being just plain "VC", after the abbreviation of his name

, i.e. Vincent. He was not only a good and kind teacher but a good disciplinarian too. As one can imagine, he rated high in my mother's book, as she was herself a well-known disciplinarian in the township. VC respected African traditions but knew enough about street language not to be trivialized by students. He excelled in the classroom and was a gentleman in behavior. I say this not just because he later became my relative as the maternal uncle to my wife, but because I schooled at Cowan for three years and got to know him. When he encouraged us to write articles to be included in the school magazine called, "The Cowanite', I wrote an article with the title " We Love Him". I had mentioned in the article some word which was modified by the teacher who edited the article. I had written "We wish we could bop him on the head" which he teacher kindly modified to "hop him on the head"!

We had to do Latin for two years of schooling and "VC" in that time, taught us how to greet him in Latin. He would say " Saluete discipuli!" and we would reply "Salue Magister!"! Mr. Qunta did not tolerate misbehavior and showed the students both boys and girls that he could use tough street words if he wanted to get them to straighten up.

Besides being the Netball Trainer to girls, Mr. Qunta was a great athlete to the boys. Not only that, he spent time advising the boys how to behave as grown men. At a time when drinking was the norm, he advised the boys to grow up not to be too attached to spirits but rather drink something healthier than that. Himself a non-smoker, he never mentioned that to the boys. When I had a slight swelling in private parts he was the one who volunteered to examine me before sending me off to a doctor, where it was determined I had a slight infection. He had to make sure there was nothing serious, as this could and did occur in those days.

In those days , teachers were congratulated by parents when children did receive a pass in the examinations, especially external examination which were conducted by the Department of Education. My mother got to know more about our schooling and Mr. Qunta, because four of us in the family attended his school, and he would sometime pay visits to my home to encourage us. African mothers worked well with teachers in our time.

Though some of us were glad when Mr. Qunta was appointed an Inspector of Schools and had to leave Cowan, we were also sad that he was leaving the school at that same time.

When I grew up to serve on the Bahá'í National Assembly I met a teacher, who was also a member of the Assembly, Stsnlake Kukama, who mentioned that when he was in politics in South Africa, he used to meet Mr. Qunta at their meetings in Johannesburg. In a way that helped, because Mr. Qunta turned down becoming a member f the Bahá'í Faith because he wanted to follow a political career. On discovering that as a Bahá'í he would have to abstain from political involvement he decided not to join. I remember him with mentioning *sine qua non* and *quam primum* in the Latin class! In that way, he had his priorities, which were different form my choices in later life

Educationally, "VC" was very encouraging and often applauded when we made good choices of books to read at the library. He would mention that when one starts reading a book , it may not sound interesting at that point, but develops with more reading into the story. His wife, who taught English, was no less serous in her teaching habits and encouragement. It was no surprise to me that she eventually became a Social Worker in the Cape Town area..

Firing Interest and Enthusiasm

The days of entering junior high were days of mystery to me. At this time I had learned that I live on a Planet and that day and night were caused by the planet turning in circles. This was fascinating! Besides this I learned that my school had a whole lot of books in a library. To boot, science was telling me that everything was made of chemicals. This opened a new world even religiously. Somehow it meant there was no heaven in the sky. Where then was heaven? My very existence was challenged by science.

It was at this time that I turned to science as being more logical. It was hiding nothing form me, I was free to investigate and prove. This is the time I met a man who was not just going to be my teacher but my good friend. This was Jerome Tobigunya Galo , my science teacher, "JT" Galo for short.

Mr. Galo was a new teacher just out of college and he was known to have graduated with Honors in Chemistry. Each class had to have an assigned class teacher, and my assigned class teacher at first year in junior high was Jerome Galo, my future friend.

On the first day of his arrival, early in the morning, he came into class and as we stood up to greet him, and said through his teeth:" Get a broom and sweep this class room!" and walked out without another word. In those days school children at junior high had to clean classrooms and polish them every Friday afternoon. It was after the class room was cleaned that Jerome came in and taught science. He was to be the Mathematics and General Science teacher for years in that school. Later when I was a working man "JT", as we called him, became a principal of a school, married and had a number of children, and also became my neighbor in residence.

I remember him clearly in the class about Archimedes' Laws saying as he strutted up and down the floor :" Archimedes said :' Give a lever, a place to stand in space, and a fulcrum, and I will move the world!' " A very fascinating man to be one's teacher in science! I remember well also that, though in science, JT was a Catholic and a devout one at that . Before a meal , he never forgot to make the sign of the cross and mumble a prayer. At weekends there was not much to do for teachers except get together and chat. I had to be present at some of these meetings at his home . That way I got to read most of JT's books that he had. It was his book while I studied Zoology, that I read most especially on the concepts of Evolution, and the book was generally called " Grove and Newell" after the authors. It was far easier to follow than the one by "Thompsons" assigned at my school or any earlier one called " Borradale". I got more familiar with Grove and Newell while I studied Zoology at a college, for it was used there.

It fascinated me to learn from JT's books that the human was regarded as a piece of 'clay' crawling on the surface of the earth!

All this opened such a new world for me that when I got to reading books in the library I found favor with the librarian who was to be a of great assistance in my life, and a very good teacher to the young man I was, and that was Rosemary Sala.

I tend to lump the two meetings together in my mind when I think of my youth; that of meeting "JT" and being associated with Rosemary.. It begins to be understandable even to me why "JT"'s wife, Julia, should want to know where I resided in the USA by coming on a visit once in the past five years on the island .

JT was a very young teacher, and Julia his future wife had just graduated from junior high and had started working when he arrived at my school. I have no idea how else they met, but know that they were neighbors in residence, and Julia was herself quite an attractive girl in her youth and still is in adulthood.

After years of teaching and living far away from his home on Harlem of Langa Township in Cape Town, JT passed on in Port Elizabeth a well known figure in the community, for he also served as some kind of deacon in his church. His son , who happens to have a twin brother now works as a Medical Superintendant in a hospital in East London, South Africa, and has made quite a number of visits to the United States, including one with his mother on Washington Island, WI. To me JT has served not just as a teacher but a resource and more in the caliber of a big brother. In my life as a young man, we socialized with him such that I would often accompany him on some nights when he sought to see his future wife at her home. To him she was " Julie".

This is the teacher, who in our last year at Cowan High taught us how to dance for the final party and farewell, to the music of Benny Goodman and Glenn Miller. I still remember him putting on " Stomping at the Savoy" from a very small record player in class, one afternoon and asking us to practice dancing for the final party we were to have with parents present. All I can say is : "JT was good company!" On attempting to tell part of my story I requested photos from Julia his wife and following are pictures she sent:

Mr. J.T. Galo , my science teacher at Junior High, whose wife, Tabina Julia, his wife took the trouble to visit me on the island to see how I was settled down.

(R-L) Julia, a graduating friend, and "JT" Galo, at a graduation ceremony.
(Contributed by Julia Galo)

A group of students and teachers at Cowan High, JT is the second teacher
from the left in front sitting position.(A gift from Julia Galo0

Firstly: He lays stress on the search for Truth. This is most important, because the people are too easily led by tradition. It is because of this   that they are often antagonistic to each other, and dispute with one another.

But the manifesting of Truth discovers the darkness and becomes the cause of Oneness of faith and belief: because Truth cannot be two!
(Abdu'l-Baha, Abdu'l-Baha in London, p. 27)

Two statements that legitimize a perspective of science and such a an attitude are in the Bahá'í Writings. I found that in later years :

21. O MOVING FORM OF DUST!

I desire communion with thee, but thou wouldst put no trust in Me. The sword of thy rebellion hath felled the tree of thy hope. At all times I am near unto thee, but thou art ever far from Me. Imperishable glory I have chosen for thee, yet boundless shame thou hast chosen for thyself. While there is yet time, return, and lose not thy chance.
(The Persian Hidden Words)

15. O SON OF UTTERANCE!

Turn thy face unto Mine and renounce all save Me; for My sovereignty endureth and My dominion perisheth not. If thou seekest another than Me, yea, if thou searchest the universe for evermore, thy quest will be in vain.
(The Arabic Hidden Words)

The Scope of Study
In those days all Africans studied at school under what was termed the "Bantu Education System" which was quite different to what was offered to the rest of the race groups in the country. For an example, at completion of junior high we were offered the Junior Certificate which was different from the Cape Province Junior Certificate. This also applied to high school, for then on completion one had to have the certificate of the "Joint Matriculation Board"

which was not the same as the Cape Province Senior Certificate offered to other race groups. Another example of classes taught was that instead of Physics and Chemistry, Africans were taught the "General Science Subject" which included parts of Chemistry and Physics; and instead of History and Geography what was offered was the Social Studies subject which included parts of History and Geography. In the Matriculation certificate one had to meet certain criteria to have a passing certificate. One had to pass two languages, two science classes and two arts classes. Any deviation would have one receive a School Leaving Certificate which was not acceptable for university degree classes but would be accepted for employment.

JT then taught General Science to us, and a certain Mr.. Ian Sogoni taught Social Studies. Repetition of classes to attain the matriculation standards was frequent as students wished to proceed to universities to study.

What really helped in opening the doors to the outside world was the library and books sold there to students by a Librarian. Most books were from Canada and USA as the Librarian had ties with several libraries and organizations there. This was the case in the time I schooled there. Foreign magazines were attainable in the library and that helped students find out about other countries and their educational standards.

Study at JT's

When I left junior high to study at Newell High for the Matriculation Certificate , I tended, many times to study in the evenings at JT's home, for , not only was it quiet there , he also had many books to look at as a reference. However, being there taught me a lot about JT's life.. But then I also found out that JT drank sometimes. This involved my being present at times when other teachers came to his home. They would however depart soon and go into the township and would leave me to study.

JT made a point of keeping his liquor in his wardrobe, and it had me mystified. Not that I did not know that this was liquor but why he kept it there. Perhaps he wanted it out of the way, but it made me curious.

Once, when I was alone I ventured to take a sip from his bottle, for the wardrobe was not locked. It was "gin"! JT did not ask any questions about the bottle until the next day when I came back to study. He mentioned noticing that somebody drank his liquor and I held my silence. For years after that, JT remembered this in my adult life and would require remuneration as , he said, I was then a grownup man and circumcised and must take responsibility. I paid for that double, until JT stopped the request.

It is strange that in those days he called me by the name of "Mousie", and yet, as I grew up he changed that to "Robbie" a name he used until we parted in 1987 when I left the country. Yes, indeed , up to that time I visited JT and has wife Julia, as his home was the only home where I could be comfortable at the time I was applying for a visa to enter the United States, for he understood that. Many friends I had queried the fact that I wanted to marry outside the country. There was always the insulting remark that I preferred like others they knew , to eat "White Bread". This was insulting in that white bread was known at school not to be nutritious! But I bore that with some pride. For, I had done what was laudable in some quarters and got in "import" from overseas! It had been regarded as a good thing to marry one from out of town to avoid marrying one of the same clan, now I had gone off the continent to look!

The Last Task Performed

On the very last day of school in 1959, when we had had both the Prize Giving Day and the Completers' Ball, we were heading for the summer vacation and to wait for the results of the External Examination. The External Examination was when our papers would be corrected and graded in Pretoria, the then capital, to determine as to which students would attain the Junior Certificate in order to proceed to high school to do the Senior Certificate classes. The results for the examination would be obtained sometime in December and mailed from Pretoria, to our principal's address or the school. We would then hear of them at that point and would visit the principal's home for confirmation.. There was, therefore , very little to do except wait at this time. For, one could not really plan until the results came out.

On the day when we closed school, JT asked me to kindly report at his home as he had a task I should help with.

That afternoon, before going home, I went to his home, only to find that he had bundles of the marks and grades from the whole school for all science classes, that he wished me to help total with him. The job was that he had an adding machine, and mine was to call out the marks and he would add them up on the machine .There were no names , just numbers. Somehow the totals

, at the end of the day, had to make sense to him . I never knew how, but proceeded with just calling out numbers. This became a full afternoon's work,
and I wanted to go home and enjoy my music and prepare for the December's
fun. In order to get the encouragement not to flag, JT bought some fruit but
did not engage in much conversation. Apparently this was a bind to him too,
for, there was nothing he could do about anything until the totals were done.
There was then some urgency about the work. He wanted to go on but I
wanted to go home. At last we completed in the late afternoon, and JT
thanked me profusely. These were then my last impressions of Junior High
School, for, the next year , I found out that I had passed the external exam
and moved on to Newell High for the Senior Certificate offered by the Joint
Matriculation Board, which, as I said was termed by students as being The "
Just Meant for Bantus" Certificate., for only Black students studied under
that Board which was operated from the offices of UNISA or the University
of South Africa in Pretoria.

Learning To Be, or Learning the Blues

I place this comment here, because it was during the years at junior high that these thoughts became so important, and were further developed during high school years, culminating in present beliefs. They are as important as one's education, for they, in many ways, determine one's destiny as a person. If one never learns how to deal with them earlier in life, it might be too late to do anything about them later, and yet, they stay with one all life through.

This is the part that concerns men and women. As one grows up, one has to come to it and act or not act. It is very true that when my friend named me "Solente", at circumcision, he was right, I knew very little about actual contact between men and women, but I had read quite a bit by then, enough to know that there were dangers I had to find answers before getting into the act of that contact.

The problem of that issue was developed by my teacher later in Zoology, a class I loved as I learned more about the human and science in it. My teacher, a certain Mr. Vinqi, who is now deceased, put it very simply. During physical contact, there is an area where reason and figuring out do not come in. So before you get there, where you lose reason, think clearly what you might be doing. There is your future and there is the future of both participants. Think in terms of the real aftermath. Can you really handle progeny at this stage? What of your future, where would you stand afterwards? Therefore, if you come to the issue of being married, you have to ask yourself the real questions that pertain to your living with the person. Can you handle him or her without the body? Can you deal with who she or he is besides just being a person of a sex? Can we grow together in the direction of really knowing each other, body or no body? One in this area has to think of the movie experience. It is very well to see a lovely attractive movie star, but taking them into your life, how would you start to live with them if you actually knew them as real people and not bodies on the screen? Every person has some kind of baggage they go with: do you I know what baggage this person who looks so attractive has? If then I know, how would I deal with them in the long term?

In order to make this very clear, Mr. Vinqi said to try to understand the trip of the sexual act. For once the chemical trip reaches a certain area in a man's of woman's body, one can as well forget all reason . It does not work to try to be logical then. So before one gets to that stage, one has to know what one is doing, with whom one does it, and what might be strategies in the case of a serious outcome that requires a life commitment. Without this thinking only fools would get involved. Once you reach that stage in the actual act, you do become a fool. No doubt about it. My teacher even said you would even promise to give what you do not have!

It is then not surprising to Bahá'ís that the Guardian of their Faith advised the young to avoid even the holding of hands in courting, for there is a trap underlying that from which they might never be able to escape or extricate themselves.

To illustrate this and bring the point home, Mr. Vinqi told the boys in class to consider that when the cells in their body travel out, they have to reach the area called the "caput epididymis" and the "cauda epididymis", and when they do , they forget about what others told them about avoiding trouble, be- cause by that time they will be in an iron grip they cannot loosen themselves from .At that point, he said, to hear the boy say :" Honey I will buy you Paris on a budget!" is very easy, when in reality that cannot happen.

Later in life I was treated by an Indian doctor, who had done Medicine with my younger brother. We became such friends that he advised in the fol- lowing manner. :Since one is married , one had rights in bed, but must try very hard to avoid antibiotics." I could not, for a start see the relationship. Then he explained that the chemicals seek all the little cells in your body and kill them and do not discriminate between the useful and the dangerous, and one may find after a while, that one cannot produce any progeny! Veiled but clear...

The Pharmacist decorate adverts on medications and they look ever so lovely. But to ask one's self what the drug contains and what it does to the body and what side effects there might be, is very wise. For then one knows what is coming and how to handle what might be adverse. If one decides to kill the Minautor, one has to know how to get out of the labyrinth., otherwise , please do not to make the attempt. For killing that animal, might be minor compared to how to figure ways out. There might not be cause for celebration at all. One movie actor called an event of that kind : "A one night stand" of a show....

My Sociology teacher put it differently. She said that the sex event takes a very few seconds, but not the aftermath if it comes, and that is like rolling dice. There are no guarantees even with protection of sorts.

This would then brings us to the issue of a very angry world, the result of activities that were never well thought out. What then should be the future of an angry world, that no longer can see reason? For being abandoned or being a being of an accident is no pride. In other words .no one wanted you when you came. What then? Do we get surprised? Yet we breed this, and we want the world to be complacent. How many enemies do we create if we consistently do that and keep all queries of our behavior on leash? We have to remember that we are the human race, that the word race, does not really mean "running". Can we sustain this going forwards? If so , until when? Are we not warned now? If we the humans , who live now take no cognizance of that, who do we expect will?

To many of the boys I schooled with, conquering the next beauty become the thrill. Sometimes the reasons for this are that "She flies too high" ,and someone has to make her land. The sad part is that such women have for nine months to be out of action ,and for a long time out of view while they nursed. The boys on the other hand go on to make another conquest. This is the culture of mounting the next hill.

I have experienced this personally as a person in my youth. While you may be interested in one girl , she may fall for the guy who wants to conquer because he talks a, little better than you. After the conquest he then drops out of sight, and sometimes, you who were so keen on the girl have to take care of the leftovers the person has dumped. If one reads some book by Edgar Wallace, one sees how this affects humans in very adverse ways. The slogan we carry that : " It is a man's world", has to somehow be dumped, for it does the human race no good. In fact it is a reversal and not progress. We spend more time wiping the dirt we leave instead of moving forward, and we are proud of this. Many girls I really liked, never got educated, while the boys who took them over, went on to graduate and marry into very lucrative families and became standards of society. I ask myself concerning our standards and values: Where are they gone now? Perhaps, the above is the one reason that created my lonesomeness as a boy and resulted in my taking up a religion that honors both women , children and men. I felt it far safer, and relevant to the issue. Here I could find something to dedicate life to for , it deals with all the issues I had mentioned and went through in my life and offered some solutions I could not but admire.

To claim that such strategies are for the young and growing would be a great fallacy, because it would legitimize an attitude that virtues cease at one point or another in life, and that none is really accountable for any deeds. Virtue stays whether one makes progeny or not. Besides, one has to be an example to the very young we bring up. For, to merely say " Do like I say and not like I do", would be very lamentable. This is the challenge the religionist faces today in the world. In life one has a number of people who might take one as a standard of some kind or another of virtue and when one falls, those persons will surely all fall too. What of our world then?

Those who no longer bear the responsibility of bearing children still remain humans with all the responsibilities entailed in that. They have no intrinsic right to live immoral lives, just because they are old. Besides, what is the age of a mere human in the face of the cosmos that ever existed? Old or young we still are all humans with all the responsibilities that apply to being human. We surely would never like to be called 'inhuman" at a certain age. Each one of us has to have a story to share with the young to caution them on what they might meet in this life, and thus would civilization grow, as a determinant of being civilized, and thereby forming a link to 'survive together". For, what else would civilization entail , but to go on surviving together as a group? None is excused. None can find a true right not to be human in behavior or not to care for the fate of humankind just because they have reached a certain age. Why would that apply?

I would not live another day, if my very life would be a legitimate insult to my progeny! Perhaps, that is being very strong but needs the statement that we must all make an effort to care in one way or another and never leave that care to progeny, for they will have challenges of their own, for sure, for we progress towards whatever we as humans must eventually be , a perfection that would manifest the real image of who and what we are. Each has to try, hard as it might be, and there is no time at which to relent.

Our questions whenever an advice comes are more like:" Who is he to advise us?" That has nothing to do with the logic of any argument. It in itself is an ingrained prejudice, which vehemently claims that we are not guilty of anything. A mother gives advice to the young boy, who soon will declare that " My mother is nothing but a rib". How that happens always amazes me. For, what one is, is actually a multiplication of what must have been the qualities of the original unit. Is one amoeba different from the mother amoebas? It is we the higher order and species that find this distinction necessary. Witness even among locusts, the mother locust is much bigger than the male, and at fertilization she has to carry him on her back! We may find this funny, but do we learn from it, is the question? The locusts, nevertheless , do not seem to separate in a very distinct way into male and females of the species,… we do that. This is what we as humans say, is a lower order. We who have the intelligence to observe it! In one instance in our studies, we honor this, and in another in our lives we do not. That is called consistency?

Viewed in a sense then we are true to ourselves when we are true: We make the vow, we keep it. There is no one who is the true watchdog of the other, for none can tell the true intentions of any other. To be true in a vow then means to be true to o one's own self. We never can account for one the other,… just ourselves. If I detract from my own vow then I detract from what I truly am. Actions are originated from intention. They do not occur on their own. A child plays while learning, and so learns. A grown person relaxes and plays. What then if a grown person decides that all activity is play? Can he or she then say his whole life is play? How really does the person view the self as an irresponsible mass that has no direction?

Many a time in the country I come from, a person plays with another and the other actually dies from the play. Does the issue stand that the other was playing with him when he spoiled the game by dying? Most of the time, such injury accrues and plays a part on both parties, they both in one way or another, do hurt, even if the hurt does not become immediately visible or felt, for the souls and minds do not forget experiences. Sometimes a regret hurts more than the actual action , for it lasts longer and sometimes hard no remedy until, one someday finds a way of looking at it otherwise than negative, as a life experience maybe, but does that take in both sides of the equation? Just because one finds some sort of justification for an action does not force the injured party to abide by a decision that the other comes upon. Perhaps even into the distance separating the two later ,the issue is still hurting. So to say " I am happy with myself ",may not mean much ,if out there is someone hurting form my action without relenting. There is no case of : The end justifies the means. That, would be irrelevant and very hurtful. Much more should one consider the intention than the end. To be accidentally right is not viable. One learns very little in the experience, for it never was it their experience. The intention was never there. How then does one celebrate a victory never won? In plain words to be accidentally right with bad intentions, serves no good purpose for the individual, but to have a good intention that fails, it still remains a good intention and not punishable in essence. That is my thinking. If they ask :" What were you thinking?", I could explain.

It is a wisdom to teach these things to the young at an early age and in the initial building of life, for one cannot begin building a house by erecting a roof. It is the laying of each brick that matters so much. It is not even wise for one to talk loud on democracy on a pedestal when one's life at home is based on dictatorial authority. A social order built on bad ethics and morals is guaranteed to collapse. The life of individuals will reflect the success of the civilization. Survival of the whole project depends on the dedication of each doing their part in the whole.

> *For in him are potentially revealed all the attributes and names of God to a degree that no other created being hath excelled or surpassed. All these names and attributes are applicable to him. Even as He hath said: "Man is My mystery, and I am his mystery."*
> *(Baha'u'llah, Gleanings from the Writings of Baha'u'llah,*
> *p. 177)*

Fascinating Books of the Time

Below are some of the books I read and found so fascinating, as I grew up into a high school student at Newell High, New Brighton, Port Elizabeth, South Africa. In many ways these books shaped my attitude in life, and led to the investigation of many avenues, social and otherwise, in time.

On Morality by Francis Bacon
(scanned from cover of book)

This was a book which surprised me by dealing with moral behavior, which , after being momentarily debunked by my student friends at college, took on a grave importance in shaping both my moral priorities and social involvement , after much meditation, and , of course , much traveling in the world of mistakes. For through it, I soon realized that no social order could stand without collapsing if it were populated by persons of no moral or ethical code. That naturally led to religion.

On a political angle by Father Huddleston
(cover scanned by author from original)

This book written as it was by a person of religious belief, came to be more of a handbook, for many of my friends who got into a political careers. It was offered to me to read, but I never got too far with it, though I appreciated it much. The reason was that ,at that time in my life I had never seen persons of political inclination immune from some kind of immoral behavior. Politics then did not become my priority in life. Mine was a search for a proper social order that could help man and the African involved , survive without self destruction. To me that did not depend on political stance but on human behavior in general. Thus morals and ethics became more of a priority. The books: Holy Bible, Qur'an , Baghavad Gita, abound in that. Thus , they became my prime concern. For civilization has to do with getting together in order to survive together, and religions, a term that mean s 'to put together' does just that. Hence all civilizations have that incorporated as a guidance for behavior. I had seen in my youth many organizations fall apart because the participants could not adhere to policies that respected one another, or one another's properties. That was not then for me. Such fallacies carried to extremes make life very unsafe and difficult to handle or live. For how does one live in comfort when lacking all trust for neighbors? I can then be blamed of non-participation , but would avoid being one living in foolishness .I found that to be below the dignity of the human, and one recognized to be of a more sophisticated intelligence. I revere fighting for the rights of all as a human family, but do find behaviors one towards the other appalling to say the least. Liberty of man from the fetters of oppression is very good and commendable, but what if the human is tied up with so much immorality that the human can no longer be deemed human in behavior? At the very onset of interest in political activity in my town, we also watched the degradation of human standards of moral living. My friends at my college always referred to their behavior ,if immoral , as being caused by being " oppressed". This became an excuse for many behaviors which were untoward for a person of some culture , education and moral norms. I could then never become a proper politician, for in politics I would have to change the stance of what I defend with the change in the direction of the vote. Where will my consistency be then? How do I find credibility for myself as purely a person and not a political cog? The slogan is :" Man if born free by everywhere is in chains". It strikes me that the worse chains are those we set on ourselves, that do not present us as thinking humans, but those centered on some material goal. To me that is a limited goal, for, I know not what placed man on the planet, or whence he goes when he departs. Why would he have a dream in his sleep and find it a reality in a few years? Where was man? Who does he speak to when he shuts up and thinks of ideas? It is very much harder to change how people think than to determine how they will be governed or will govern, for the latter action depends of the former not the other way around. The priority of how to behave matters in the equation.

On why to be, by Corelli.
(cover scanned by author from original)

I found this book in my father's shed. It was torn but still readable. In the area I found it were my grandfather's books. My grandfather had been a priest in the Presbyterian Church, and lies buried in far off Lesotho, because he could not abide the rejection of his Xhosa wife by his Zulu relatives. I never met him, for he passed on when my father was only ten years in age but I do have a picture of him in my house and so have my relatives.

Reading this book came at the same time when I was trying to decide what to do with African beliefs as related to my religious belief. First of all, I wondered just how heaven was divided. Did we have sections for different Gods? Or are we all worshipping the same God? Why then would my ancestors have the right to depart from there and haunt me in my dreams about what might or might not happen? What right did they have that they did not in this world.? How loose or controlled was then the Next World? The whole issue clashed with what I thought was accepted reasoning! Ghosts wandering around at will, with a lot of evil spirits? Who was in control? It was in reading this book that I finally came to the conclusion that , if God wanted one to learn anything from one or cause one to act in any way in accordance with His Will, at any appearance ,He would not try to scare one out of one's wits, but make one understand what He wanted one to do. Why would He scare one and what is to be gained by that? Thus it is I found that belief could only be by reasoning and not by being scared. Being scared has no guarantees that I would stay in belief. Also in this book, I learned how powerful the human can be and what power lies hidden in him After many years of wandering, belief in a Deity began to be a reality. The whole idea of being was in control of behavior, and how one saw the universe as related to a world we do not see but perceive. I was adamant in thinking that religion was not a scare. It had to be something I can relate to, something tangible and worth working towards, not perhaps in anyway physical, but very real. Coupled with Bacon's thoughts on morality, this was sobering. The one problem was what moral code did one have to adopt. I had departed from fear of hell, and was looking at existence ,perhaps of a different type, but existence, whether I died or lived in this world. I would go in depth with that in explanations now that I am adult, but feel it can wait. Let it suffice to say that towards the end of that sort of reasoning, I met the religion called the Bahá'í Faith, which helped a lot in that direction. Suffice it to say that I viewed worship as an action that is based, not on just fear, but reason.

On debunking witchcraft by Dennis Wheately and opting for science and religion
(VCR Tape cover scanned by author from original)

Reading this book by Dennis Wheatley, was quite an experience! That one reading led me to also read one by the same author called:" Three Inquisitive People". In one way it made me look at life as being very mysterious .In another it changed my thinking about many issues especially in African life, or in consideration of what the world has come to know as Alchemists .I came to understand the meanings of two words " Black Magic" and "White Magic". These are two entities I needed to understand. One reason for that was that my father was himself an herbalist. I came to understand that "White Magic" had to do with using herbs and other chemicals to cure sicknesses, it had nothing to do with color but the effect of light, for then one can actually see. "Black Magic", on the other hand has to do with using herbs and other chemicals to kill life. It dawned on me that the Alchemists were the ancient scientists who wanted to find the cause and end of things. Their antiquated ways have now been superseded by what we call science. It also became a truism, after reading the story, that belief in God was the greatest protection one could have. No matter how great a force that is on this earth, it cannot go beyond what the Maker of this earth can do. If evil spirits or whatever, wanted a dominance over my person, they could not do this without His permission, for was He then not the Creator of all? In the story a verse from the Bible kept occurring which is from the Psalms " Even though I walk through the valley of death, I shall fear no evil". Why would I fear anything that did not really control the universe? Why would I, who has the designation of being the image of that Deity live in fear of such? I do know that poison can kill anybody, but somebody has to decide to administer that before I can die; so that could be attributed to their decision and not magic in the concoction they prepare. If I die , and am a believer, I then die to the Lord and not the one that caused my death. Life then does not become our game; it is His game. I live a mere eighty years and the universe persists! Then do give me any evil spirit and I would tell them that! This stance helped me survive living in "roundavels" in rural South Africa and Swaziland without ever beholding any evils spirits! I lived in Africa for over forty years and never saw anything the like of what they tell me I should see on reaching the Western World!

Teaching my Faith in rural Africa was a pleasure, come night or daylight. This of course does not mean that there are no minds that think nothing but death of another, no, they abound in all societies, and take up many a mode. The greatest magic one can find is in religion, for it can change an attitude completely, and cause one possessed of no power to achieve the insurmountable. Think of Christianity and how Jesus without a home or possessions, conquered the world, such that many centuries later people still live by His Law. Behold and wonder! Look at Each of what Bahá'ís call Manifestations of the virtues of God, how they lived and how they triumphed. The world itself is in darkness just as the universe is and probably would remain so, and were it not for the shining of Those Souls . It would remain in darkness and not know the Will of its Lord, and what the Suns of His reality symbolized!

The 'fear of God' spoken of in the Holy Books, appears to be a different kind of fear altogether. It causes one to face all calamities with courage; if helps man to withhold his hand from doing evil; It helps man to realize there is no power or strength except in God: **"I verily proclaim: There is no power nor strength except in God, the Help in Peril ,the Self Subsisting"**(Gems of Divine Mysteries, p. 76)

"In addressing the people of Constantinople Bahá'u'lláh makes His own position clear to them:"

> **Whoso hath known God shall know none but Him, and he that feareth God shall be afraid of no one except Him, though the powers of the whole earth rise up and be arrayed against him.**
> **(Adib Taherzadeh, The Revelation of Baha'u'llah v 2, p. 318)**

I can but quote the two examples here of that fear:

> **WORSHIP thou God in such wise that if thy worship lead thee to the fire, no alteration in thine adoration would be produced, and so likewise if thy recompense should be paradise. Thus and thus alone should be the worship which befitteth the one True God. Shouldst thou worship Him because of fear, this would be unseemly in the sanctified Court of His presence, and could not be regarded as an act by thee dedicated to the Oneness of His Being. Or if thy 78 gaze should be on paradise, and thou shouldst worship Him while cherish-**

ing such a hope, thou wouldst make God's creation a partner with Him, notwithstanding the fact that paradise is desired by men.

(The Bab, Selections from the Writings of the Bab, p. 77)

God testifieth to the unity of His Godhood and to the singleness of His own Being. On the throne of eternity, from the inaccessible heights of His station, His tongue proclaimeth that there is none other God 87 but Him. He Himself, independently of all else, hath ever been a witness unto His own oneness, the revealer of His own nature, the glorifier of His own essence. He, verily, is the All-Powerful, the Almighty, the Beauteous.

He is supreme over His servants, and standeth over His creatures. In His hand is the source of authority and truth. He maketh men alive by His signs, and causeth them to die through His wrath. He shall not be asked of His doings and His might is equal unto all things. He is the Potent, the All-Subduing. He holdeth within His grasp the empire of all things, and on His right hand is fixed the Kingdom of His Revelation. His power, verily, embraceth the whole of creation. Victory and overlordship are His; all might and dominion are His; all glory and greatness are His. He, of a truth, is the All-Glorious, the Most Powerful, the Unconditioned.

(Baha'u'llah, Prayers and Meditations by Baha'u'llah, p. 86)

ABDUL BAHA: When the devotees of religion cast aside their dogmas and ritualism, the unification of religion will appear on the horizon and the verities of the holy books will become unveiled. In these days superstitions and misunderstandings are rife; when these are relinquished the sun of unity shall dawn.

(Abdu'l-Baha, Divine Philosophy, p. 153)

"Religion must be the cause of affection. It must be a joy-bringer. If it become the cause of difference, it were better to banish it. Should it become the source of hatred, or warfare, it were better that it should not exist. If a remedy produce added illness, it were far better to discard the remedy. A religion which does not conform with the postulates of science is merely superstition.

(Abdu'l-Baha, Divine Philosophy, p. 82)

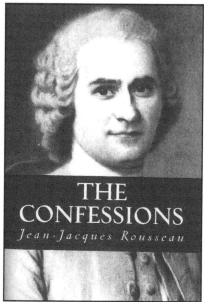

On liberty of ,mind and freedom of spirit.
(cover scanned by author from original)

When I entered high school at Newell High in 1960, the first class in modern history we had was on the French Revolution, and not on the American War of Independence that my big sister had to start with before my day. This class happened at a poignant time in South Africa, because this was the very height of revolutionary ideas then. Discussions were not only on democracy and its slogan of "One man one vote" but on communism and what each stood for. There was however a clearer idea at that time of what democracy was and very little trickling through about communism, except that Fidel Castro was in it and nobody in South Africa's government wanted it. As students we wanted to know. So the French revolution was somewhat a good start. It took many years before I could understand that communism was merely that the government controlled industry and all other beneficial activities in a country, and resultant enforcement of such ideologies , lacking also in any religious belief. This probably could not work with many Africans for their life on earth was centered on life with ancestors in another world; so it would have been hard to give up ancestral belief for a belief in mere land.

In talking of that revolution at school, we had also to distinguish later between that and the industrial revolution, which, though doing the same thing we were but was not actually alike in activity.

In the study of the revolution three names of so-called "Free Thinkers" were observed, and these were Jean Jacques Rousseau , Montesquieu and Diderot.

It is not as if Jean Jacques Rousseau was a favorite that I have his picture. It is because he is the only one whose history I read while I was a first year student at Fort Hare University College in 1963

I do not at approve of Confessions as such as a Bahá'í, because in that Faith, sins can only be confessed to God alone and not to other sinners that we all are. The only reason then I was attached to that reading was that as a Bahá'í , I could not join a political group but was known to be able to carry a point and argue it, hence many times I was more or less referred to as a "free thinker", that term to us, indicating one who can think but is not attached to any organization.

The other reason that, besides finding the book on confessions by Rousseau, in the library, was that I was in those days more wont to discuss with older women when it came to serious ideas, instead of younger ones of my own age. It interested me that Rousseau was known to have affairs with older women instead of young ones. That way I felt relevant. The truth is that, though I studied the book , outside of a syllabus, I never did complete reading it, but found it necessary to buy it twice for my library , both in South Africa and in the United States. I found what I read of Rousseau's history interesting to read about. Coupled with what I read at the time, which was "Les Miserables" by Victor Hugo, it made sense. One can point out that those were the days following the "Treason Trial" in South Africa, a very hot subject of the times. Also at that point we had had a visit in Africa of a man who was the Secretary to the United nations , who on visiting spoke of the "winds of change" in Africa.; that also following the Mau Mau wars of the fifties. The reason the topic of Fidel Castro came up was because, even though from a smaller country, he had a say in the political field of the time. The Africans were at that point looking for someone to relate to who was in international politics, as they found themselves on their own, without the Western World in the stand against apartheid. One has just to study those times, and the occurrences which attended them to have any understanding of that. I have been asked in the United States if I was in the struggle in South Africa and what part I or my Faith played in it , by persons who have never been there and who do not actually know firsthand the situation of that country, and I had then been blamed of not having taken a responsible part therein. Rejecting that accusation I still find that futile, because the state of affairs in South Africa has not even reached the state of being understood , and yet it has pertained since the time on of the World Wars. Therefore, to a certain extent, my ears are deaf to all accusations, and to all claims of sympathy, as it is the way of this world to allow a dangerous situation to persist, aid it, and then feel very sorry that it took place only later!

This state of affairs was witnessed at one of the Xhosa wars when they were encouraged to fight by someone who never turned up at the battle field: a very well-known story. This was deplored and is part of the idiom today..: the coming of the help that never arrives. It is as if one kills another intentionally and then tearfully cries that they are very sorry one died. Can they raise one up? Is their end achieved ? Yes!

I shall then desist from writing on Rousseau, for coming to that subject has many unpleasant memories attached and this is the time we should talk peace, before we destroy the only home we have, the Planet.. It is hoped that past events are teachers and that we should learn from and not repeat the same.

Bahá'u'lláh has written:" **Glory is not his who loves his country but his who loves mankind"**

This to me indicates that national patriotism is no longer viable in the face of the impending destruction of life on a planet. I have seen the movie : " The Day After "and do not wish for us what is in it, for how are you to claim a home when all is gone? What piece of land will be safe for humans? Shakespeare has also written:" Let me not to the marriage of true minds admit impediments" , if that is what we want to for ourselves and our future. That is the reason I work for the safety ways for humankind, and not for any creed or color. If then, the ideas of that revolution are merely European, what then is that to humankind? Are we distancing ourselves from humankind... and standing , where, I ask? All that we find on this planet was found out by mankind and none of us are foreigners there. If not, then I do wish I knew the indigenous persons of this planet. If it blows up , we all go, civilization or no civilization. Who will want to claim responsibility for that and then claim to be a responsible being? Will it matter when none are there? Perhaps as a question in the Next World…?

> That one indeed is a man who, today, dedicateth himself to the service of the entire human race. The Great Being saith: Blessed and happy is he that ariseth to promote the best interests of the peoples and kindreds of the earth. In another passage He hath proclaimed: It is not for him to pride himself who loveth his own country, but rather for him who loveth the whole world. The earth is but one country, and mankind its citizens.
>
> (Baha'u'llah, Gleanings from the Writings of Baha'u'llah, p. 250)

On the angle of avoiding the bias and the clash of religions
(cover scanned by author from original)

In this clash of principles from different religions of different times and strategies, one perceives that, though the merchant is not quite right in holding such a grudge for so long, there is yet something to be learned from the statements Shakespeare attributes to him.

In one he says:" I am not bound to please you with my answers", which is right. How can one ask you a question and expect that you will give that which pleases that person? How then can one answer that? We know now that one of the laws of the Torah is an eye for an eye, and we have forgotten that people were brought up on that principle, for a while..

If we claim righteousness, let us turn that to other Faiths. How do we cause ourselves to abide by those principles also and still be right? It slips us that justice is relative, and so are laws that preserve humankind. They depend much on time and circumstance of humankind. How does one account for a man who kills ten persons, and is hanged. Does that bring back the ten? Rather it is a warning to the living that this was not right, but cannot be reversed. We have to have justice, but let us sometime or other look at the times, and find the Divine injunction for that time. It is not our game , but His. Always He changes it in view of what we have to face. How many times has the earth turned and buried everything under? Yet we feel we absolutely will always be here! Is it our universe?

I can understand my teacher in school for refusing to take this play as an example of a true tragedy. Were it not for the accidental moments of the story, one would easily point out a setup! I am African and have been setup many times and found to be guilty over very predictable circumstance. I do not talk blame but accept the nature of humans, for none are perfect. I would, they would attempt to obey the Law of a Book with more diligence.

Events of modern time can bear me out, we have done this many times and remained very innocent and uncommitted to the result, when they are actually known in detail before they even occurred.

I have listened to this play on audio, because, on the celebration of a Shakespeare Day at university, a part of this play came up, and was staged by students.

It calls to mind my little brother and his quip about a cowboy movies that I shall not even explain. Very innocent but guilty totally! A little voice asks me how vendetta is based. My little brother asked me who we cheered for when we had cowboys and Indians on the show in olden cowboy movies. When I answered that it probably was the cowboys. He then remarked that we knew not what we were doing...and that is a fact... How then do I cheer for Antonio or Shylock? The matter remains unresolved and needs different eyes...

2. O SON OF SPIRIT!

The best beloved of all things in My sight is Justice; turn not away therefrom if thou desirest Me, and neglect it not that I may confide in thee. By its aid thou shalt see with thine own eyes and not through the eyes of others, and shalt know of thine own knowledge and not through the knowledge of thy neighbor. Ponder this in thy heart; how it behooveth thee to be. Verily justice is My gift to thee and the sign of My loving-kindness. Set it then before thine eyes.

(Baha'u'llah, The Arabic Hidden Words)

Activities of Youth

A Deviation

Before going into this issue a word on my sisters has to be inserted. This does not mean that my experience with the people of female sex is dependent upon knowing them, however some parts of my experience are reaped from them, ,as they, as my sisters, remain the closest people I knew of that sex, in my youth.. It seems proper and fair to make mention of where they stand.

My sisters

Thus far, I have only barely written about many of the women who aided me on the way to becoming a being in the world. It is said that for a being to have meaning that being must have a becoming. What I am today and will have a becoming, whether I am on the earthly plane or not. This is a belief I adhere to and that gives my life a chance to continue in hope and not in anxiety..

There are two persons in my life who are close to my beginnings and they have to be mentioned . They are my two sisters. Both of them in one way or another have been companions my on this journey. They are women who subsisted despite many disadvantages on the way, in a land where their worth was, for many years not recognized except for being marriageable, and bringing up children.

My eldest sister grew to be a hospital matron, and graduate from university with a degree in nursing. I have told her that her action of worship was in her work. As Bahá'í I believe this entirely. My big sister was for many years a nurse in the pediatric ward and knows many a child who has passed through her ward and her clinics. As the eldest sister she had to act as a guardian to all her younger siblings. This meant having to learn , at an early age, how to cook , care for children ,and care for a home, as both her parents worked all day in the city. I could write a book about her but have chosen here to make a mere mention of her. As a believer, I know that all her work is known to her Creator, and can say no more, except where I wish to prove a point on a theme I might choose. Here I make the point that she has mothered many a child she was not even related to, and got educated despite the conditions of her upbringing. The little township of New Brighton offered no safety for boys how much less then did it attempt to offer any extended care for any girl? Besides that her culture offered less of an advantage of survival to a girl than a boy. Perhaps African culture did not bury girls alive at birth, but they did far less to give them any availability of better conditions of subsistence. At least, this was the case in my time as a youth and as an adult.

Picture of Eucinia Thobeka Melane (from private collection). As a Matron in a hospital My eldest sister , who worked in the Pediatrics wards of the hospital, attaining in later years the status of a Matron in the hospital, after privately studying for a degree in Nursing. Both sisters still reside in Port Elizabeth, but my younger, travels most of the time to different countries giving some talks on Economics.

My youngest sister was the last born child of my parents, and I was twelve when she was born. The task I performed in bringing her up, is perhaps more than equaled by what she did to bring up her nephews and nieces in the family. As she grew up ,when there were already grown children in the family, and most of what she got in teaching came from those who were older than her . Even though cared for adequately by both parents, she was given less care as, by then many problems had to be solved more for the grown than the younger children. Regardless of that her strength of character , growing up in New Brighton propelled her on her way. Today she is a university professor, and has travelled the world for her profession in Economics. I cannot say much of her except to point out that in my religion teachers take a very high position as they, like mothers, are first educators of children.

Dr. Eileen Noxolo Mazibuko.
This perhaps when she first graduated in Economics, she has by now gone on to attain a doctorate in her field at the Nelson Mandela Metropolitan University in Port Elizabeth, South Africa.(from private collection)

It is therefore clear that the education of girls is of far greater consequence than that of boys. This fact is extremely important, and the matter must be seen to with the greatest energy and dedication.

('abdu'l-Bahá, The Compilation of Compilations vol. I, p. 285)

My Years of Youthfulness

Having dealt with my two sisters I then turn to the task of association with the opposite sex, outside the home and how this played out in my life. Though I had good friends who were girls in my neighborhood, my first serious 'affair' was later in life when I entered junior high school. Most of my earlier years were spent in other boyhood activities. Prominent among those activities was in trying to understand many themes spoken of in my family about the afterlife and being 'a good child'. One has to remember that my mother had already expressed a wish to which I wanted to rise up, that I become a minister of religion in my adult life, as my grandfather had been..

Junior High and an affair

At junior high, I had gone to some trouble to hide the fact that I had a girl-friend, but my mother sensed it. With this in mind she issued a warning which was so direct it was embarrassing . Her words were:" Do not sleep with her. She will get pregnant, and you will have to leave school and work for your child!" This sounds innocent enough but it was a big issues for a boy at seventeen. It was only when I turned twenty that my mother openly encouraged me to find a girlfriend. Even though we disagreed in the method to adopt achieving this, for by then, times had changed and so had wooing strategies. Now that I am grown up, I appreciate her advice much. I hope by now, where she is, she finds reason to understand why we disagreed on the matter. She had been giving me what had been advised her in her youth, and, unfortunately, I saw the matter from the rock 'n' roll era, in different perspective. I was to struggle with this issue for many a year. In my day, I believed that one had to sense love and not negotiate it, and in hers there had been a mixture of both. However, one had to progress towards marriage once one had definitely chosen and was in love. Regardless of that she taught me that there was an age when one had to start looking for a partner, but one does not have to start too early and forget the responsibilities of learning, schooling and working in the home. This latter part has been inculcated into my progeny

A Preamble

By the year I reached junior high, I had had no real girlfriend, but had had girls as friends that I appreciated and actually loved. The first was a girl who was always dressed in pink, in my kindergarten class. We never mentioned anything serious but I liked her. I knew she lived outside of New Brighton and a place called Daasie Kraal, near Korsten ,where my parents originally resided before being moved to New Brighton. Maureen was a sweet girl, but we never talked much. I could not even get the courage to go to her and tell her how I felt. Thus, by the time I got into higher primary I no longer could see her.

Ethel lived with an uncle who was a Caretaker in a cemetery. The cemetery was located near the plant Ford Motor Company , near the area called Neave Township in Korsten. It occurred years later to me that my grandmother had been buried in that cemetery. I have tried to locate the grave long distance, but it would take a long time to trace. It is something my youngest brother is working on. The area lies outside where I grew up in New Brighton, but many times had my father in moments of frustration referred to his mother as lying in a grave in Korsten, This was the only possible burial place for Africans living in Korsten at that time.

It is painful to know that I had been so near and yet so far. For I had been there in efforts to try and see Ethel, unsuccessfully on Sundays in that area. The problem was that no young man was allowed to blatantly visit a young girl, unless marriage was imminent in those days. All I could do was circle the place and hope against hope to see Ethel. Only once was I ever inside that home, when elder people were home. Once on a night after an event at school I boarded the bus with Ethel to her home as I did on days after school. I was caught in the act by her older cousin who gave me a hard time. Nevertheless, with all that time after school, Ethel and I avoided too much intimacy .I was always conscious of jeopardizing my schooling and hers. It was a sad moment to part but by then I had lost all reason to be intimate and was more concerned with finding myself. I tended to study instead of dating. This is the time I finally got interested in the Bahá'í Religion. However , it took me another two years after junior high school before I could make a commitment of becoming a Bahá'í. My affair with Ethel lasted about a year and a half and by the time we parted, much against her desire, I was I a different school doing the last two classes of high school. I loved Ethel but after junior high I was a changed person and desire more to study than play. Hence some people would remark about myself becoming a dull boy for not playing. I could not honestly account for that change. Over December of '59 I found I had lost interest in even being in rock 'n roll! This was , however , an important time of my life and I took time to go into the detail of that time in an earlier book. i.e. "This Side Up"

The Detail of The Love Affair

In 2010 a book was published with the title:' This Side Up". In this effort the author attempted to establish some of the ideologies and events that led to his becoming a Bahá'í, but , as it transpired this tale did nothing in detailing how much the author was at all committed to a search for a partner, in his later years, nor did it mention any of those many blunders he had as a young man. An esteemed college friend who is now a doctor in Physics vowed he would not read such an autobiography, until and unless the tales of an amorous nature, which he knows must exist in the time he has known the author, have all been touched upon. The author has then decided he will try to satisfy this desire, not to just get anyone to read the story, but to prove that he has above all tried not to fake his life story, and that all events are actually a reality of what he has lived through.

I shall, therefore state that from the time I entered college until the year I left, I did not have a a girlfriend at college i.e. 1963 to 1964. I cannot try to prove this but can present my life for any investigation in that direction. Outside a short affair I had outside of college in my youth, which lasted less than a year, and the friendship I had a with a school friend who had taken up a nursing profession in another town, I had no serious love acquaintances which would could concern anyone, or had proven to have lasted more than that , at least a month on the whole.

Ethel

In my youth at junior high school I ventured to have a love affair with a school friend which lasted about a year and a half. The girls name was Ethel and her African name was Thobeka, It may be curious that both her initials and actually the African name were those o f my eldest sister. However, this was not planned. I saw a face and liked it. I shall recount how that occurred for the record so no mistake can be made now or in the future. The following is more or less a repetition with more detail of how exactly I met Ethel.

This occurred in my third year at junior high. It was during the period between sessions , when we waited results for the different mid-year tests. We were then not really occupied except to loll around the school while papers were being corrected and graded. I had no girlfriend and most of my friends had. The part that teased the other fellows in my class was that I was a sort of a rock star in the school, and a great rock 'n roll fan. My repertoire at that time included some Presley songs , including" Wear My Ring Around Your Neck" and "Teddy Bear". Of course we would also do "Gum Drop", "Ko-komo" and "Two Hearts", some songs by the Crew Cuts and Mills Brothers, which were popular among the fellows in my school.

A friend I knew , during this interim period, asked me if I would like to show him a girl I liked and he would get us introduced. I did not know Ethel, but had seen her around, and I so I zeroed in on her. We were introduced, but she was not interested in a love affair. Over a period of a whole two hours I managed between me and the friend to persuade her that this would be no problem . When she did accept this deal offered, I had to walk her home. She lived outside of the township and had to board a bus to go home. This walk became an every-school-day thing, until I found out I was being tracked by another fellow. It soon turned out that this was a circumcised man who had been in love with the girl and he schooled in nearby Newell High. Getting rid of him took some doing, and I had to act tough. But then he soon gave up and went for another girl in the school.

Thobeka and I had this ongoing love affair which sometimes ended up with me taking her right up to where she lived. We had no problem with initial intimacy but anything serious was not in sight, partly because I was not at all initialized into that, though she admitted having tried it. When she did even-tually express a desire to go into a deeper relationship, I decided not to venture into that, because I had already been warned by my mother not to attempt leaving school too early, and that the one thing that would achieve that destination if I wanted it, would be to cause a girl to be pregnant a. By this time , my mother had perceived that I had someone in the opposite sex in my life. No one should ask me how, and when they do I shall refuse to tell! But a taste of the truth was that I had a girl's girdle in my wardrobe, and someone must have seen this or perceived perfume in it!

My affair with Ethel ended when I reached high school at Newell High, because , by that time, I had left rock 'n roll, and took on a serious note of life, while she saw me as a the rock star and no more. I then drifted away. She on the other hand, wrote me countless times to try and return and I never returned any answers.

In the next two years , I tried for another serious love affair but that did not last because I found out that the girl was also in love with a friend of my little brother, and that to me was below dignity, that is, going for little brother's friends' girl. I left that too. After that two years I met that girl's mother, who sadly told me that she became pregnant through some fellow who did not marry her, and instead pursued a college students' s career. That angered me, but by then I was on a different tack in life altogether. On reaching college I was told the same girl had mentioned my name while schooling in another town. I attempted to visit her by hitch-hiking to school and failed to meet with her. That sealed the affair then, even if I had any desire to revive it.

At high school I had a friend schooling in a far way city, but I would see her twice in that time, during her leave. When the affair took on a serious note on her completion of studies, I did not wish for any commitments, the reason being that I was broke and could not really support a family or even pay her dowry. Also I was suffering a disappointment with myself for not having completed the degree I wished to start at a college.

It was two years after that I then decided I wished to marry, but that story comes later.

> **Strive, then, to abide, heart and soul, with each other as two doves in the nest, for this is to be blessed in both worlds.**
> (Abdu'l-Baha, Selections from the Writings of Abdu'l-Baha, p. 122)

School Friends at Junior High and Comments

A Picture of Rosemary Sala with her library helpers at Cowan Secondary in the 50s. (L-R Eunice Fikiswa Kabi (Magongo); Rosemary Sala, Robert Mazibuko, Dr, Angelinah Yaliwe Jiya (Bomela). The fourth helper, Daniel Budaza was not present at the time of the photo.(author's collection)

On extreme left is Eunice who later became a trained staff nurse at the Livingstone, now retired. Eunice or Fiikswa and I were very close friends as we did the first year in high school at Newell later together before she went on to Johannesburg to do a course in nursing. She is the one girl I could have spent life with , but she got married just when I had thought of it, only too late. By the time I got to her house to let her know and check up on her, it was on her engagement party day. We, as old retired persons are still in touch by telephone and email since her husband's death which occurred on my arrival in the United States. On my left if Angelinah, with whom I schooled at Fort Hare in later years. Angelinah became engaged to Dr. Zin Jiya, and both were professors at Fort Hare, Jiya in Physics and Angelinah in Education. The one event that saddened Rosemary about Angelinah was a visit she had planned to the United States, and which Rosemary had looked forward to on the possibility of her making contact with a friend she had in the there. However, the contact with the friend failed. And.. What went wrong I am not to know, for I got the message from Rosemary second hand and never mentioned this to Angelinah. However, the failure saddened Rosemary.

The one person missing in the picture is Daniel Budaza, who though the nephew of a teacher at Cowan, did not go far in education, but decided to work and help his family, though offered a chance of study by Rosemary at her expense. When he failed to accept the offer, I was then asked to be that person to take that advantage an event which I accepted with mixed feelings, for Daniel was my friend. Later Daniel and I found mates in marriage, and we both lived in the poorer area of New Brighton, until his divorce. I subsequently moved away from that area to an area in New Brighton which had better priced housing and lost touch with Daniel.. By then I was a Quality Controller in a well known Pharmaceutical company in Port Elizabeth and could afford to move.

Meeting with Angelinah as an adult

*Robert at home of Jiyas' in Fort Hare University,
recovering from police questioning, and visiting*

The above picture taken during a visit of recuperation. I had had a questioning by police, at which time my doctor, Dr. Manga, sent me out of town with a prescription of Valium to be taken every day, for the questioning had not been easy. It would be, when you wished to be very brief in every answer, and mention very little under pressure! At the time I was also divorcing and wanted time away anyway. Besides, at the time I had a very brief friendship which threatened to be an affair with a girl who was schooling in Fort Hare. It was a friendship which refused to flower in any way and I eventually had to abandon nursing it towards anything serious. I never married the girl, because she was also committed elsewhere. By the time I was free to marry I was on my own, looking for a partner.

By this time in the late seventies, both Jiyas' were professors at the university and I was their guest. It is perhaps a shame that Jiya, the man , never understood that Angelina was my good friend and no more. Perhaps our being both under the great concern of Rosemary Sala gave the wrong impression. At this time, I am only in touch with Zin Jiya, my Iona House friend(both of us were housed at Iona House, Fort hare, for a year) , and very little with Angelinah; in fact I only hear about her now and then from Zin or Sipokazi Mampe (Mtsaka) my cousin, who lives near them in East London. Sipokazi was the one person who enabled me to keep in touch with friends at my college after I left. Since she was from east London where Jiya was born it was only natural that we should be in touch.

It should be noted that Sipokazi was one cousin I communicated with when I had a problem of housing in my attempts to obtain a visa to enter the United States. Even though she was a neighbor of the Jiyas', I chose her for as a confidant. Today we are still in touch.

Cousin, Sipokazi

In the eighties Sipokazi and her husband visited me many times in Port Elizabeth as relatives from Fort Hare.

The good part is that I was invited by Sipokazi to live with her when I was applying for a visa s to enter the United States, at a very dangerous time in New Brighton, as no one was keen to support one who intended to marry a White girl at the time of the riots of that period. I stayed with Sipokazi until a call from my sister in Port Elizabeth informed me that lady called Judy had called from Cape Town to inform me that I could go for an appointment for the visa, at which point I had to hurry to Port Elizabeth and get funds organized for that trip to Cape Town and the visa! Sipokazi's invitation and the free ticket to East London she had offered me helped a lot in this critical period of waiting.

She was instrumental in my learning of the passing of my brother, Donald in the early 2000's for she knew he lived in East London. Also when I attended that funeral of my brother , it was she who made the arrangements for housing at her home until I left to visit Port Elizabeth, after the funeral. In this sense, she is a valued cousin.

Sipokazi Mampe, graduating in Social Science at Fort Hare U niversity with cousin Kholeka Nondlwana and Sipokazi's son, Sishe.

Details of High School Changes: A Comment

The time of high school at Newell High from 1960 to 1961, was probably the greatest time of my school life. However, it has to be known that, at this time, Newell High did not have such a great reputation as a school, but it was the only daytime school I could go to if I could not afford a boarding school. One had no options if one was not one of the richer families, and that is exactly where my family stood. At this time I had much help from a school teacher who knew me from Cowan secondary. I shall not go into the story of how I was taught by her, but perhaps later, will limit story of to how I shifted into coining my way to an ideology I took up for myself and my future.

The name of the teacher was Grace Makhuluma, my English teacher at junior and high schools. Grace a great disciplinarian was nicknamed by the boys in my class as " The Girl", because she had no known boyfriend, and was very strict about moral principles. In her way she was more a nun than an ordinary person, which is the reason she got the name she had among the boys, for nuns were said to be girls who did not know much about the other things the boys thought were valued in life, which of course is a great fallacy. As evidence of my belief, up till today I hold on my computer, a picture of "Mother Teresa" who passed some years ago. She had shown that what most men and women would die for, was not worth as much as human life, and human dignity on the planet. To me that is greater effort to be respected than having children, for many have them but fail to make any worthy persons of them ,and rely on the chances of the world to educate, when , in fact ,they had brought them to this world , with not so much as a serious thought of what the consequence might be; just for a mere second's enjoyment ,which brought them no peace of mind, at all after it has been done. This disgusting behavior is regarded as the pinnacle of earthly existence! I fail to see how it can be, when it has brought such anger and disgust to many children born of an unwanted results . For, they ask : " What was the purpose, if I was not?". When the mother who brought me up instilled this issue into my mind it took shape in my refusal to have any child until I would be ready to do something about marriage and bringing that child up; and that is not a boast, just a statement of fact. These were part of the reasons that made even circumcision so abhorrent, for I saw it a passport to irregular and irresponsible behavior by those who felt they were entitled to cause pregnancies on any girl , jut by virtue of being circumcised men, as if animals do not have sex in the same way as they do and still care for their young in a much more better way. For, do chickens lay eggs without a nest? It churns the blood when this kind of irresponsibility of bringing young to the planet, without a single plan of their security in mind, just because of nothing but an emotional and passionate urge! Grace stood this in her youth, and only came to an active participation in marriage in her older age, and as far as know, had no progeny.

I applaud her. For many older persons take it as a right to even perform it in front of their children, and do that knowing that, they themselves could not bear children because of age. When this is copied by progeny, they fall in all kinds of abandonment dangers for which their parents are entirely to blame,... and guess what? They wonder why there is bad behavior in the children's lives! Do I like to be such a man? No, I want to be the man my own mother taught me to be, who cares how he behaves, and how much he endangers others , born or unborn. Nokhaya cared about that and I could not let her down as a son! A man, I was taught, is he who watches where he goes all the time and does not act without thinking. Neglect of this thought has even obliterated all thoughts of decent morals in even the best of races ,if there is such races.

What are we today? Less than animals! For they, at least mate at the same time each season, while we do it winter ,summer , spring and fall, and care very little about the resultant situation we have in the world today. All is joy for the present! Then we claim to know better. Do we then feel insult at such disobedience in our day? We are now known for exactly what we are, lovers of the pleasures of the flesh. This is called group behavior by current standards. All that matters is :" I got that girl!" or " I got that man!" At what price? Think again before you condemn the nun! How many sons and daughters are today, sure of their parenthood? We have come so such a pass! May Grace, rest in her tomb in great pleasure for she denied herself this until we were all married, even though we were just children she educated. If any person accused her of looseness, let them first behold the plight of our world today, a world they played a very active part in destroying life for future generations, while maintaining a mockery of responsibility and aloofness. If then , they recall that, let them turn to the Holy Book, and realize that Sodom and Gomorrah are no longer in existence.

I do owe much to her encouragement for most learning in English and literature. She was the one teacher who gave me a great credit for an essay she had assigned, where we were supposed to write on a subject called simply :" The Drum" . The essay I wrote at that time, was so good in her eyes that she read it n class to all the students. The essay dealt simply with the importance of the drum, from giving messages in the jungle, to encouraging soldiers at wars in the present world. I was really proud of myself then, even though I had never realized that the essay would be so important to the teacher. It was also at this time, that I got interested again in studying more about religion a course I had given up at fifteen due to problems I had and I have explained elsewhere, which, of course, I am not going to repeat here. One has to note that, even a rebel I was at that time, I was to her a "great asset" to my parents" . This was because Grace, got to know that I was not only able to cook and look after children, but also was able to cut lawns and do gardening outside. This pleased her.

I shall say one thing, Grace tried very hard to get me to understand more about religion at this time, than most African friends I had. However, I found out she was committed to a religion; that she was a member of , the Jehovah Witnesses group, which I had met earlier in my youth, through friends whose parents were in that. Even though Grace got me to study the Bible again, this did not go well, because there was always the science angle which I was struggling hard to relate with the religious thought, and at that time, I could not find satisfactory answers, even from her.

On the last year of high school, , when I had toned down most of my behavior, Grace wanted the class to understand the meaning of a book called : " Murder in the Cathedral" by T.S. Elliot , which was part of our set-work for the class. Without passing English, and that book ,we would be in serious trouble. Grace then wanted us to stage the play to get to know it better. In the enthusiasm of the time, I got the school Librarian who functioned both at Cowan and at Newell high scools, to come into play, for I had known her when I was a library helper at Cowan. Having heard the initial rehearsal of the class, the librarian then recruited two persons who were in the acting business at the time, mainly Eve Tate, and American lady whose husband had worked in Siam for the United Nations, and a local person who knew more about drama, and that a was a certain Mrs. Peterson of Port Elizabeth. Even though I actually visited the Peterson's' once and had lunch with them,, I do not know much about them even to this day. Eve, who passed away in Newlands near Cape Town later, was a Bahá'í and so was her younger daughter, Rosemary Tate, who was a god-child of Rosemary Sala's. The Tates' and the Salas' were old time good friends from the Americas.

As mentioned . elsewhere, the play was actually staged at the Crispin Hall in the city of Port Elizabeth, but the cast then separated to different towns and the play was then never staged again. One of the players eventually moved to New York and stayed there to the present day.

Scene from the play " Murder in the Cathedral", by T S Elliot)
The scene of the martyrdom of Thomas Becket in the play
(L-R) Knights: Mafa Sonjica, Benjamin Hewu, Leslie Ngqoza, Gladman Nghona.
Archbishop: Ferdinand "Pitso" Mafata. Play staged in 1961 at the Crispin Hall in
North End, Port Elizabeth .Producers: Peterson, Eve Tate.
Advisor: Rosemary Sala. (from private collection)

The Fate of Actors in Life

Mafa Sonjica moved to East London and became a businessman and is seen occasionally in East London and Mdantsane.; Gladman Nghona worked in the Maintenance and Disability Grant Office of the government until he qualified as a lawyer and passed on later in Kingwilliamstown; Benjamin, Hewu, worked as a clerk in Port Elizabeth and died in a car crash in the late 60's; Leslie Ngqoza moved to Northern Cape's Graafreinet area, because he could not live in Port Elizabeth, outside his designated jurisdiction, and has not been heard of since.

Miss Grace Makhuluma the English Teacher became a Mrs. Grace Duba after marrying Monroe Duba , a Medical Doctor qualified at Fort Hare University College and Natal University.

Sydney Lucas who acted as the messenger worked in the Tax Office until he qualified as a lawyer.

Thembisa Hlekani , one of the ladies of Canterbury tried a degree at Fort Hare, went on to nursing but finally graduated in Pharmacy and now works in the Transkei area.

Sydney Mbayise who acted as one of the public from Canterbury, became a Medical Doctor qualifying at Natal University, worked at the Livingstone Hospital in Port Elizabeth until his passing recently.

Edmund Mooi who acted as a one of the sentinels went and completed a BS. in Fort Hare University and worked as a teacher until his passing recently.

Duma Luke who was one of the tempters did not complete his degree but worked in Queenstown at is possibly still there. He received top grades at high school, more than three times, but could not do university because of ill health. His uncle, Mr. Vinqi was our Zoology teacher and a great advisor to our class. He, the teacher, held A BS.. degree from Fort Hare and he has also passed on. His wife a nurse from Johannesburg is still in Port Elizabeth.

Grace (Makuluma) Duba: My English Teacher

Grace had taught at Cowan Secondary ,and as part of the English set-work for the year, we had to study a play called: "Abraham Lincoln" by John Drink-water. As a result of this, Grace asked the class to prepare the Gettysburg Speech, by Lincoln, for the final presentation before the Inspector of schools. She had it typed and handed out to each one of us to memorize for the examination. As we know , this is the speech :

> *Four score and seven years ago our fathers brought forth on this continent, a new nation, conceived in Liberty, and dedicated to the proposition that all men are created equal.*
>
> *Now we are engaged in a great civil war, testing whether that nation, or any nation so conceived and so dedicated, can long endure. We are met on a great battle-field of that war. We have come to dedicate a portion of that field, as a final resting place for those who here gave their lives that that nation might live. It is altogether fitting and proper that we should do this.*
>
> *But, in a larger sense, we cannot dedicate — we cannot consecrate — we cannot hallow — this ground. The brave men,*

*living and dead, who struggled here, have consecrated it, far
above our poor power to add or detract. The world will little
note, nor long remember what we say here, but it can never
forget what they did here. It is for us the living, rather, to
be dedicated here to the unfinished work which they who
fought here have thus far so nobly advanced. It is rather for
us to be here dedicated to the great task remaining before us
— that from these honored dead we take increased devotion
to that cause for which they gave the last full measure of devotion — that we here highly resolve that these dead shall
not have died in vain — that this nation, under God, shall
have a new birth of freedom — and that government of the
people, by the people, for the people, shall not perish from
the earth.*

Abraham Lincoln
November 19, 1863

All this time, Grace remained very appreciative of the time we had studying and was very encouraging up to the time of any stand I took. When I made
a decision of becoming a Bahá'í she had had a wish that we stage an African
play, but by then I had lost interest in acting. However, I became at college
interested in acting again, and found myself being voted Chairman of the Dramatic Society there for a year.

Like myself, Grace did not see eye to eye with the custom of circumcision
and what it taught the young men at our present time, even if it were better in
olden times.. On that we agreed, but I was the one who would lose status
among the Africans if I did not go through with the custom. That did not
mean that I went into that with a willing heart. As it were I was never advised
when it would have to be done, but was suddenly taken in after school one day,
when it became known that the high school examinations for matriculation ,
were over, and hustled into the bundu overnight, before I could think. Thus I
went through circumcision, like all African fellows of the Xhosa, and Mosotho
tribes do. I am not sorry, because I learned much about that, and was able to
react to it positively , after learning just what it was in social terms, and in
other individual ways of knowing exactly where I stood as a young man among
the Africans. Had I not done this, I would probably had had to move to some
foreign town ,and forfeit having family in my town , at all.

Grace and Marriage

To tell the next part of the story involving Grace, I would have to tell another involving other persons, in the hope that when these are combined, then they would make some sense.

When I reached Newell High, there were senior students studying the senior certificate I had to study for. Some of these people in senior class, were grown men, who wished to get to qualify in something in their lives. I say "men" because they were much older than I and any of the high school students in my class. However, we got along. Two of these older students became medical doctors . One of them, I believe still lives, and was to my knowledge, a friend and colleague of my younger brother, who also did medicine with them. All these fellows started studying in the Alice/Lovedale area of the cape Province , South Africa. Two of them graduating at Fort Hare, before moving on to Natal University where they then qualified as medical doctors.

The one we shall be concentrate on at this stage is the one named Dr. Monroe Langa " Bro Lanks" Duba. Duba worked for a while before returning to school and graduating in the MB Chb, a qualification medical doctors have to have in South Africa in order to practice medicine.. Monroe has ever since passed on in Port Elizabeth , South Africa. Monroe must have had a kind of related family with Grace., or was familiar with her family, for he boarded in her house for a while. When "Duba' as a we called him , graduated in Fort Hare, I was at that college. A very humorous man , Duba majored in Chemistry and Zoology in his BS degree. When he moved to Natal University, he, because he was from Port Elizabeth, became friends with Donald Mazibuko, my younger brother, who was also schooling there.

After graduating, at the Fort in the BS, Duba who intended to be a teacher, became closer friends with Grace, and from there they got married.

After leaving teaching, Grace became a Social Worker for the Municipality. She is also reported to have passed on , but this has not been confirmed . But her husband passed on earlier in Port Elizabeth after establishing a medical practice there. Even though Monroe was older by far than I, and had returned to school after working for some time, he completed medicine with my younger brother at Natal University. Duba, as we called him at college, was adjustable and full of fun. Asked what he wanted to be called as a doctor by his friends, he replied that they should call him " Dr 'Bro' Lanks Duba" after one of his African clan-name which was Langa or of the Mbhele clan.

After High School and College
My struggle in High School

In the two years I spent at high school I battled mostly with cultural ideologies and some problems with figuring arguing out why one had to be a believer in religion. These thoughts came to invade my life. That was the time I lived a very reclusive life. I studied alone every Saturday at school preparing for exams, and would , in late afternoon take a trip to the movies. The movies that I distinctly remember having a meaning and bearing on a serious life were movies on the nature of " An Affair to Remember" and "High Noon", for there I saw purpose and a victory. One taught me the patience and perseverance of love, and the other, that reason one has to have towards a purpose beyond just personal enjoyment in life. I valued that. That is the reason I still have copies of those movies in my collection at the present time.

Covers of two movies seen by author as a student, after an afternoon of study at high school, on a Saturday afternoons, at the " Rio Cinema" in New Brighton.

Cover to DVD of movie "High Noon"
(scanned from cover)

Cover to DVD of movie "An Affair to Remember"
(scanned from cover) Activity After High School

Robert Mazibuko at twenty one, entering university at Fort Hare University College

When I entered university at Fort Hare, I had made a unilateral decision to further my studies. It had nothing to do with a decision from my parents. I had a high school certificate but it did not allow me to continue with a degree but to pursue a course in a diploma. I decided to choose a Diploma in Agriculture. This was because, first of all the first year would be courses in Chemistry, Zoology, Botany and Geography. I loved all four courses. Secondly I had in my youth gardened a lot with my father who was a Gardener and a herbalist and my first job had been in gardening.

On reaching the university I faced controversy. My friends at school thought it would be a waste to do Agriculture and felt I should try for a degree. I found I could go for a degree in Agriculture. I therefore approached the Registrar with those thoughts of majoring in Agriculture. The Registrar informed me that the degree was not being offered at the university, but if I went home and registered the next year it would be available.

I decided to stay at school and complete the four courses I had registered for. I did and by the end of the year earned all four. The next year I did not go to second year Diploma in Agriculture but decided to pursue the degree in Agriculture, however, it was still not available. By the time I had to register after much wrangling with the Administration, I was late for registration in the second year. Therefore I took a registration in the South African Teachers' Diploma. It was possible to convert courses done under that diploma into a degree. This was a viable option but it meant I could not register my courses for that diploma but had to repeat them under a separate diploma.

At this time I decided to get involved with college activities. I joined the Dramatic Society of which I became chairman for the year .DRAMSOC or Dramatic Society was part of SOMFAD or Society of Music Fine Arts and Dramatics which had encompassed a number of activities on campus in olden times. At this point SOMFAD was well nigh nonfunctional whereas DRAMSOC was , mostly under the English Department..

It took all effort to put plays on stage at college, but I did what was expected and got the shows on stage by end of the year. The reason for the difficulty was not that the plays were hard to do but the atmosphere at the college. Neither the students nor the administration wanted the plays on stage for different and divergent reasons.

The university was not keen to support plays suggested by students as this would not promote the Bantu Education System. The students did not want the plays performed because this would support the Bantu Education System.

The staging of the plays was a student activity and the students had sworn earlier not to partake in any social activities that seemed to involve the administration or otherwise tend to show that the students were happy under the system. So the staging of the shows was open to a lot of criticism on both sides. Meanwhile many students were suffering from nervous breakdowns because of too much work and no social activities .However, we staged the shows even under protest from the student body with a success.

Later we required funds to stage the plays at other universities in the country, however the university administration did not support that . So, that plan fell through.

All this did not do much for my academic improvement. However, I was doing the same courses I had done before except I had changed from Geography to Physics. My passing grade was not high at the end of that year. There was also a strong argument from most students that I could not do well in Agriculture anyway because it was the domain of the Afrikaner farmer. It was hard to continue unless I changed to something else altogether different before I was acceptable to students.

After high school I had worked in a hospital assisting both the hospital and the Social Worker provide for families afflicted with the Tuberculosis disease.. I had even been offered education In Typhus Diseases in the UK, which I had turned down and opted for local university study. I had many other reasons for that which I shall not share at this point.

Faced with my predicament , I asked myself just what difference it would make if I became a Social Worker instead. All my life as a child I had prepared myself to become a minister of religion. Now I was at a quandary having become a Bahá'í instead. It just occurred that I would do well in Social Work. So I registered and was accepted at college for that. However a few days before I could board the train to return to Alice where the university was, I received a note from the university that I had to support myself in fees entirely. I realized that this was another way of asking me not to go back to university, since this was days before opening school and I had no contacts for financial aid except a loan from the university which would be a loan from the government. Also I had not registered under my parents' name at college but under the librarian from my high school, who was supplying my other needs. This was Rosemary Sala. For that financial reason I could not return to university. A few years later I again applied and offered to pay all fees myself, because Rosemary, who was then in Canada offered to pay. When I applied to the university my application was not acknowledged.

Hence I could never go back there to study again. This was a situation which was known at college as "Shit Street".

My Victory and Failure

I was twenty years in age when I got to the Fort and turned twenty one the next March. It was hard to celebrate my twenty first because I was far from home. My sister had had a very large celebration when she turned adult, but I was to celebrate with a few friends invited. My parents never even acknowledged this event but I had received a sum of money to celebrate with from Rosemary Sala. Hence I was able to purchase a cake and call together a few friends. I was housed at Iona House but my friends were in Beda House. So I went to their room to celebrate.

After a few speeches from friends, we turned on the only radio that was in the room. A song came through. It was Cliff Richard with "Bachelor Boy". There were some remarks for I was not known to have a girlfriend and was not known to be trying to have one.

Some of the fellows were quizzed about my situation. Here I was from the city, being able to dress well; speak English well; have knowledge of ballroom dancing in waltz, foxtrot and quickstep; being able to argue a point to a conclusion: Why was it with all those "bowling aids" that I had no girlfriend.? Bowling aids were supposed to be such qualities or abilities that made a fellow an acceptable, even marriageable boyfriend. Failing in this area was regarded as "starving in the midst of plenty".

The answer to that was simple: I could not bring myself to announce to a girl I did not even know that " I loved her". This needed time and getting used to the girl. However the attitude of announcing this was different at college in my day. You bowled a girl until she said "Yes" to you..

It must have trickled through to my aunt in East London who was a minister's wife that I had not taken on a girl because I heard her address me as her "Bachelor Boy'! This could be taken as a victory that I was at college two years and did not have a girlfriend. It could be taken also as a failure to be unable to convince one to be my girl. I had given that up in the end and turned out to be very cynical about the process of finding a love. Hence in my second year there I tended to be more of a rebel and that carried through to my time as a working man the following year.

Some many years later when I registered for studies in the United States, the University of South Africa acknowledged my having completed the first year of the degree in science in Fort Hare, so that I could eventually graduate in Information Technology.

*Robert Mazibuko after graduating in Information Technology
in the US at Franklin University*

*Robert Mazibuko after graduating as Office Technologist, Medical Assistant and Certi-
fied Nurses' Assistant working in Joliet, IL. (photo by his wife G. Misselt before work)*

Belief and Character

Very few of my friends at college knew I was a Bahá'í. This was at the beginning of 1963 and I had declared as a Bahá'í in August 1962. I loved being a Bah'í and today I can find no other course in life I could have taken than that and it has brought me solace of heart and mind. At the time I knew very little about the religion but adhered to it for its principles of a social nature as well as those of a moral disposition. Being a student and being involved in daily arguments brought about a situation where I had to resort to a more rebellious kind of life. It took time for me to reconcile the inward belief with the outward expressed life and the clash of the two can be disastrous. For a while I was not aware of the nature of my own belief in the Faith. However in travelling through the country with a Radio Announcer who also happened to be an American Bahá'í, I came to learn more than I had ever known. It was a good challenge for, the man was a Jazz Fan and I was at that time also. The vastness of the belief and its international principles brought me focus of ideas.

The meetings with students at the town area of the college , especially at "Ramona's" were a Saturday activity which one could not miss, yet meetings at the hall with students on many issues were even less forgettable. They could not be matched by any other experiences I had had in the past with my student friends.

Ramona was the spot for socialization, but the Christian Union Hall taught one all the philosophies that were present in the college.

Occasionally there would be talk among friends of "Radomsky's" but that was always besides the main point , for "Radomsky's" was for those who did partake of strong drinks. Since I was not one of those until a year I left college, this did not matter. What mattered was being in touch with the changes in social order that I saw before my eyes while I was at college. As I could hold my point in an argument, and because I adhered to a principle of non involvement in politics, I was regarded as more of a 'free thinker'. I was no free thinker because I was aware of some of the all encompassing teachings of the Bahá'ís which involved a change in the whole world and not in just one country. I was learning this and was not at a point where I could expound on it. Later when I was on the National Administration of the Bahá'ís in South Africa, I could explain a few themes of my Faith. This is no excuse nor is it an apology but a statement to all my friends who might not even today know what the Bahá'í Faith stands for, and let them know that as far back as1962 I was a Bahá'í.

For years after I had become a Bahá'í I was declared as a 'lost child" by my mother but it is gratifying that before I left home and after I arrived in the United States my mother and I were closely reconciled. I left for the States from her home which was my home by birth. Anything to the contrary of the above would be misleading and false.

Education and Health

At the time I was at college there seemed to have been an interplay between getting educated and keeping good health. On my first year there had been a number of nervous breakdowns , and some occurring at the time of examinations. When a friend I had was admitted to hospital with a psychological complaint, I approached the doctor on the Psychiatric Clinic and asked what could have been causing the breakdowns in the college. She replied that when students study they need moments of relief which could be provided by some kind of social activity to relieve the intensity of study.

The resolution by the Student Body stood that no social activities would be undertaken by students on campus. This was a protest against the government's decision of placing the university under the Bantu Education System with no university autonomy .This decision then was backfiring into bad health for some students. The idea of the protest was encouraged with the words:" Get your certificate and get out!". There were to be no participation in the trappings of a graduation ceremony.

Since there was no ending this protest as the government was not changing, a group of students and lecturers especially Nonwhite lecturers were concerned about the health and the quality of graduate we would produce at college. It was a wish to revive art, music and the kind of activity among the students but most of that would have to be unofficial without an endorsement from the Student Body. There was no Student Representative Council, so decisions had to be handled in a Mass Meeting of students. For holding that, a 'legitimate' reason had to be given to the college administration, otherwise meetings were not permitted.

Nevertheless, to some extent the college had a choir, a jazz club and a dramatic society all without the approval of the whole student body.

I as a student became one of those who joined the choir, the music club, and the dramatic society because I could see no good end to the protest. This did not mean then that I was a favorite of the politically inclined but I proceeded rebelliously to pursue the course of introducing some sort of student activities in defiance of both the administration and the student body. My activities had some success, for we staged plays and had choir activities, which would account for my being debarred from the college the next year. The college administration sought some approval for some actions and it was not helping them for the students to go independent without seeking some aid form them.

This was the state of affairs when I left college in 1965. It gratified some of us when the university was granted autonomy in a few years.

After College
The Change Effected through Music

(Picture downloaded from Amazo.com 2016) Cover to LP "Love Supreme" by John Coltrane
A copy of LP by Coltrane when the author awakened from a long stupor which lasted almost two years and started a moral existence based on the Bahá'í Teachings. LP was played more during the first Bahá'í Fast undertaken by author in 1966.

An Affair of a Transition

At this point, we come to the love affair that took a great toll on my life. I was working as a receptionist in a hospital, which is a great position for finding partners. In the first month of employment I had ventured to try for love again, only to find a friendship that would last no more than a couple of months and petered out. I then stayed for a year and months without trying again. It seemed to hurt too much to try.

One night , while on duty, I conversed with a student nurse who claimed she "believed in what is right". That raised an old questions: What was right in life anyway? In the two years of leaving college, I had lived a more or less hazardous life in other ways, which , thankfully, did not involve wanton sexual activity, but I was what one would call a "rebel". On most days, I would have a beret, slanted on the head, and pants rolled up once; a t-shirt draping over the pants, a cigarette in the mouth, and listening to jazz songs in all kinds of places one could imagine in the township. My mother had come to describe me as an "IDC" which stands for : " I Don't Care".

The question of being right, brought me back to the question of right and wrong. Yes, at this time, I had ideologically accepted being a Bahá'í, but behavior was not anything I paid attention to. I had even argued against keeping the Bahá'í Fast, because there was a statement in the Books , that said that a lady in her turns and a person over seventy could not fast, why not then, I asked, not add that a student must not fast? Pondering on this question, had me trying the fast for the first time, and making a decision to stay more at home and do any listening of music there. I even bought a slide viewer and went around town showing pictures of my religion. That very statement of right and wrong, from a nurse, had meant a lot to hear!

In my excitement I decided to introduce the girl to my family. My mother liked her so much, an unusual disposition for her, that she was planning marriage long before I mentioned it. Perhaps she had thought the change in behavior had to do with her too.

However, the marriage was not to be. When I broached the statement to the girl she had doubts. Instead of coming through with a definite 'no', she fell in love with someone else without any warning. From a distance I can now understand that, even so. She was Catholic and wanted me to change religions, and I was refusing. She went to the extent of introducing me to her fellow worshipers, some of them being nuns, and I still refused. I however, kept that secret of the separation away from my mother, hating to disappoint her, which was the cause I refused speech at all and ended up depressed. I kept the secret of my own disappointment to myself through many a question. Not even a doctor could make me talk! The doctor I saw even declared me mute.

At recovery from that depression, I still kept faith with my idea of marrying the girl. The waiting took no less than six years, at which time I gave in and married a girl from out of town. All that time, I kept my belief intact and could not see any other way of looking at life.

The Awakening

When I came back from university in 1964 and did not find admittance into that same university in 1965, I had taken the stance of being more of a rebel; this manifested itself both in dress code and in language. It was at this time that I was learning more of the music called jazz, and it did me no good to be told about anything for I wished to find out for myself and make up my mind about each involvement. That meant that to a great extent I was on my own. The reason I was on my own was that I had taken a departure from accepted norms and developed a method by which I would decide behavior , not from a traditional standpoint , but from the point of how I was to view things now that I had taken up Bahá'í norms .For by August/September 1962 when I had left school I had joined that Faith.

It took the greater part of a year before I could come to terms with most issues and I found them confusing. Besides African tradition were accepted norms in the Western world, and given that I was living in the Apartheid environment it was hard to be objective without taking up behaviors that I deemed unworthy.

At this time of total mayhem in the political and social world I could only keep in touch with Rosemary Sala, mainly through Julia Tabina Galo, the wife of my Science teacher who had schooled in the school where I had done junior high education , and who knew Rosemary from her time at school. Julia would and occasionally visit Rosemary and acted as a channel into my other life.

When I did awaken from that stupor of investigation of a personal nature, which found difficulty in explaining itself, I found Julia to be good company.

Julia Galo as a student nurse, at the time of early marriage to Mr. J.T. Galo my Science and Mathematics teacher at Junior High. A good friend in critical years. (Gift from Ilona Sala)

Conscious Acknowledgement

When at last, I decided on attempting the Bahá'í Fasting Season in 1966, a decision I shall not explain at the moment as it entailed my whole change of attitude, which would benefit no one, I turned to Julia as a friend. It was then that I turned also to Rosemary Sala, for a leadership in the fasting event. It was the fast of 1966 which altered my life, for , this was the first time I did something so obviously Bahá'í and different. I had to keep explaining it to myself as an endeavor I would be involved in all my life. This all arose because the question of right and wrong had again presented itself in my life. What was right and what was wrong? I was a Bahá'í and had declared that to all my friends at college, but what about behavior? Where did I stand there?

At this time Rosemary Sala had been banned by the government from entering African townships ; and had also been elected to the Bahá'í National Assembly of South Africa a national Administrative Body of my faith. It is poignant that at this time also, a man who was Afrikaner in background decided to join the Faith. This was Don Fouche whom I befriended later while travelling with Lowell Johnson in 1969.

To keep me going during that first Bhaá'í fast, I was fortunate to find LPs of Duke Ellington that belonged to Tabina Galo(Julia), that she had decided to loan me. These I played, while I was on night duty at the hospital where I was employed, while also learning to prepare my meals at my home each dawn and evening as a prerequisites of fasting. The music was an important entertainment and relief. It so happened that I was on night duty on some of those weeks and would play music while washing up for work and meals.

This is decidedly the very change of life that made me what I know I am today, a believer. I had to learn to take up Bahá'í behaviors amidst a generality of norms that were quite different from the Bahá'í attitude to life.

Years later, I learned from Lowell, that during that period, Rosemary Sala had taken pilgrimage and met with Don Fouche. To prove this he showed me a picture which I later acquired while I resided in the US from a Canadian who was a niece of Rosemary's, and that is Ilona Weinstein-Sala:

Don Fouche, Rosemary Sala, and Lowell Johnson on pilgrimage in Haifa, Israel in mid 60s (gift from Ilona Sala)

The Realization

The realization that it was not all the wonderful social teachings of Baha'u'llah that mattered to one, and not even the declaration that one is a Bahá'í that was important, but the change in the moral and social rules of the Faith fostered with diligence, wherewith one followed every precept of the Faith as portrayed by the Guardian, that made one a believer,… the reality of one's conduct and behavior. Thus when after some months, I picked up a picture of the Master from Emeric's office, which I had returned to Rosemary when she had offered it as gift and took it back.. It mattered at this time much more than any possession. I had returned that picture to her because, in my mind, it showed agreement with all the all old folks who were wont to tell me that age was always right and that I should obey their ruling. This time I held onto the picture for dear life . I had kept it to the extent that I had that same a picture in my room until it was time to depart from my home when I married, and still had it next to my bed all the days I lived in South Africa , for behind it Rosemary, on returning it to me , had attached the following statement by the Guardian. This helped a great deal as a remembrance where I had been in faith before that time:

> **Not by the force of numbers, not by the mere exposition of a set of new and noble principles, not by an organized campaign of teaching — no matter how worldwide and elaborate in its character — not even by the staunchness of our faith or the exaltation of our enthusiasm, can we ultimately hope to vindicate in the eyes of a critical and skeptical age the supreme claim of the Abha Revelation. One thing and only one thing will unfailingly and alone secure the undoubted triumph of this sacred Cause, namely, the extent to which our own inner life and private character mirror forth in their manifold aspects the splendor of those eternal principles proclaimed by Bahá'u'lláh.**
> **Shoghi Effendi**
> **(Bahá'í Administration, p. 66))**

It soon became so clear that my life was not at that time in conformity with the above standard nor was I even making the effort, but insisted firmly that I was a world citizen in my attitude. The above is the standard set in the Books of the Faith and no less. Today that same picture stands hanging on my wall where I live, perhaps old, but still makes the point, that I should never forget the Perfect Exemplar established by the Author of my Faith all life through.

So while travelling with Lowell Johnson in the sixties and he made the point that spirituality was a practicality, I understood perfectly.

A scan of a picture of the Master, 'Abd'ul-Bahá, the Eldest Son of Bahá'u'lláh and the Center of His Covenant, given to Robert Mazibuko in 1966 on his first fast as a Bahá'í, by Rosemary Sala in South Africa

The Transition

Knowing that an event occurred may mean that one has to take action; believing needs actions of belief; a conviction cries for expression: these are thoughts that went through my mind at this juncture. I realized that talking about the teachings of my faith was a far cry from living those principles. One great stumbling block was that at my college I could argue in an academic way about my faith, but how does one do it to the local person who had nothing to do with colleges? It occurred to me that the source of religion to the common man was the Bible and that if I wanted to get anywhere proving the point of my religion I had to go to accepted terms and norms. So it became a reality that the Bahá'í Faith had to be argued from the Bible and not really from science and religion, for the common man. The common parson wants to survive and wants to deal with things he knows about.

What bothered me with that was the fact that all the books I had read about science , religion and the Bible were in English. I did not have a leg to stand upon using English as a medium of instruction. It had to be the African language. Therefore, I had to translate what I had learned in the English language to an understandable language that was African. Knowing that I could not explain what happened at college in any understandable way to one who had not been there I realized that the commonality would be belief and the Bible. Fortunately, the Bible itself was available in African languages, but the Bahá'í Faith was not. My first task then was to translate the literature of my faith, from English to the African language and let minds digest on their own what was in the Bahá'í Faith. In this way began a journey to the mind of the person I dealt with from a very young age, indeed from birth. I found it to be escapism to want to resort to English explanations even when I was talking to one who understood an African language.

In translating I found I had to face parts I understood and parts that made sense to someone else, and perhaps not to me. I even began to find a broader view of what I thought I believed in. Out of a loneliness I was now finding ways of expressing myself to anybody, no matter what their calling was.

There were several hurdles to be faced, especially when it came to norms and customs. One had to have a logical explanation for many things that people do without thinking anymore. Finding those answers in turn, made it possible to be able to find alternative behavior for many customary things and yet be logical and acceptable .I had for many years avoided many traditions because they were illogical, now I had to deal with them and find their logic of application. A solution to problems needs a mode of application. It cannot remain a theoretical entity with no practicality.

This helped in an in-depth acceptance than one that depended on the person one spoke to, but remains fact in the absence of all. This attitude helped not just my finding more answers for myself, but in finding strategies for building a community of believers. For, one has to be involved with the community to have any impact at all.

On parting, when she left for Canada, my spiritual mother had told me that I was going to be on my own and with no company and will have to work on whatever good I could find by myself. I realized I had found a good to work with and for and could and could augment it into something bigger that approached the reality of a dream.

A Vista Opens

After travels with Lowell in 1969/70 it became much more easier to talk openly about the Faith to friends. At this time , I befriended a Colored man by the name of William Benjamin who was a machine operator in glass factory where I worked as a quality controller. After a short time of meeting, we were discussing religion . Billy accepted being a Bahá'í. This in itself was momentous because it meant that, if Billy were willing, we could have meetings at his home in the Colored area. The advantage of having meetings there was that both Blacks and Whites could enter the township whereas Blacks could not enter white homes, nor did the law prohibit Whites from visiting Colored homes. Billy's declaration marked a change of strategy. Thus it was that after that period we could meet several visitors from everywhere without interruption from the police.

(Front L-R) R. Mazibuko, Faith Mazibuko, Bernard Benjamin (Back L-R) Sadri Farabi,, Ronald Fudu, Peter Simon. In Salt Lake, Port Elizabeth.

A comment on Marriage in My family

Though my big sister did no willingly enter into wedlock, nevertheless she stayed married and gave birth to three children. After the passing of her husband , a little before I left the country, she remained single to the present day until illness overtook her after retirement from working as a matron at the hospital's Pediatric Block. She and Donald, my younger brother, were the only ones in my family who had wedding that were large and publicized in the 60s.

Donald on the other hand got married while still studying as a Medical Student at university, but that marriage did not last very long, however, while I travelled in the late 60s I found out he had already undertaken to remarry another lady with whom he settled for more than a decade as is evidenced by his video of his : "13th Wedding Anniversary of Donald and Valencia Mazibuko", taken on that very day of their anniversary in Durban South Africa.

As there are no records of the marriages that are immediately available and the author is not willing to request them at this time, there is available a picture of Donald marrying for the first time in Port Elizabeth,… and a big wedding in New Brighton it was too!

Donald and Nomble married for first time. Donald was a medical student and Nomble a nurse at the local hospital in which I had worked in previously.

Front, Third from right: Robert Mazibuko attending his brother's wedding at the St Stephen's Church, New Brighton, Port Elizabeth, South Africa

Wandile , my youngest brother, and I never had big marriages as such in the 60s, but mine had some publicity in the 70s as it was celebrated at the Civic Center in Mdantsane., near East London. None were big weddings in the style of Tumana's, that is , Donald, and my big sister, Thobeka. Hence for both our early marriages(Wandile and I), there are no great available records

(Extreme Right,) Robert and Faith Lulama Mazibuko with first child Emeric in the lap of one of the believers in a Bahá'í meeting, possibly a convention or conference.

In the late eighties I did have a larger wedding but not by arrangement, even though it was performed in a public place, mainly the Bahá'í House of Worship in Wilmette ,IL. The persons who attended the wedding were those who saw the marriage being performed and decided to join in, to the extent of moving to our home in Evanston , IL , for the celebration.

(L.-R) Dr. Maren Anderson, Robert Mazibuko,Gretchen Misselt, and a member of the Bahá'í Local Assembly of Evanston Lee Anne Olson,, during the signing of marriage documents and finalizing of marriage in the House of Worship's hall, under the Temple, where the marriage was conducted.

My little sister, now a professor in Economics at a local university in Port Elizabeth,, never married, and remains the one center where some of the grandchildren of the family find a home and care. However she remains committed to her profession , travelling the world and writing papers on Economics. She has students in different countries in Africa.

(L-R) Robert Mazibuko, Gretchen Misselt and a friend, Emeric Sala, Robert's spiritual parent, at the House of Worship Wilmette, IL on Emeric's last visit to the United States, after the wedding to see the bride, Gretchen. Emeric was pioneering in Mexico at the time, where his wife Rosemary had passed on earlier in 1979. (Picture taken in 1988)

Emeric is the author of the book " This Earth One Country" and a speaker recorded in a famous talk of his paper : "Shoghi Effendi's Question" now available as CD at the Archives in the United States. Emeric and Rosemary Sala's activities as Bahá'ís , are recorded in a the book recently released i.e." Tending the Garden" by Ilona Sala. The book is not to be mistaken for " The New Garden" by Hushmand Fath'eazam, of the Universal House of Justice, published earlier. The second edition of this book by Ilona, has a fuller measure of the story. Both titles of the two separate books occur as imagery in Bahá'í historical stories.

The reason Emeric had to be invited from Mexico, over to the United States and the reason he willingly came over was because , he and his wife Rosemary had been teachers to Robert Mazibuko and had seen him through turbulent youth years of his youth in South Africa where they had pioneered earlier between 1956 and 1968. Part of their story is told elsewhere in another book. i.e. "This Side Up" by Mazibuko. Emeric, in the process of his visit was invited to give a short talk at the House of Worship in Wilmette ,IL. As he and his wife, Rosemary, had served on the first Bahá'í National Assembly established earlier in the United States and Canada.

The Dilemma of Language

Because of the high school tendency in using English at all arguments and interactions, time came to define identity, because one has to take stock of where one stands especially in matters affecting one's cultural stand. In acculturation this becomes an obvious hurdle. To me part of it came after attending college. For interaction at college was all English. This attitude was taken up by students to counteract the insistence of the government that all Africans be educated in their vernacular languages. We did this because we wished we could interact with the outside world at one stage or another and sticking to vernacular somewhat prohibited that. With language diversity, there also tended to be separation of cultural background, for, each language was attached to a culture, some of them very different one from one another. Students wanted unity and a difference from the so called "Bush Colleges" established later. The beginnings of change of language came at high school. Hence the story begins there:

After high school, I had a good friend who would often visit my home and with whom I had schooled. He was Ferdinand Pitso Mafata. At the end of the year of the schooling period ,we had staged a play which was all in English, at the Crispin Hall in the city. The name of the play was no less than " Murder in the Cathedral" by T.S. Eliot. As that was the last major activity we were involved in at school, outside of the final year school examination, it left us with a feeling of great interest in drama. To encourage us to keep in touch and "avoid boredom" , Rosemary Sala decided to invite us to see a play by Athol Fugard at the Feather Market Hall in the city of center of Port Elizabeth .

As this play was to take place at night, we had to avoid being arrested for being in the city after 6:00 p m without the documents called "night passes". These passes had to be arranged for by Rosemary. This event lit up more enthusiasm in us to be in drama, because, after seeing the play called " Blood Knot" at the Crispin Hall, we formed our own group of a dramatic nature and aimed at staging "Hamlet" by Shakespeare. However, this latter wish was not to be realized, because, Ferdinand, who was to act the main part of Hamlet, soon left for Johannesburg , to do further studies in drama. Someone had seen how superbly Pitso had acted the part of the Archbishop Thomas Becket in the play we had staged earlier , and had decided to advance him in that direction of acting. Thus, then broke up the endeavor of staging the play "Hamlet".

By the time I came back from university two years after this in 1965, where I had been elected to be chairman of the Dramatic Society , and had had to act in one one-act play, I found that in New Brighton, the very man I had seen in the play "Blood Knot" was then involved in drama in the township. I attempted to join the group he had formed, but found that the only part left in the play was that of a sentinel. Out of respect for my colleagues at my college, I decided not to take up the position of acting a 'sentinel' in a play in a township, as I felt they, the colleagues , would blame me of having insulted them. College at the Fort was proud of itself!! How could I degrade them by taking up a part as a 'sentinel' in a location play, when I had been a chairman of their dramatic society at university? Would that not be agreeing with the prevalent thought that educational certificates of Africans was more like the worth of toilet paper?

The main difficulty again there was that Athol thought my English accent to be false, for it is neither British nor American, but lay somewhere in between. In years to follow this was to get me into some trouble, but all was worth it, for, I found I had found an English accent of my own! Bastardization of the English tongue had once more occurred!

Athol would have been right in saying that my accent was fake. It was very true and this has been observed many time in s my life, not to mention involving me in many unpleasant or pleasant situations. I shall explain.

From the time I learned to read and write English I found that I had a great difficulty in speaking the language so that I was understood. What was the good of learning any language if one is not understood when attempting to speak it? For, are not the sounds we utter which we ardently call our language merely expressive of thoughts in our minds? Much as I attempted to speak the language I found the same difficulty, sometimes aiding in my being derided for the pronunciation. My difficulty was perhaps simple: I could not reconcile similarities in pronunciation in many words with the difference in meaning. Some examples were: How I do I express a word like 'grey' when it is the same as 'gray'. How about 'fest', 'first'; 'fust' and 'fast'; 'bed' and 'bad'? There are many examples. I found the differences indistinguishable and making no sense!

In listening to different English speaking races as they spoke, I found that there was even a great difference as to how an English speaking person from England, and an American pronounced the same words. If there was a mixture of these race groups I was speaking to I found I had to hit a compromise somewhere in between. That is exactly how I learned to speak English. I had to switch between the American and English pronunciations in order to be understood at all. That , of course, renders me as a foreigner to both race groups. It was more viable to use the American pronunciation for some words and the ordinary English accent for others in order to be understood and make sense to my own self.

The result of the above in the present day is that I find myself in the United States carrying the question of "Are you from the islands?". For, a while I could not figure that out until I found out that the English from the islands was closer to British English than to American English. Hence, when I am in South Africa, my accent is determined to be American, and when I am in America it goes elsewhere! I have lived with that and am unable to change, because it is the only way I can be more or less understood, in reality. One uses what works anywhere! So I can easily say that I have a workable accent. Working in public places on the island, I often find the question of "Where are you from?". My answer usually is that I am from South Africa but learned English from Canadians , Americans and the English! Make sense? One could trill all the "r's" but then the meaning would be totally lost!

In general, therefore, Athol, who was used to many accents was correct. My accent was a bastard, a brand of my own! By it and through it I communicate with the world successfully. I am happy with that…

Athol Fugard as he looked earlier in his life. (Google Images)

Attending Events

Return from university was not a happy time, because I was myself embarrassed that I did not achieve what I went t out to reach out for at college. Also , by that time, I had learned some habits that would befit one who lives a night life and very little daylight life. I then separated myself from friends I knew and joined in with new friends who were agreeable with my style of living.

Towards my last days in 1963 I had spent an evening with a Demonstrator in Botany, who had invited me to dinner, a dinner he had prepared himself, Indian-style. This was because the Boarding Master had by then closed down the dining room and I was the last student to leave the house I resided in.

I therefore, went over on that last evening to the room of my Indian demonstrator, and found that he had cooked lots of Indian foods. We had a lovely dinner, and before I could even think of going, he reached from under his bed and produced a bottle "Olde Meester", a brand of brandy, which students always referred to as "the Old Teacher". I was not much a drinker then but accepted a drink. We got underway discussing our separate cultures and voicing just how much we regretted some issues in them. I went into a long explanation about mine, and he was just about taking off on his, when the Radio Station we were listening to suddenly went dead. Instead of Rock, there was classical music on. He then tried several stations and when he was just about to give up on one that also played classics, a voice came through announcing the death of President Kennedy.

He then concentrated on all the details coming through the radio and I was disappointed that we discontinued the subject as I still had not voiced my actual stand. I immediately left him sadly and unceremoniously and crossed over the hedge to my house to sleep. The subject of the death left a huge hole in me, for that very year I had been entertained by a US Consul who had taken me to the Seminary in Alice for the opening of same. I had friends I knew in my town who would want to view all this with a concern I knew so well, and I was far from home. Would my friends understand that? There was in my mind, really nothing to discuss but much to think about. So, to my room at Iona House, I went, for at that moment. We had been at Beda House where my Indian friend resided , just across the fence from Iona House where I resided. I had to return and ponder. It did not help that I was slightly tipsy at that point but that indeed made death easier to countenance......

Several weeks after this, I found the story on a newspaper, the Saturday "Evening Post" in Port Elizabeth. That story ran for several weeks to complete a book written on the event. called "The Death of a President" by Manchester. I could never read all the story from the newspaper at that time, but was later able to purchase another book called "A Thousand Days" by Schlesinger. I no longer have the latter book, but the first was purchased second hand from a library in Ottawa , IL., and that I have. I valued it because , the first US Consul who picked me up at college in 1963 was under Kennedy's regime, and he had been directed to contact me by friends in Port Elizabeth, because , in those days, there was a US Consulate in that town and there I had friends who were American. Clearly remembered is that the Consul spelled his name as Horace Byrnes. Again the question of pronunciation did come up, for was he Bens of Burns ? Good times and horrors of the past do stay longer!

(Cover scanned from original by author)
*Book published in entirety in the " Evening Post " of Port Elizabeth, for weeks after
the death of President Kennedy.*

**And among the teachings of His Holiness Bahá'u'lláh is
the origination of one language that may be spread uni-
versally among the people. This teaching was revealed
from the pen of Bahá'u'lláh in order that this universal
language may eliminate misunderstandings from among
mankind.**
(Abdu'l-Baha, Foundations of World Unity, p. 29)

A Second Death

About three years after that tragic event, another of a government figure occurred in South Africa. I was on my way to a vacation to East London on the
train when I heard that one of the Presidents of South Africa, had met his
death , stabbed by a page in parliament. The one thing I remember about the
man was that when he was about to take office, he had made a statement about
putting the Blackman in his place. I probably could say no more than that, for
at the time of that statement, the man was a Minister of Education. I could
not comment then because it was dangerous, and cannot do much now because
I know that the people of that country are doing their best to merge efforts in

becoming one country. One does not dare dwell on past events but look forward to changes in the future, so that the unhappiness of the past becomes the happiness of achieving a union and resultant felicity, where possible. This attitude would be applauded in the United States , because with all the differences that may pertain, one man, Lincoln, did sacrifice his life to see that this was achieved i.e. the uniting of the whole., regardless of what it might and did to his own life. That is to be applauded as a sacrifice of modern times. I , as one individual person can stand identified with those who strive for unities in the world, for we do live on one Planet, and should it suddenly explode we all would disappear.

Prevalent Attitudes

At university, it was very necessary for one to avoid being called a "mass", because a mass was recognized as someone with volume and weight and nothing else. They could not be used anywhere except as mass. Also this term related to one being merely one of the masses instead of being an academic in the true student sense. So, one got involved in arguments to prove one's stand in life. These discussions and arguments which were frequent and all over campus, would sometime go deep into the night or rather into the early morning with no sight to a conclusion. Somehow I made it into becoming a member of NUSAS or the National Union of South African Students, from which I had to eventually resign when the organization was banned as a political organization,. I remembered I was Bahá'í and Bahá'ís do not get involved in political organizations at all. One can have a point, but one cannot be in a political group or political party. This is known.

At this time mentioned above, a friend I had in Port Elizabeth who was a Bahá'í was arrested for political activity and spent ten years on Robben Island. This impacted on many Bahai's because he was a Bahá'í. Of course this meant that Bahá'ís would be under surveillance in the town. It helped therefore, for me to lose myself in jazz for a while and join in visiting 'joints' like all the young fellows in town , especially those from universities. However, the desire to visit such places came as an automatic reaction but suited the plan in retrospect. This was at the time, when a trial had placed many political leaders on life sentence, and we knew many of them in my college, and had followed their activities. It was a serious blow when they all vanished into the cells., not to mention some suddenly falling in bathrooms and cracking their skulls.

It was at this time of return, that I made a visit to Rosemary, and because going there was another automatic response defining one's stand in the issue in the atmosphere of the times. Taking a stand at college was necessary instead of being a fence-sitter. Because the Bahá'í Faith was unknown at my college in those years, my stand had been defined as that of a "Free Thinker".

On a particular occasion of a visit , I found Rosemary preparing to go out. She had a visitor. It was the wife of the American Consul. I had been told earlier that the Consulate was moving from Port Elizabeth, at the time of the end of the Kennedy rule. The new Consul had visited our university to explain the take over and swearing in of a president so suddenly after one died. I had then met him and his wife there, though they knew very little about the visit of the former Consul to Fort Hare at the opening of the Federal Theological Seminary the previous year, or so it seemed, for neither recognized me in an way. For ,at that time in Fort Hare , I met them and inquired about the former man. One never knows what answer to expect in political fields! For some reason my inquiry went without a definite answer. So, I tried to be a gentleman and let that ride without pursuing it.

As it were, at the time of my visit to Rosemary I was in casual clothes and they were dressed formerly. I therefore, rode with them to the opening of the Centenary Hall in New Brighton a center that had newly been erected, and they dropped me off a few yards from the entrance of the hall because of this difference in dress code. I was, after all, in jeans.

Soon after this event, I learned that Rosemary had been banned from entering African townships. However, for a year she was elected and served on the Bahá'i National Assembly before she and Emeric departed for Canada to eventually depart thence to pioneer in Mexico.. After those years , I do know that it made sense that she would attend the event at the Centenary Hall with the Consul's wife!

An Impending Second Awakening

Employment After University

Employment after university was very hard, because at this time, the city of Port Elizabeth, which had been criticized as being British was now targeted for change to a more Afrikaans-speaking city. This is my perception. First, the university on Bird Street then called Rhodes University which was very English and was near to where the Tates', my American friends ,lived was renovated and altered in name to become the University of Port Elizabeth, and what they called a "twee taalige Universteit" or "Two language University", with Afrikaans being predominant because most of the workers were Afrikaans-speaking. Secondly, the statue of Queen Victoria which had stood on Market Square in the center of the city was also removed and placed in the suburbs .Somehow, these two changes never went unnoticed by myself and seemed to be related. Port Elizabeth seemed to be under reconstruction with the coming of freeways on the roads. Building brought all sorts of very strange people into town. The Mayor's Garden at Market Square was replaced by a bricked pavement

I had never been, at that time, been employed in a strictly Afrikaans company , but now there nothing but that available. The very worst situation which one could not escape was to go and wait for one's name to be called up at the Labor Bureau/Influx Control Offices and be told where available work was to be found and sent there with documents from the Bureau to be signed at the employment as a "work seeker". It not to be forgotten that when one I was employed one had to have the Reference Book signed by the employer every month or end up in jail as unemployed, not to mention being arrested for not having a paid tax document on the book one carried. As student I stood a chance of a certificate of exemption from taxation.

There were several job situations I was sent to. One was in a construction company where they said they could use someone with a high schools certificate, where I ended up being the clocking machine for workers. Another turned me down as too educated. Finally , because of the education complaint, I was sent to Port Elizabeth University to work in the library. However, my supervisor an Afrikaner, was a maintenance man whom they called the 'supervisor'. He spoke some English, but did not approve of my accent, and was angry if I showed an attitude of "rolling eyes at him".

I was , however in the library, and he could not do much except come in now and then to see if I was working. As is the case, when somebody does not want you on the job, there usually are many complaints which are vocalized loudly, so that when you are sacked eventually , it is approved all round. I had that problem with this man. Soon the clerks in the library warned me that they felt he was actually gunning for me to be terminated.

The problem was that I was friendly with the Assistant Librarian, who was Belgian, a certain Mr. Hostene. This was not good news to the Afrikaners because this was a foreigner. Secondly my Afrikaans was not as good as my English; another bad point. Thirdly the Assistant Librarian spoke some French some of which I knew ; that also did not help. The man had only to find a legitimate excuse to exercise his right as the boss; and I waited.

The actual librarian was said to have gone on studies to New York and would soon be back. When he did turn up, I did not see much of him but heard that his name was Kirsten where the Assistant was Hostene.

A few days after the arrival of the librarian, whom I did not even know that well, he called me asked me my name. I then told him and his response was : " Collect your pay and do not come back" . End of story ; the man from New York was back!

In that library however I learned some things. I learned about the film photo copier with what the librarian called 'the blink side" which had to face down to copy on the machine. I also found out that the library had a whole dictionary of American Slang words.

My job had been simple. First see that the library is clean in the morning. Then spend time separating paper pages that are stuck together with a paper knife, in all new ordered books for the library. I was given a table, a chair, and a place in the corner of the room. Thirdly I had to be ready to make photocopies for professors for all items they wanted to use in their classes. The last was to help in the distribution of journals to different professors' offices, with a white girl who, thankfully was brought up in Cofimvaba in the Transkei and knew Xhosa. The thrill was to secretly talk to her in Xhosa which she pronounced very well too. All I really knew about her personal life in the conversation was that she resided at the house on campus called *Felsted*.

I sorrowfully had to leave the university before I knew anyone better. That chance led me to working at the Livingstone Hospital, a job I found by deciding on my own to visit the hospital. The thing that got me promoted at the hospital from a Porter to a Receptionist the ability to pull indices from files needed for patients so fast from the cabinet at the registration window that the supervisor was impressed and recommended me to be registered as a receptionist.

The Belgian Assistant librarian had taught me to appreciate one French philosopher, and that was Balzac. I was covering one book for the library with the title "Bazac Que Voici" , and he happened to be around and we talked. Hence I found later I had to buy the book for a friend from Haiti who spoke Creole, and who resided in Evanston IL. USA.

Also Hostene and I spoke and discussed which Psychoanalyst was best, and he happened not to like Freud at all, and I had by that time read a little of C.G .Jung. There we agreed totally. His argument with which I agreed was that one could not legitimately say that in humans all responses and adjustments were centered on the sex of the person. There had to be more.

It was years later while talking to a teenage girl visiting the museum on Washington Island and was a student that I learned that Belgians also spoke Dutch. That then cleared why the Assistant Librarian spoke of "the Blink side" for "blink" in Dutch is "Shine" or Shiny. So the shiny side was to face down on the copier. I learned that from him without even knowing why he said that when he spoke very little Afrikaans! One has to understand the language spoken even if it is not a legitimate language in the book. It works. If I was in Johannesburg I had to know that, for they had "Tsotsi Taal" which is not in any book. Tsotsi Taal really means in English "Hooligan's language". When they talk of the "Fast Move" one has to know that the fellow has got to find you the trick in doing what he is doing or a way of a fair deal in what he offers. If one wanted to be fancy one could use a sentence like " Kai kai mafatseng" In Sesotho meaning : " We are far from home among nations" but actually means " "Can you do me a trick on this one?" While I was in construction the fellows from the Transvaal would use this last phrase, and if it was after a public holiday and we had worked they would then add "Five hours over time", even if they were not at work on that public holiday. They would then be asking for five hours overtime! I had to always refuse and they knew it. This was because I was known to speak "George's language" and in that crowd that George's was English.. It amazed me that even though those fellows thought that , because I caught onto their language, they also thought I was also some kind of a hooligan!

Hosten the Librarian, knew how things went. One does not always ask questions, one learns what has to be done with each move and performs a task! It takes a lot of "move reading" ..Listen to the song that has the line "Find me a find!", and you will know what I mean…

Musical Tastes

I may never have mentioned this, but I am aware that the time of my sudden return from university without qualifying, was a turbulent time for me and for many young people of my age. I shall go into a short explanation.

In my younger age , I had been very interested in music, an attitude that has extended in existence into my adult life. The kind of music I grew to like as a young student was varied in genre. I would listen to anything I could lay my hands on. As we progressed to junior high, the music of the young became Rock 'n Roll. This of course got one to watch related movies at the theater. To mention a few we watched besides deep rock, were movies involving instrument players like Glen Miller and Benny Goodman., the others of course were strictly rock, for example "Rock Around The Clock"; "Loving You; "The Girl Can't Help It" , etc. It took years for any change to this to occur. That happened when I left school and worked in a hospital

The popular dances at my school were strangely enough not rock but ballroom dancing. At the hospital where I was first employed, they had invited a group to play for patients, for it was a long term facility. The group that came were just about four fellows, playing drums, piano, saxophone and string base. This was a jazz combo. The radiographer in the hospital was an American girl who also was not only interested in music but in many subjects such as philosophy etc, but she was Catholic and at the time I was studying the Bahá'í Religion. However we shared much in common. As she was somewhat friends with the people who taught me religion, and her mother and sister also belonged to that religion. I would sometimes visit their home which was in a prestigious area in town, and near a university.

I soon learned from my friend that she also liked jazz, and from her I received my first *avant garde* LP by Miles Davis playing at the Black Hawk. Two songs attracted me in that LP: "Walking" and " Bye , Bye Blackbird". This LP record, was my parting gift from my friend when she suddenly left the hospital and eventually married to move back to the United States.

When I got to college the following year, I got into jazz very much. On leaving university, I became one of the few *avant garde* fans in my town, for there they knew the jazz of Duke Ellington, Ella Fitzgerald and Louis Armstrong, but at that time no one even spoke of Thelonious Monk, Miles Davis, John Coltrane etc. These persons were unknown then. This was in the early 60s.

Rosemary Sala and I never talked music. So my interest in jazz was of my own adventure. It took time for me to try to introduce my music to them, i.e. Rosemary and Emeric, because up to that time, the only records I had got from them were those of Ella Fitzgerald and "Satchmo". Now, I was playing Brubeck, Mingus, Miles and Monk of whom they knew very little. I took pride in showing Rosemary one LP I bought by Les McCann. It was called "Oh Brother!"

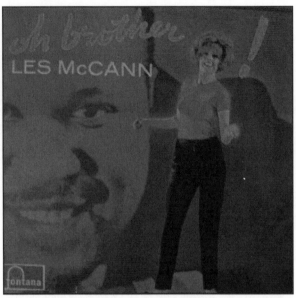

The cover to the LP I bought and showed to Rosemary. Cover of LP by Les McCann purchased from a local store , "Master Keys", of Port Elizabeth owned by the Gunstons'. A copy of LP loaned to Rosemary Sala for perusal and appreciation.

The setting of the picture must have interested Rosemary , for she kept the LP for some weeks before I went back to pick it up. No one of those I was associated with knew where that path was going , and paying dues in jazz can be a dangerous and deep task to undertake until one attains a way of personal appreciation of the music, not tainted by any of the situations people usually associate with it. I perceived this kind of music to have been born in very difficult circumstances in the States, admittedly. If one has doubts about how dangerous life can be in these situations, think of one getting a Mickey Finn or a whatever in a glass and waking up in late morning,. That hurts even more if one remembers that one entered the place with a lady! Need I explain? It just hurts and leaves one devalued for the longest time. Believe me! Regardless, when dues have to be paid, one pays.... One is lucky if life persists. To go into the subject of the message of this music would be different subject, and can only be undertaken at a future time; for it has a definite message, which must be eventually appreciated as real American music ,not attained in Europe **or** anywhere else.

From Rosemary I had later received the music of Handel, Schubert and others. A far different musical LP was received from my Radiographer friend and that was of the title "The Mikado", by Gilbert and Sullivan. As one can perceive these gifts had a deeper meaning and were not shallow.

Because of this sad difference in musical types and tastes, there was a brief separation between myself and the Salas' while I tried to figure out where I stood with it. My real help in understanding this occurrence came when I met Lowell Johnson, in later years, for he was a Jazz Announcer on Radio at the time I met him and a Bahá'í. I had to align the two involvements..

Learning New Languages

From an early age in junior high and high school, I loved different languages, and Rosemary helped much with this by supplying grammar books which she would sell for about a tickey each at the school. After paying her a number of times for the books, she would forgive the debt without completion. It seemed she just wanted one to show a willingness to pay a debt. From her I received a French Grammar book, and bought for myself a Spanish Dictionary, for she and her husband spoke both languages. At the time, I did not know that Emeric Sala knew many more languages and spoke them fluently.

It was during these years that I acquired a number of books about languages.

The result of my interest in languages was that I went and bought a set of LPs that had lessons in French, from a store in downtown Port Elizabeth and started my own lessons. That in a way brought me back to getting more involved in humankind and religion again. This is a long story and I shall not tell all of it lest I embarrass myself! The road to straightening up can be long and involved and I took it.

From this point on I found it easy to know a few words in varied languages , and this has helped greatly as introduction to people I might have never known at all. Learning to greet in German, Italian, Hebrew, Russian , Polish, and eventually learning to chant some words in Arabic an Farsi became much easier to do. Of course, several persons were met along the way and they assisted greatly.

Set of LPs for French lessons purchased at the OK Bazaars in Port Elizabeth, South Africa. (cover scanned by author from original) A box of four LPs of French Lessons purchased in 1966

Improving or upsetting the cultural balance

In my humble opinion I feel the balance in African culture in South Africa was greatly affected by the girls getting educated, especially as regards the nursing profession. The reason for that thought is knowing that in nursing, girls had to go out of their cultural background and train in various towns and cities where the culture was far different from the one of their origin. So ideologies from different cultures flowed around all over the land. Besides this there was marriage into different tribes and cultures and the gene pool was greatly variegated. Considering that nurses at that time earned more than many men, there had to be changes in many a custom, for in most cases the women held the purse for the performance of each ritual, and therefore had to have a say in how money was spent and therefore how things were done. Their presence could no longer be considered as minor. This also meant that women could choose who they wanted to marry, and not be married off to any man of parental choice. This was a drastic change!

Of course women like my mother enjoyed this as she always abhorred being bullied by some man in her house about things she felt she knew better about. Hence there were women at this time, who were great advisors to young girls and women, about how to conduct themselves with the new options. In my street the two women I knew who did this very well were my mother and a lady called Nosidima Sishi who was a Sister Tutor at the hospital. On my last visit in April/May 2017, I did notice several changes in attitudes of the time. The third lady was the one who taught me better music while I was in junior high, and she was also a nurse on my street. One obvious change is that some women have advised successfully that, during circumcision some methods of checking medical preparedness and medical attention of a modern nature be utilized on their sons, who are due for the custom. This was unheard of in the past. This had been a men-only endeavor!

Incidents and Accidents of Life

My Second Employment

As mentioned in the book "This Side Up', my first employment was in a hospital and a Tuberculosis hospital at that. I learned much at this hospital because I had to work with the Influx Control Office, across the street to confirm employments of workers, as a General Office Worker , and had to be in touch with Department of Bantu Administration and Development to apply for Disability Grants for patients in long-term sickness in the hospital, as well as a social worker for families involved. This also meant that I had to be in touch with the companies employing blacks who came into hospital to make sure that patients had received their pay due for periods already worked. This stance became useful when I was in a larger hospital in helping to distinguish Motor Vehicle Cases from IOD(Injured On Duty) or Workman's Compensation Act Cases later. For a certainty, the clerk at the Bantu Affairs who attended to Disability Grants and payments thereof, was a certain Mr. Nkomo, and the man in charge of social work was a certain Mr. Bokwe. This was fact for I dealt with both of them in preparing Disability Grants for patients..

Having left work and gone study in at college I returned one summer to find no employment for December. However, I discovered that four of friends I knew at school, had jobs with the government in the Tax Department, the Welfare Department, and the Deaths and Births Department. Having found nothing to do, I was invited by the friends to join them. Two of these friends subsequently became lawyers ; the third became a mayor of an African township in Uitenhage, i.e. KwaNobuhle Township.

I then joined the Additional Tax Office, which dealt with companies that had to pay tax to the government for all Black employees on their staff. It was the first time I learned of that tax and never knew it was applied. I had the job of informing such companies to pay tax and if delinquent to issue summons to court.

My friends in different departments were James Tini, who became a mayor; Nghona, a lawyer; Lucas another lawyer, and Zigqolo, a clerk who soon left employ through sickness..

I had to leave work in December after working for about a month ,to do Bahá'í work in the Transkei. That work that had to do with electing delegates for a Bahá'í Convention which was going to be held that year in Swaziland. . Subsequently I returned to college to continue with a Diploma in Teaching. Before returning to school, I again turned up for work at the Bantu Affairs, and was told they could not accommodate me there. I guessed that story of my teaching the Faith in the Transkei, and the fact that the Faith taught oneness of the human race, where the law of the land adhered to Separate Development, had got through to the department. Hence the denial of employment..

The head of the Tax Department then had been a certain Reineke, and the coworkers I had were a certain Johaan Van De Berg, and Snymaan. Handling taxi was no problem and we all kind of got along.

Employment there helped a lot in understanding how things were run in the country and gave me firsthand knowledge for the future. It however, puzzled me why Reineke thought I was foreign to the city. But I soon knew more about him when he became a Commissioner and performed my second marriage in later years to his apparent amusement, as then he was a magistrate. Before then he had been a Police Captain or Sergeant. I knew this because a man who later became a Radio Announcer, and was then a police constable working in the Tax Department, referred to him as " Sosaant" or Sergeant and whenever Reineke called him he would command with the words "Konstabel!" or 'constable'..

It is enjoined upon every one of you to engage in some form of occupation, such as crafts, trades and the like. We have graciously exalted your engagement in such work to the rank of worship unto God, the True One. Ponder ye in your hearts the grace and the blessings of God and render thanks unto Him at eventide and at dawn. Waste not your time in idleness and sloth. Occupy yourselves with that which prof- iteth yourselves and others. Thus hath it been decreed in this Tablet from whose horizon the day-star of wisdom and ut- terance shineth resplendent.

(Baha'u'llah, Tablets of Baha'u'llah, p. 26)

An Arrest that Defined a Path

When I was a student at Fort Hare university college I learned of a technique students adopted which is called steamrolling. Steamrolling in argument means that you hurry the person to make a very quick and immediate decision or answer, such that the person never realizes they are making a very big mis- take. Take for an example the question of person who knows very well that you are careful about grammatical mistakes and wants you to quickly tell him the difference or correction of this sentence:" The yolk of an egg are white or the yolk of an egg is yellow". You are now tricked into looking at the grammar and reply" The yolk of an egg is white" and you are caught because the yolk of an egg is yellow!

A Fort Harian avoids steamrolling and I do because I am a Fort Hare stu- dent. When they hurry and say: give us an answer, you pause and ask yourself "Why?". You then think it through and do not answer . .. not then anyway. At that particular time a trap is set!

The story I am about to tell may be short or long depending on how one looks at it:

In 1965 I was arrested for not having my 'book' on me. One may find that funny. Well, it is not. A book was an identity book a without which in the streets landed one in jail. It contains many details about a person from address , workplace, payment of tax etc. If you did not have the book it was jail and if again you had the book and had no tax stamp on it , that was also jail. I did not have the book on me. I was caught at the weekend and had to stay in jail and wait for the case on Monday.

In court I found that my younger brother who had been looking for me all over was present. I was sentenced to ten days in jail but there was a fine. My brother came up to assist . Then he was a student in Medicine in Natal University and did not know much about the streets and arrests and the procedure at that time for attaining release for one convicted.. I asked him if he had brought bail, and he had not. I then instructed him to hurry before I was transferred to "Rooi Hell" Prison (Red Hell Prison), to go the Sala and Company , and ask Emeric Sala to hand him some money to pay for the bail, for Donald my brother had just arrived from school and had not found any financial situation of his from which he could have obtained any funds.

Fortunately he made the trip and returned with the money just before we were transferred to a van to be transported to jail to serve the sentence, and thus I got me out.

However., on collecting the items that had been taken from me when I was booked in, I noticed that my arm watch was not there. I took what I was given as my property and left for home. At home I could not rest knowing they had my watch.

I set down to writing a letter in a formal manner asking them to find the watch. Sometime later I received a note asking me to collect the watch at the police station at the New Law Courts in the city. I did and that and was grudgingly given the watch and asked to sign for it.

Time passed, and then in 1967 I was arrested again for being in the city without papers that gave me permission to be there. This time no one came to the rescue. I served the whole five days ,partly at the police cells for the weekend and the rest at Rooi Hell.. The funny part was that I was arrested near a light house in Summerstrand very near to where I used to take a swim in the old days when I used to attend classes on the Bahá'í Faith with Rosemary Sala, and across the apartment where she lived. This had been my refuge in the past, before starting off for home in New Brighton. That weekend I again stayed in jail and waited for the sentence on Monday. After sentencing of course I was transferred to "Rooi Hell" or "Red Hell" Prison.

The saddest part of the jail sentence, was being taken in to the cell. First I had to get rid of all belongings including the same watch I had claimed from the police station. This watch found in my pocket among my clothes, was recognized and it was set aside for more questioning. That was when I got the beating of my life from a policeman dressed in plain clothes. I was not sure if he was a "reservist", but the beating left no reserves in the body. He did a full pounding while asking me to hold the watch in my hand. I guess that this was one way of legitimizing the beating. I had the watch in hand , whatever that must have meant to them, for they were three of them working me over. The excuse was that they had found me smuggling a watch into a cell.

Later I was then handed over to some Colored fellows who were to cut my hair. They had a hang of a good time ,cutting my hair on one side of the head and showing each other just how funny I looked.

I got through that , and had to face up to some guy in the cell who wanted sexual relations. I sat up all night watching him and thus avoiding a rape.

Fortunately the days I had spent in the cell waiting for the trial had short- ened my stay in the jail and I was soon out. A very unforgettable time, indeed! Imagine then, walking from the city with that kind of haircut that had been done with a pair of scissors,, with persons in the buses who knew me as a clerk at the hospital, staring in wonder and amusement. Somehow I survived that too…

By that time a depression was setting in. This again was caused by a dis- appointment in a love affair. I had fallen in love with a Catholic girl who wanted me to convert before being involved in anything serious. I had refused, and without any warning, she had fallen in love with a porter working under me in the Casualty Reception Office . That had hurt, and I had refused to talk about it ,not even to my mother who had met the girl and liked her very much, something not quite like my mother, but she did.

When I did not respond to my mother's inquiry about the girl, and just shut up ,she thought I was being cheeky. The result of that was that she felt I had to find a place where I could stay and behave the way I wanted to behave. As there were no such places for single people in the township, the alternative I was given by Rent Office, was to find a bed at the Single-men's Quarters, a buildings occupied by workers recruited by the government from the rural areas workers in the cities. That then was my estate.

I refused to live there but not overtly. I just swore I would not live there. So I would come into my home, and take a nap on a bed which had neither a pillow nor a blankets on it ,just on the springs of the mattress.

The result of that was an increase in the worsening of the depression and I was soon to see a doctor in the police quarters.

Having been admitted I spent seven weeks in hospital until I had a sneaky idea that the Head Nurse would talk for me if I somehow communicate with him and negotiate a release from the hospital. One day I just walked up to him and said in his ear" Get me the heck out of here!" Some hours later I went up to him again and said "I meant what I said earlier' .The very next Monday following that weekend I was out . I was discharged from hospital.

My troubles were not over just then. I had to travel home from the hospital. That meant boarding a train. I was given a loaf of bread and a bottle of tea for the trip. Guess what? As I sat waiting for the train, I chanced walking away from my seat, and two little White boys dressed in very neat school uniform came up to the bottle and kicked it over, spilling all that tea onto the platform. Lucky me!

However I got home , and started work as a Batch Charge Hand in a glass factory. I was later promoted to a position of a Quality Control Clerk.

My victory in that stay in a hospital is that , though they queried and persuaded me to talk they missed asking me the cause of the depression and, under all that treatment, I refused to talk and not one knew what the problem was. I accepted treatment withheld all chat. After all, what was in my mind was my business and I , no one else's ,and I had to find a solution, and today I am certain I am able to write about it and laugh at it all.

The girl I wanted to marry passed on a few years ago from a cancer situation and that occurred while she resided in the United Kingdom, working as a nurse. I am proud of myself on this that , I did not trade my religion for marriage and shall not do that now anyway . Age and commitment do not allow!

The very next year I attended a Bahá'í National Convention in Soweto, and that is when I met Lowell Johnson. The rest will be history if one reads the book " In Spite of All Barriers" by the same author

Robert Mazibuko after second questioning by the Security Police in South Africa, taking a vacation in Alice at theuniversity as advised by his docor.

Early Bahá'í Years

Frederick Gqola, married in later years(Google Images, 2017)

Frederick Bafana Gqola was my first Afrian Bahá'í teacher. I was nineteen when I visted him at Kwazakhele in Port Elizabeth after obataining his address from the Salas', however on my return for vacationin 1964 I understood that he was in jail for political involvement. I could understand that, for South Africa in those days was a hard and difficult country to live in for an African. However , in order to survive that, one had to constanlty remind one's self of the Supremacy of our Creator and realize that His Plan never fails. In the environment I lived in at the Fort Hare University College, this was even harder to do, that is keep in faith, but there were several minsisters and several gentlemen who stuck to religon, and I was one of those. One of them ins the well-known and late Bishop Sigqibo Dwane., whose good friend at college had been the Honorable Consul for South Africa in Norway, Mr. Stephen Pandule Gawe who always addressed him by his nickname of "Sgqi" . I would see Bishop Dwane at the airport in Johannesburg many times in later years, and would avoid greeting him as a past fellow student I knew, out deference for his position as a Bishop. However, he would , were he alive, testify that we have met. The other prelate I met once o twice, was the Cannon Reverend Mbopha, who would sometimes chat with me as we waited for flights in Port Elizabeth. Once he asked me where I was bound and I let him know that I headed for a Bahá'í Administrative meeting in Johannesburg,, whereupon , he replied that he was going a church meeting in Durban too. He had been the one to question me on my belief when I left the church, as that was reported to him by my mother. The pleasant thing was that I showed him, at that point of discovery, literature of the Faith and he had seen no harm in it. Of course, that had not been easy to accept form my mother!

The last I heard of Fred Gqola, was from his ex-wife, a lady called Winifred who was a Bahá'í in Port Elizabeth . I later while I was in the Sates, understood that he was out of prison on Robben Island where he had been for ten years. The surprise was seeing his picture on the net, as above,, and know that it is covered by copyright . That is acknowledged by the author, but he will only use the picture in the format it is in , in recognition of copyright rulings.

Fred was my friend and I met him through Rosemary and Emeirc Sala, both , at this time deceased, after pioneering in Mexico's Guadalajara, and Chapala. Their niece has written two books on them , one updated from the other and they are both called "Tending the Garden". Ilona Weinstein Sala, the author, is a Bahá'í in Canada and wrote this book on her relatives, updating it a few years ago, through a publisher in the United States. Fred might want to know the fate of our two friends. We have no differences, and are even willing, should we meet once more, to talk, for the Xhosas believe things are fixable only through talking and perhaps an agreement or decision found that way.

A lady of African American race group once gave me a tape recording of a talk by Emeric Sala, called " Shoghi Effendi's Question" given in Canada after the Salas' return to that country, where he states " Adolescent boys cease to fight when they reach maturity and dispose of their problems over a table".. We surely pray for that, for a bloodbath was avoided in South Africa through eloquence and strategy. We thank the Lord for that! I still treasure some of the correspondence we had while Fred was away in jail, for it manifests something of what we wish as a better quality of life for ourselves and others.

After College: Lessons Learned

As one progresses through the trip of life, one learns some things to do and not to do, and also how to do what one then decides to do. I shall site only one example of that in case someone wants to take advice and learn through what would appear to have been my folly or lesson.

Unguarded Drink

In the early days after college, there was much experimentation with behaviors and I was part of that. However, one sometime or other wakes up from the stupor. The challenge would be choosing future friends who may no longer be in that stream of life one has experienced prior to change. As always the past will always haunt one and want one to go back to old standards. This in a way happened in this instance. I had decided to stop the youthful frolicking and concentrate on more serious and urgent matters like settling down, an issue which entailed partly, finding a partner.

While vacationing in East London, a time which coincided with the death of a South African President and resultant funeral, I chanced to meet a girl I got interested in . Of course, when I returned home I invited her to visit me. I found my mother was not in favor of the girl because of a report she had had from my aunt in East London. The report had not recommended the girl as a worthy partner. To me that did not matter much, I liked the girl and that was all there was to it.

On the girl's first visit to Port Elizabeth I took her to a movie, after work, a movie I scarcely can remember. By the time the theater show was over it was more or less after dark.

My status at this time was that I had ceased to visit old friends at Jazz shows or 'joints' etc, however, on this occasion, when I found myself with no friends, I decided I would take a chance and visit a 'joint'. All this seemed to work out well. At the place I was offered a drink which I refused. There was a medical doctor at the joint and several girls who were nurses at the local hospital with a number of local guys. I adamantly refused to partake of any drink. What I looked for was a private moment with the girl, an event which was not to take place for a while. However, my mistake was in accepting a drink of orange juice. I learned the principle of never leaving a drink unguarded, for I accepted the drink at about 7:00 P.M. and got up at about 9:00 am. What can one do but leave the girl after that, especially if she had no complaint in the morning. Somebody had spiked my drink out of spite or anger that I did not drink. My prime suspect was the doctor. But I said nothing. That however, ended my affair with the girl. For, after that it was impossible to continue.

The Defining Change

Change of Life-Style: Sickness Strikes

Between 1962 and 1966 I had not had a steady love affair, not an affair that would have been said to last more than a few months anyway.

At this point in my life, a period after 1966, I was again beginning to look for more answers in my religion. To boot, I had stopped any late nights and had for the first time started observing the law of annual fasting that I found in my religion. Because of these drastic changes and because there was no advisor I could turn to, I tended to be a recluse. Perhaps the worst of that stance was refusal to communicate my thoughts to anyone but a few of my friends, even with them ever so cautiously. The reason for the caution in speech was a fear that I might reveal the hurt I felt over the loss of a love.

This silence itself did not bring good results but that did not deter me from keeping it. It became far easier to speak by symbolizing than open speech. Therefore , at this time, I was a very silent person.

Having decided to fast and keep to myself, I met a good friend I knew at school, who was now friends with my junior high science teacher, and that was Julia Galo. To keep me company during the fast I borrowed from her some LPs by Ella Fitzgerald and played them as I prepared for work each evening, before starting off for night duty at the hospital. Julia had borrowed from me some Jazz records and loaned me hers. Although this helped a little, it did not do away with my problem.

Admitted in medical hospital

It was after the fasting season in 1966, just after Naw Ruz that I found I had a problem with my bladder. To help with a persistent headache, I had started taking a pain killer that was a mixture of chemicals that, though they helped had a side effect of drying my systems and induced constipation and loosening of the bladder. For that reason, this also had a side effect of constant urination. So I saw a doctor who advised a cystoscopy. The cystoscopy procedure yielded no results as it proved that my systems were fine to the frustration of my Urologist. Having been exposed to that I went further in refusing to discuss anything with anybody, for both issues were disgracing in my thinking. It was just about at this time in 1967 , that I resigned from work and stayed home. Such an issue surprised my mother, for earlier I had talked marriage with her about a girl, the which girl I had by then lost. The resultant period between 1967 and the beginning of 1968 was for me a period of sadness, for these were the months I had to deal with a serious time of depression. A depression which could only be attributed to lost love and a drastic change from a lavish life to a more stable life. I had managed that change without the advice of any doctor or social worker. It took me, however, sometime to transition to anything that I could call stable, for I had been used to a life of a night-lifer and daylight life was quite different. Somehow I had had to start my life all over again.

Work and Developments

It is kind of controversial that my next employment at the beginning of 1968, that lasted some two years was as a Quality Controller in a glass factory, and that my next job in the following ten years, was as a Quality Controller in the Tablet Department in a prestigious company in South Africa. During employment which entailed examining tablets and capsules for defects or quality, I found I had an eye problem. I had had an eye problem before but had ceased on my own from wearing glasses until this time. I saw an Ophthalmologist who tested me twice and came up with a surprising answer. He felt he could not give me proper glasses because the treatment of the tranquilizers I was taking tended to interfere with my sight. He promised to give me a proper prescription for glasses once I ceased taking the tablets. I had to continue with the old glasses I had acquired from an Optometrist earlier. After that year I never went back to the Ophthalmologist even though I ceased for years in taking the tranquilizers, for my medical doctor did not see the need for any concentrated treatment but rather wanted me to occasionally take a mild tranquilizer for depression.

More than fifteen years later when I was residing in the United States, I saw a doctor to resume treatment of tranquilizers, which I had not taken for some five years ,and he refused to treat me unless I had a full examination. Subsequent to that, I was seven years later I was again diagnosed as being depressed and was taken off any medication for anything else . Another ten years later I again was taken off all medication. It was around 2017 after I had a had a car accident that I was requested by a local doctor to take a nightly dose of a tranquilizer. At this time I was in the United States residing on an island. , which is where I stand at the moment without much complication to the story. I am now in my seventies and do not require that much monitoring by medication. The important thing to note is that throughout that period I refused to mention the original problem of a lost love which had been my issue, to any doctor or person. The one person I found inescapable to keep talk about that was and is my present wife, Gretchen Misselt, whom I acquainted with all related problems; and not a doctor. The drastic change of lifestyle that was complicated by a disappointment in loving, had combined to be a problem that dogged my footsteps for years! The loss of love as a reason, blurred all other involvement I might have been in either as a worker or as a student, and that had become my safety, for I did not have to make any other major confessions…

A Set of LPs borrowed from Tabina Julia (Ntsuka) Galo, I used each night I went of duty during the Bahá'í Fast of 1966, my first. (from cover of CDs purchased by author in US.)

Loving and Leaving

Regarding the involvement I had , one may want to know just what happened in one's life, when we know that all have faults. This is a huge or simple question depending on one's view. It is well known that in the young age, one is tangled up in a many a liaison before a final decision comes into view. I was no less involved in that. As a result, after my first book i.e. "This Side Up", was published my friends felt it covered very little, for they felt they knew more that does not come into light. I agree to an extent. I made a decision to recall my experiences and not to write a confession. That has to be clear.

Where I am residing at this time, they talk of " one night stands" which my little brother called "Hit and runs". I rather defer to the song " Traces of Love" or loves that fizzled out, many of which are not worth the mention as in a story for they did just that, fizzled out! There are those which took some time to actually fizzle out, and may be part of one's perception of one's self. Those need be mentioned. I have also been asked why I had such young wives to start with. The truth is I have had loves affairs with women who were much older than I was and even older than my eldest sister, and they knew somehow that a love would not last or would mean delivering a long explanation to me, an issue which would cause me to become disenchanted with an association.

Before telling of that story one needs to explain a few things which matter in the issue. Traditionally African girls seldom gush at you with: " I love you too". One has to figure that out in how and what they say or do. In olden times, before "sugar daddies" and "sugar babies" girls spoke in a lingo one had to know. To do that one had to engage an older person , preferably an older woman to interpret words and actions of a potential love, so that one knew where one stood with a girl. Besides this one could not be in love with a clan sister or any relative unless it were an in-law or that level of relationship. There were therefore, many times one abandoned an affair and was abandoned in a affair because one did not understand the lingo. To the girl it would be a case of " If you do not get that, how do we begin to live together?". Sometimes the man kicked himself for not catching something the man should have caught and left too early in an attempt to clinch a liaison with a girl. The thing required not just feelings but brains. In that case one has to tell one's self that if one wants to catch the bird one has to wake up earlier in the morning. and that is being wise much earlier in one's life. It is a fact that in 'girl talk' there is much meaning, It not just prattling, and one has to learn to get to the truth of things. This I fear, is the case in Western Civilization too, I had to learn. The fight begins much earlier than when it starts. What goes on has roots elsewhere and one had to find them to quell a dispute of heart or even in married life .

One girl I met who was under counseling and once made the statement " Tread carefully, it is my heart you step on". Because I treasure that statement I shall not name any names but will describe in general some of the things one goes through in getting established.

When I was twenty one, I was introduced by a friend to a girl who was much older than I , and possibly than even my eldest sister. I found her hard to track down and get her into a commitment. Later , many years later, in which time I was associated with girl, I got to know why. She was being very decent with me, for she knew that at twenty I did not know she had been married before, and that by the time I reached thirty six she had a son who was twenty one. All this came out in small bits, much later with time. I then understood her reticence to engage me in an affair.

I had tried hard to impress her even at a time when she was physically incapacitated after a vehicle accident, by bringing not only flowers but cards and the like, while she lay in hospital recovering. At the end of that period which took years , she finally came around to my thinking, for she had discovered that my background was Zulu and Zulu take any age for a girlfriend in her thinking, but by that time I had other commitments and could not duly respond. We stayed friends through a very difficult time for me, but soon I found I could not commit either because of my own personal reasons .The one mistake I made was leaving the association without explaining myself. I now recall my aunt , who lived in Johannesburg's Soweto, saying that, when one wants to leave a love affair, even in Johannesburg, one had to explain to the partner that the interest was no longer there, before engaging another love. I did not do that, and that remained a sore with her for some time, and l learn that she has now passed on. One has to listen to the song " Down the road of broken hearts where nobody's hiding their tears" (Patti Page), to get that.

I was divorcing at the time we had made contact , and had to care for two children in the process. I know there must have been an expectation to commit but I found it hard to decide that then, and there was much that was in the grapevine about my situation too. She would probably be blamed for all sorts of things. However, as it were, by the time I was free to marry I was really free, for I had no affair in view. I lived for a while alone. She herself must have lost all interest in anything I did after that, for she never knew when I married a second time, and only learned that I had moved out of the country after a second divorce, when I visited from Swaziland.

The delay in African girls in committing in olden times was to give time for both parties to investigate one the other and know what they walk into when establishing an affair. This took time and effort and one could not be overt in many cases. By the time that the statement of love was acknowledged both parties knew one another thoroughly.

One lady I knew said "No" to every advance I made, and I later learned from a friend after the attempts had been abandoned that sometimes an African lady says " No" when she means " Yes" and one has to check other reactions to establish the true response. I could have hit myself, after years! I had to live with Xhosas in their domain to get to know this. "No" may mean " Think".

As Medical Assistant and as a Nurse Aid I have learned this, sometimes the hard way!

Losing the Trend of the subject

In this vein, there are two times I felt in one instance perplexed, and another wondering why people do what they do. While I was on vacation, from college once, I visited a shebeen or a home where I could meet a lot of fellows from college and girls from the local nurses' home. As we all sat talking on a sofa, I got into a discussion with a very pretty girl, and this was on a subject matter I wished to discuss. It was a medical and scientific subject. I got into it hard and produced all kinds of proof to prove my point. I even went home which was located down the street from where we were, to fetch a book of psychology by Carl Jung on the subject of " Dreams , Visions and Reflections" to prove a point. I totally forgot that there could be another subject the girl wanted to discuss. She was a midwife and ready to acquire a home. This latter fact escaped me totally. Finally under what I now feel was desperation , she disappeared into a room and came out in her night clothes. I still had a point to convince her. Sadly she looked at me and said:" Some other time then , Robert" . That took me pretty much by surprise because my mind was not there yet. So in embarrassment, because I knew I was too late, I said also:"Yes. Some other time" and left without my book which I never got back.

The second time, I again got involved in the same house with another girl, seriously in an argument. There happened to be a government dignitary in the house, but to me these were just folks in the house. I had been invited to go out by a college friend. After some precious minutes of discussion, my friend came over and listened. While I was talking one man I now know to be a government dignitary reached into his coat, and took out a firing weapon and asked one of the girls to put it away since he did not wish to use it. I was somewhat surprised at this show off of power from a man I did not even know.

My friend hastily said:"Robbie, let's get out of here!" On reaching the street I asked him to explain the rude disturbance of a good argument. He replied that the man from a government was angry, that I had been talking to his girl! ! I did not comment or ask questions. I found that safer...

Many times I had found that the best way of not being tangled up in some ugliness is to bow out of a situation where one has to compete for love. I cannot do that... A woman should only love like a man and not ask to be competed for. That is my motto, after years of disappointment and pain in loving. Twice I found that the girl I loved was also in love with my younger brother's friend. Under that discovery I would then leave, for I cannot compete in loving with my own brother. It does not seem right or moral. In my own little book, a person respects a younger brother's view of one's self. What is he supposed to think or do when his friend competes with his elder brother over a love affair? If we have to do that, then we might live by the motto of " dog eat dog" and that to me is not even human.

I feel and believe that it should never be a necessity to aggrandize one's self at the expense of one's brother, be they a relation of not. Also one should not feel it a need to kill just in order to mate. Animals do that, and humans live under a different code. That is the reason they are called "human" and not just animals. To find sheer animal love, if there be such a thing and not depravity, is not a *sine qua non*. It is never a waste to live without sexual contact, for humans are made to do a lot more than just reproduce themselves, they have to grow in other ways. There is want and then there is need. It is better if the need can be all encompassing than limited to the self. In some societies even marriage has been deemed more of a strategy in times past. Today it is a choice of a partner to travel Eternity with. It is no bond to be taken or dropped lightly for with it comes a vow before the Deity and His witnesses. If we then wish Him to trust us, He must find reason to see that we trust His law and pay respect to any promise we make Him. If that is not the case, then we take the stance of the animal, and are not being His Image.

The Challenge of Our Day

Again, regarding statements made above, it would seem to me and to many others that today there is a blur between that which a human can do and what the animal does without effort out of the dictates of nature and the surroundings. When I was about sixteen I attended a class in the Xhosa language in South Africa. My teacher would describe African life in olden times and show us how things went very wrong with the coming of modernity, and he would then with a very bitter tone address us with the comment I now translate" I have an undying grudge against the Whiteman". The reason for that may be likened to the reason England had a social problem with the coming of the Industrial Revolution of the 1830, a breakdown in manners and the first existence of the squalor of crowded homes, all for the profit of the industry. It is very true that Christianity brought a good redefinition of norms in Africa, but , considering that it was introduced at a high price of loss of material gain, it also brought mannerisms that were not there to the same extent to Africa.

There is no sense in crying "Foul!" every time we see anything bad accruing from the behaviors we introduced in Africa, when we know that we created the opportunity for them to exist. The past industrial progress has been in a way a sabotage on manners, and we did this for the sake of profit, when morality, the very aim of existence, suffered and languished on the bed of material gain. All that while, when we look at our situation we claim that man has got to be free: liberty, ladies and gentlemen, when liberty without any control has allowed us to exist, not as husbandmen for the planet, but as co-equals of the animal, when we are not even equipped for that. It is come to such a pass that the loss of life on the planet by humans has far less an urgency than the hunger of our pets!

In so far as we are concerned , we have reaped that gain even from Africa, and time enough has come to hand Africa back for them to govern. That is called just and proper today. To top it all we make a big issue of Africa not catching up with democracy when we know we have not handled that too well ourselves for several decades of war and pillaging. We name this struggle with such beautiful terms that it has become palatable to exist in our debunked world with an air of superiority that we are above the animal. I ask : "Are we above the animal, or do we envy the animal?"

> Liberty must, in the end, lead to sedition, whose flames none can quench. Thus warneth you He Who is the Reckoner, the All-Knowing. Know ye that the embodiment of liberty and its symbol is the animal. That which beseemeth man is submission unto such restraints as will protect him from his own ignorance, and guard him against the harm of the mischief-maker. Liberty causeth man to overstep the bounds of propriety, and to infringe on the dignity of his station. It debaseth him to the level of extreme depravity and wickedness.
> (Baha'u'llah, Gleanings from the Writings of Baha'u'llah, p. 335)

Were even I, to write down graphically what we do endeavor to do today in exact and fair terms, I would never find a publication, and that how free our world is today! We sanction all things we feel are an abuse of our laws of existence as stated by ourselves, and find reason to forgive and live with others because of their origins which are truly related to ours. That is called justice and not justification. My own relatives passed on, on farms dug out for them by hands that cared not, while many a dog lies in a beautifully made coffin and tears shed for it to boot! This is called human empathy and sympathy. It is true then that the law in South Africa was cockeyed for years! It would seem that the world has taken up that cause now.

Returning to the Work force

By the second week after my birthday in 1968, I found work in an electrical manufacturing company which was part of Phillips. However, this time the major part of employers were neither Afrikaner nor English, they were Dutch ,and spoke no Afrikaans I could recall.

The company manufactured glass bulbs and tubes, both clear and fluorescent. This meant working with furnaces and the like.

My first job in the company was feeding glass and sand into the furnace using a hoist lift and drums of prepared materials. After about a month of that I was employed as a Quality Controller, reporting to a supervisor who was partly German and spoke some German, Afrikaans and

English. I know because I found I had to ask him the proper German pronunciation for 'Wagner' and he let me know very easily. I later met that supervisor while he was employed as a salesman for a pharmaceutical company I worked for, only to find that his wife was a staff-nurse. He was known to know some German.

The foreman in my team was a man of Belgian origin, but brought up in Scotland. He was a good, kind ,man to work with and between us we had a friendship, for he found to his surprise that I knew some French a language spoken in Belgium. Also the man was an artist, and would spend hours painting nothing but birds. Hence, among the workers he was known as "the bird".

It was exactly at this time that I decided to go to Bahá'í Convention because , by the end of that year, the Salas who were my support , left the country for Canada. At that very time I then met Lowell Johnson of whom I wrote in the book " In Spite of All Barriers" later.

There were many other African friends I met at this time, some of whom became Bahá'ís with me. Two of those who are now late are Thomas Luthuli, who became a general supervisor later, and Christopher Songongo who later trained as a Male Nurse in Johannesburg and practiced in a local hospital.

The other man who featured greatly in the country later is now called Reverend Welile Kani. Welile was a relative of a school mate called Harry Kani. Harry who had an interest in my Faith but never joined, later got involved in activities and spent some time on Robben Island. Later still, after independence Harry then became a member of the Advisory Board and of a higher position in the municipality in Port Elizabeth. He has also by now passed on. Like a Fort Harian Harry had some cynical jokes about life. Once I let him know that my little brother was then a medical doctor, and his reply was: "You now bathe in his sun like a moon." I never appreciated that but kept my silence. The last song he reminded me of at my last meeting with him after his release was " This Can't be Love". I never knew why that song was so important at that time...

Welile still subsists and is now in a parish in an area earlier known as a Colored Area, and has two wonderful daughters who sometimes write me about their father. Welile lived for a while in the Kingwilliamstown area of the country.

Reverend Welile Kani

Sandy and Babalwa, Reverend Kani's two daughters.(gift from Kanis')

Welile's in-laws were very active Anglican Church goers. His mother-in-law a Mrs. Haarmans, was a sister in the hospital I worked in, and later she became the Matron of that hospital. They attended with her husband the St. Stephen's Church in which I was brought up earlier. They were an interesting family, however, outside of working with their mother at the hospital, the only other member of the family, besides Welile that I met was a lady , a student nurse, who I saw at the hospital, while I was doing Enquiries Clerk duties. She had borrowed a book I was reading about the " Scarlet Pimpernel" of the French Revolution, a character by Baroness Orczy. The last time I saw Sister Haarmans was at the hospital I worked in later where she came in for a minor procedure.

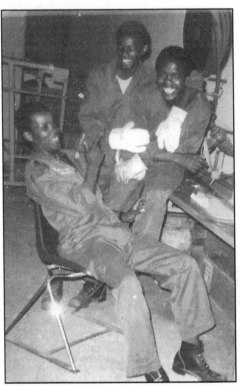

Co-workers, Bulb and Tube Sorters at Associated Glass Works. Elijah Mancayi on extreme right became a Bahá'í at this time. (gift from M'z'ubanzi i.e. Elijah, on right in picture)

My Stand and What it Entailed
It should be valued that, when one takes up a stand about what one believed in heart and soul, one should be committed to same in every principle of en-

deavor. I had, from a time earlier turned back to religion and decided to adhere to a commitment, by logic and emotion in determining my stand. Everybody I knew in Port Elizabeth knew that I had gone to pains in organizing meetings and slide shows on the Bahá'í Faith. I was then an obvious choice for one on the political scene for I knew many homes and persons I had had to deal with while teaching the Faith. Hence it was that I was approached by political organizations for support and belief. Because of the principle of the Faith, and that of non-participation in political activities, a principle lost to the Special Brach who were wont to visit me in those days, I found I could not legitimately join a political action, but could retain thoughts of what I wished should happen in the country.

The refusal to join groups at college was never a problem for I was regarded a s a "free thinker", and that left me room, for at that time in the 60s I was the only active Bahá'í on campus. There was in my second year a man I was told was Bahá'í but he would not talk about that much. Outside of that one of my friends soon served time on Robben Island, for such involvement.

At this point, this issue was a problem, as I perceived. The difference in thought played out in the work environment. Worst still, because I was a Bahá'í and a member of the National Bahá'í Administration, I was not permitted by that administration to join a trade union, as, at the time, all trade unions were in the struggle for independence in the country and were, therefore political in intent and purpose. What compounded the surprise of workers was that I had, for two consecutive years been elected to represent the Table Department, both Granulation and Compression rooms as a member of the Worker's Committee, elected by popular vote each year. When that was dissolved due to the formation of Trade Union allied group, I was asked with another Quality Controller to draft a new deal for workers which we called the Togetherness Group instead of Workers' Committee. That also ended when Trade Unions were allowable in the country

Pondering on the teaching of the Faith that humankind was one, it is no surprise that I could not very well get along with the Afrikaner worker that well. Given that my religion started in an Islamic country and had a teaching that differed from Islam, I still could not even get along with the Muslims, who comprised the greater part of the Analytical Laboratory, through which we submitted samples from the Tabletting Department before compression ensued. This issue left me only with the Jewish section of the company in the main, to be in any way close to, for the World Center of that Faith is in Haifa, Israel and is welcome there for the time.

One would then appreciate why it was very difficult when my department soon had a head who was Afrikaner, and who knew my stand in the company.

After ten years as a Quality Controller in that department, I had to leave and move to a more commercial post, further being changed there to work in a department controlled by one of the strong African men in the political scene of the time. From this time of the change in my department life became a pain. However I stuck it out and worked for years.

By the time I left the company I had been awarded an expensive watch for ten years service , but that did not seem to help, even though I held a certificate for Pharmaceutical Production Technology as the only Black who held that certificate in the company.

The injury perhaps was not as great as when the same man, who was in some political organizations, suggested that the head of the department I was now in, be the brother of the girl who had let me down earlier. Both of us knew that my time with the girl had terminated in a depression on my part. This in a sense was a mockery.

Most of my friends outside the company were amazed that this was happening, but what could they do outside the company, but try to console me with sympathy?

Perhaps this also was not enough for, within my own home I had a problem. My wife, as a high school student, had joined the same group that was prevalent in the country. However when we met she became a Bahá'í. At this point she had changed her views and wanted to know how I could actually stand working in a multiracial environment in my religion. This was an added pain in life for we dwelt in the same house. Both the workplace and the home were a painful challenge for years.

In a way I was not really surprised when my wife stayed in a hospital for over six months without visiting home. It was then that I had decided I needed a divorce badly . I had not tried infidelity for that was again against my religious belief. One had to have one wife, and make necessary arrangements for a separation where necessary. That then was my case, as I headed for pilgrimage in 1985. Plans for separation and divorce wee being arranged..

The issue of heading for pilgrimage was highlighted by comments by one of the managers in the company. She had been employed in the Influx Control of the government service, and wanted me out of the job as she felt I was a problem. However, her solution was even worse. She had heard that I was taking medication for a depression and wanted me to go to a doctor from the government who would, according to her, make sure that I never worked in the country after seeing him. I only had the option of going on pilgrimage and doing some serious thinking about what I was to do with my life at that stage. Prayer was the need. How better could I do that if I did not try the World Center of my religion? Through the accountant of the company, who knew I made trips to Johannesburg each month, and who was the one Afrikaner man I could deal with amicably, I found out I had pension money in the company. Having found that out , I then approached the CEO of the company, who offered me the money from my pension to go on pilgrimage. I was wont to cash my checks from the Bahá'í Faith with the Accountant and buy tickets through the company receptionist/telephone operator, and they all knew the Bahá'í Faith Administration to be an 'incorporated organization, not for gain' . So I had no charges on those checks as then I was traveling for a faith, a religious entity. This had worked! Contrary to expectation, I did not escape from the country but left through the Port Elizabeth Airport ,legitimately and got off at O'Hare , Chicago. I have been out to the country more than four time in the years between 1987 and now.

> **When we review history from the beginning down to the present day we find that strife and warfare have prevailed throughout the human world. Wars, religious, racial or political, have arisen from human ignorance, misunderstanding and lack of education. We will first consider religious strife and conflict.**
> **(Abdu'l-Baha, Foundations of World Unity, p. 22)**

> **How can a Faith, whose ramifications have brought it into contact with mutually incompatible religious systems, sects and confessions, be in a position, if it permits its adherents to subscribe to obsolescent observances and doctrines, to claim the unconditional allegiance of those whom it is striving to incorporate into its divinely-appointed system? How can it avoid the constant friction, the misunderstandings and controversies which formal affiliation, as distinct from association, must inevitably engender?**
> **(Shoghi Effendi, The World Order of Baha'u'llah, p. 199)**

Lessons learned from Love Affairs

The above stories have never been told until now. My mother used to let me accompany my father and yet she would receive no news from me concerning whatever we might have done or seen. As a result I gained the name of being " The Secret". I can retain my privacy for as long as it takes.

First of all. I know that one stricken with love may be or appear to be out of the logical and predictable, but I have learned to identify love and react to it normally. This can be told by a man from the perspective of being a man, and not that it cannot be equally told from the perspective of being female or a woman. It is in a man to experience even sexual enjoyment and not just in the woman. The best the woman does is provide proper attraction and proper environment, just as she does should she expect a child, just as a man has to . The biological setup of making love is not in one but in both and each provides the surrounding and the feelings of attraction. The attraction without the body reacting would never result in progeny. Hence to create a family one has to choose the one with whom it would be possible to live together in some understanding , with the hope of a continuance in the Beyond. I was once told by a friend that, in order to make a union , one has to have the spiritual understanding, and that is, have the same moral code; the social understanding, and that is , perceive more or less the same things about people and life; and thirdly the physical attraction where one is truly attracted to a certain kind of person. When any of these three lacks, pandemonium may result. Take for example physical attraction: How far does it go before old age overtakes it? If socially you agree can you develop some trust without the moral code necessary? Should you have the first two , how can one live with one that one does not feel a physical attraction for?

These above issues have made me realize the truism that one can only love God's creatures if one truly loves Him . Then one sees in the partner another creation and another servant of the Deity. If the union is to last only to the graveside, it could never have been a vow of attraction of a soul to a soul. Rather would it have been an attraction of a body to a body, a thing which ends with the demise of that body.

Today, this is my stand and I swear by it that a soul should be in communication with another soul in a union.. There are some statements in the Writings that make this belief strong and I shall quote. A clearer example is found in our daily lives. A man and a woman marry and swear to be in love eternally. In six or so years they divorce, remarry and repeat these words again only to divorce later. By the time of the third divorce the words "love eternally" have become a cliché and not worth a thing. If in each face one sees the face of the Beloved Who is Unseen, however, who shall we say is the eternal partner in these cases of 'love'.? The love which one can truly have is if one sees the Beloved in the face which is very face, but if one considers all aspects of the person of choice, one cannot easily depart from a relationship.. Some cases known to be those of love are no more than what is sometimes called friendship for advantage as in the Latin book " Cicero de Amicitia"(Cicero on Friendship). The best seems to be a choice of a partner to travel this world and the next with. Below are some criteria for love expounded by the Master :

> There are four kinds of love. The first is the love that flows from God to man; it consists of the inexhaustible graces, the Divine effulgence and heavenly illumination. Through this love the world of being receives life. Through this love man is endowed with physical existence, until, through the breath of the Holy Spirit — this same love — he receives eternal life and becomes the image of the Living God. This love is the origin of all the love in the world of creation.

> The second is the love that flows from man to God. This is faith, attraction to the Divine, enkindlement, progress, entrance into the Kingdom of God, receiving the Bounties of God, illumination with the lights of the Kingdom. This love is the origin of all philanthropy; this love causes the hearts of men to reflect the rays of the Sun of Reality.

> The third is the love of God towards the Self or Identity of God. This is the transfiguration of His Beauty, the reflection of Himself in the mirror of His Creation. This is the reality of love, the Ancient Love, the Eternal Love. Through one ray of this Love all other love exists.

> The fourth is the love of man for man. The love which exists between the hearts of believers is prompted by the ideal of the unity of spirits. This love is attained through

the knowledge of God, so that men see the Divine Love reflected in the heart. Each sees in the other the Beauty of God reflected in the soul, and finding this point of similarity, they are attracted to one another in love. This love will make all men the   waves of one sea, this love will make them all the stars of one heaven and the fruits of one tree. This love will bring the realization of true accord, the foundation of real unity.

But the love which sometimes exists between friends is not (true) love, because it is subject to transmutation; this is merely fascination. As the breeze blows, the slender trees yield. If the wind is in the East the tree leans to the West, and if the wind turns to the West the tree leans to the East. This kind of love is originated by the accidental conditions of life. This is not love, it is merely acquaintanceship; it is subject to change.
(Abdu'l-Baha, Paris Talks, p. 179)

This quote is made here because the issue of loving is the prevalent cause of much suffering in the world today. Many acts of evil intent are committed all because we love, and many a child is left without any care from parents even though conceived in an act of love.

It was through this event that I then examined myself to see just how loving mankind and loving a partner must dovetail somehow. For one cannot love humankind and be so unkind to a partner at a parting as we are wont to do today. Just as one cannot teach democracy in the street while exercising absolute power in the home they live in. It makes the idea laughable and irrelevant to issues that matter. The whole must be seen in the very minute detail. Just as the cells of the body work alone and yet form a body. The question often referred to of: :" Why should I buy a cow if I can get milk from the dairy? Absolutely forgets that the dairy gets it from the cow in the first place. In the dairy it is second hand! At most in this life we choose a partner to travel with to eternity, body or no body. Should one subtract the body what is one left with?

Some refer to the story of Samson, a true story of how the physical should not be the defining issue in any union. Purposes are such that the issue of life must attain an end and a meaning. Samson shows that by remembering the issue he was all about.

Another Love Gone Wrong

At this time I was on my return to active social life. I was employed in a glass manufacturing factory as a Quality Controller on bulbs and tubes intended to manufacturing electrical lamps.

At a wedding I attended I met a girl who was a teacher in a local school. I had grown up on the same street as the girl but in her grown up situation she looked different. It was not long before I was visiting her every day after work at her home where she lived with her parents. It seemed to work out well as a love affair ,but the problem came when considering marriage. She was as I am partly Zulu and her parents liked to have me around. The situation of Bahá'ís is to find agreement with parents and obtain their consent before marriage. Unknown to me was the fact that the girl had been in love with a married man before. This fact had become known to my mother.

While my big sister who was to negotiate with my mother found the girl agreeable, this was not the case with my mother. Her objection was not only that the girl had been in love with the man, but that she had boasted of it to all, in public .The reason I did not hear of this before was that earlier my time was spent away from my street and neighborhood for years as I hung out in a different setting altogether. This revelation was a shock to me and it meant I had to ask he girl if this was at all true. On doing so, she seemed to take pride in that fact , bad as it was.

By then she had made many a suggestion of getting married which meant that she had not seen me as just a friend but a future husband from the start.

Under the circumstances I found that I could not go on with the affair. Having informed her I then left her but not without her protests and fervent desires that we try again. My mind was made up and I could not return.

Some years after I got married to a girl from a different town, I heard that the girl had had a child outside of marriage. That seemed to settle my mind, but not without sadness on her predicament.

One Sunday morning as I left home in Zwide where I then resided, to do some errands, I met the same girl in my neighborhood. She looked very untidy but welcoming. She sadly asked if the house I just left was my present home with my wife, and I nodded agreement and she suddenly left. Later still I understood that at the time I saw her for the last, she had had a disastrous depression and left teaching. Finally as I settled in the United States I learned she had passed on at a young age. This again I carry with me, as if I had been the cause of her early departure. Such events do not leave the mind.

The world of humanity has two wings — one is woman
and the other man. Not until both wings are equally developed can the bird fly. Should one wing remain weak,
flight is impossible. Not until the world of woman becomes equal to the world of man in the acquisition of
virtues and perfections, can success and prosperity be
attained as they ought to be
(Selections from the Writings of Abdu'l-Baha, p. 301)

A simple View of the poignancy of loving

In the Writings we are taught to love all mankind, and again to love God above
all that is. Bahá'u'lláh makes the example of love with the story of Majnun and
Lyala, a traditional story in the East, of love. One can read of this story in the
" The Seven Valleys and the Four Valleys". It is also painfully true for all of us
to know that all are sinners and none is perfect before God. Further the Master
points out that we should love all creatures not 'for their sakes but for the sake
of God'

Love the creatures for the sake of God and not for themselves. You will never become angry or impatient if you
love them for the sake of God. Humanity is not perfect.
There are imperfections in every human being, and you
will always become unhappy if you look toward the
people themselves. But if you look toward God, you will
love them and be kind to them, for the world of God is
the world of perfection and complete mercy. Therefore,
do not look at the shortcomings of anybody; see with the
sight of forgiveness. The imperfect eye beholds imperfections. The eye that covers faults looks toward the
Creator of souls. He created them, trains and provides
for them, endows them with capacity and life, sight and
hearing; therefore, they are the signs of His grandeur
(Abdu'l-Baha, The Promulgation of Universal Peace,
p. 92)

In my simple mind this means we love whom we love because we love the
Creator, knowing full well that in that very person there will be faults which
we have to overlook and work towards perfecting or overcoming the problems
in that person's behavior. Never do we find a perfect being except in God's

Manifestation . Then to make the statement of 'loving eternally' must be a precondition of loving the Creator of that person.. Perhaps our mistake in making the statement of love is equating the beloved with God, when in fact that beloved is no other than another creation of the Deity. Being therefore , the image of God still in the making, that person cannot be the perfection of God whatever we may think and however we may love them. One has to admit that in the act of even that love, one is sometimes blinded of any faults, hence one man proclaimed" Love is blind but marriage the eye opener". In living with the person one sees not he romantic picture but the real one should have seen at the beginning.

There is no wrong in loving a partner and sacrificing for that partner, but one has to have the view that all are sinners before God and work from there. In the above Book i.e. "The Seven and the Four Valleys", the Blessed Beauty touches on the effect of love and the believers have to look into that to derive the meanings He has contained in that section of the Book. As it were, Bahá'u'lláh describes religion as a vast ocean from which each can drink one's fill and no more than one's capacity.

> **Through the might of God and His power, and out of the treasury of His knowledge and wisdom, I have brought forth and revealed unto you the pearls that lay concealed in the depths of His everlasting ocean**
> **(Baha'u'llah, Gleanings from the Writings of Baha'u'llah, p. 327)**

That capacity determines one's ability to manifest the beauty of God in one's own life and status as granted in mercy to every creature that He has placed anywhere in creation.. As we study creation we realize that cohesion is the making of all things , from atoms to planets circling suns.. Why would it not be that all beings circle even a greater Sun? It is perhaps our failure in recognizing that we are dependent in existent upon laws revealed by the Great Beings called Manifestations; that we are not capable of understanding without instruction; that fishes are dependent on the ocean and yet are oblivious of it and its expanse, as Bahá'u'lláh points out elsewhere.

> **"O Sun-like Mirrors! Look ye upon the Sun of Truth. Ye, verily, depend upon it, were ye to perceive it. Ye are**

all as fishes, moving in the waters of the sea, veiling yourselves there from, and yet asking what it is on which ye depend."
(Baha'u'llah, Epistle to the Son of the Wolf, p. 160)

In knowing that each person is a unique combination, that is, unique from two parents, it maybe that one is preconditioned to certain behaviors. That being the case, one becomes attracted to persons suitable to themselves just as they attract persons who love their kind of combination. Viewed from that stand point, it becomes a necessary issue when divisions come in any union to go back to what that attraction was all about in the first place, before making a definite decision to separate. The issue may not be the attraction of being able to live together but the items in the two lives that are accumulated and make it hard to get along. Reduction of same items or readdressing the same items may cause the union to gel again. In that sense the prevalence of divorce may lesson, when the past attraction is lasting and being considered. It is again then obvious that if that attraction was merely of bodies separation may ensue as bodies age and dilapidate, for the eternal trip is not there. The association of souls there may not have existed but an association of the physical may have ruled the union. Questions such as: " What then attracted me to my partner?", should pertain and the nature of :" Has he/she lost it, and how can it be re-gained?" should be a norm. In the course of life, however, alienation which is irreconcilable may have taken place, in which case would be advisable to part, as is sometimes determined in Bahá'í cases too.

> Marriages are supposed, as Bahá'u'lláh says, Himself, to promote unity and harmony in the world, and not dis-sension and alienation.
> (Shoghi Effendi, Lights of Guidance, p. 373)

But such partings should not engender enmity, for again loving the 'crea-tures for the sake of God' is necessary. Each face is the face of the Deity, but we must choose partners to travel with to eternity. As it would seem, men and women all hold a part of a jig saw and none can understand it if they all hold the pieces and do not share them.. The picture never comes together! Is it true of the different colors we have ?

8. O SON OF SPIRIT!

> There is no peace for thee save by renouncing thyself and turning unto Me; for it behooveth thee to glory in My name, not in thine own; to put thy trust in Me and not in thyself, since I desire to be loved alone and above all that is.
>
> (Baha'u'llah, The Arabic Hidden Words)

Of love the Blessed Beauty has written:

> Love accepteth no existence and wisheth no life: In death it seeth life, and in shame seeketh glory. To merit the madness of love, man must abound in sanity; to merit the bonds of the Friend, one must be free in spirit. Blessed the neck that is caught in His noose, happy the head that falleth on the dust in the pathway of His love. Wherefore, O friend, renounce thy self that thou mayest find the Peerless One, and soar beyond this mortal world that thou mayest find thy nest in the abode of heaven. Be as naught, if thou wouldst kindle the fire of being and be fit for the pathway of love.
>
> (Baha'u'llah, The Call of the Divine Beloved, p. 19)

He Who is the Center of the Covenant of Baha'u'llah has said:

> My name is Abdul-Baha, my identity is Abdul-Baha, my qualification is Abdul-Baha, my reality is Abdul-Baha, my praise is Abdul-Baha, Thraldom to the Blessed Perfection is my glorious refulgent diadem; and servitude to all the human race is my perpetual religion. Through the bounty and favor of the Blessed Perfection, Abdul-Baha is the Ensign of the Most-Great-Peace, which is waving from the Supreme Apex; and through the gift of the Greatest Name, he is the Lamp of Universal Salvation, which is shining with the light of the love of God. The Herald of the Kingdom is he, so that he may awaken the people of the East and of the West. The Voice of Friendship, Uprightness, Truth and Reconciliation is he, so as to cause acceleration throughout all regions. No name, no title, no mention, no commendation

hath he nor will ever have except Abdul-Baha. This is my longing. This is my supreme apex. This is my greatest yearning. This is my eternal life. This is my everlasting glory! Express ye the same thing which is issued from my pen. This is the duty of all. Consequently the friends of God must assist and help Abdul-Baha in the adoration of the True One; in the servitude to the human race; in the well-being of the human world and in divine love and kindness.

(Tablets of Abdu'l-Baha v2, p. 429)

This to Him was service to God and demonstration of love for God.. We take our lesson of service and love for humankind from this and more. This in a sense becomes our true ' raison d'etre"

Attempting A Balanced Life

Marriage and Hope

The girl I married was a new Bahá'í. Marriage came at a time, when I saw religion , not just as part of a social change, but as part of an ethical and moral experience. When a mind believes and a heart is turned to obedience of law of God, one doe get the spiritual experience. Without the faith, one can break laws and feel nothing. With faith one feels the ideology of good ruling in life and one's own experience thereof. That was my experience while living with my wife. We had a simple wedding, but the vows were great. . She was devoted, and I had promised myself that I would stay in one marriage, and would not deviate.

The problem came when we moved into my old area in New Brighton, and all the old friends came back to haunt me. It probably would have worked out fine, had not my wife become interested in the old friends and their ways. I knew the trail, and had avoided it for years. Now it seemed it was back in my life again. I could not have that happen another time to me. Perhaps that was selfish, but that is what I felt at the time; that somehow I would be sucked into the old behaviors again. I knew how cruel that life could be.

I shall give an example and hope it is conclusive. To me it is.

When I straightened my life in 1966, I took a vacation to East London, and the train I boarded had to pass Alice, where my college was located. Incidentally, this event occurred at the time when one of the worst apartheid prime ministers was murdered by a Greek page , during a parliamentary session in Cape Town. So there was a kind of hush all around.

On the train to East London, I became friends with a young lady from Mdantsane. I had never been to Mdantsane at the time, as that was a new area created recently..

After that vacation, she visited Port Elizabeth. By this time I had straightened my life, but she was a party girl. I thought I could get those ideas out of her mind, but it did not seem to work. I took her out to visit some jazz fans at a joint. Of course I was welcomed back excitedly, but everyone soon learned I was dry. That caused a serious problem, which I did not quite perceive on entry to the place. The result of that was being offered twice a drink , which I refused, and later being offered an orange juice, which I drank, to a great disaster. For I passed out. Do not ask me how I felt the next morning on waking up at about 8:00 A.M. Tell me then, do I wish for these people to be in my life again? Yet my wife was interested! Even though she was pregnant at that time, I decided to undo everything . That action itself, has haunted me more than perhaps should be necessary, but such old wounds and scars can be prayed about , but never really leave.

Faith, the girl who married me in spite of myself, and was prepared to return my children to me to educate when they were grown, after a divorce, and was one who had saved me much trouble and pain when I was a young man.

Picture of first wife Faith Lulama Nonyati (Mazibuko)extracted from a group picture taken in Salt Lake, a Colored township of Port Elizabeth, during a visit of Lowell Johnson (From personal collection)

The Makings of Pandemonium

In 1978, as a member of the National Assembly of South Africa, I was also a delegate to the International Bahá'í Convention, an event that took place that year in Haifa, Israel. On that one occasional I was exposed to life outside my country for the first prolonged time. I had been to Lesotho and travelled a lot in the Transkei, but until then , I had never been off the continent of Africa. That set off a period of trying to recreate my life, and live the life of my early ideals. In that way the seeds of change were planted and needed execution.

For six years I had now been married, and had on the onset of the marriage promised myself that I would be real as a husband, and hold tenaciously to my vows. I had done that. I knew the kind of wild character I could be, but the depression had seen to that flame. I was now cowed and wished for quietude. But now had come the time to express all those thoughts of radical ideologies I had in my youth. The question was how this was going to be done, so that I was real as well as living in quietude and peace.

On reaching home from the convention, , I still had those thoughts and expressed them to my wife. We did not talk much about that but I saw it is a problem.

How then was I to express these notions I had that I was not quite living the real life, and that I was faking it. It was now six years since we got married and I had taken up the character of one who argued less about every decision ,but this was not helping me stay in a relationship. I tried hard to be normal, but eventually had to voice my thoughts to the secretary of the Assembly, by pointing out that I had fears I could no longer remain in a relation with the dedication I had at the start. I unfortunately kept the note detailing this feeling on my person and it was soon discovered by my wife, however I mailed it anyway.

A week or so after this discovery, my wife then came with a very great surprise, she was pregnant. The fat was in the fire, for the Bahá'í year of patience was already set.

I decided that I would go pioneering in the Transkei. Therefore, I took leave and went in search of employment in the Transkei. I took my eldest son with me. It was probably more than six weeks I stayed away from home. I returned with a promise of employment. The promise was cancelled when the prospective employer called my then present employer. The call was taken by a present manager of my department, who answered that I was not in the employ of the company. Thus, I was seen as having lied that I was employed and therefore lost the job in the Transkei. That meant that I had to return to a job I had planned to leave, and the Director of my company knew that I had this plan. Thus return became a misery and a torment, because I was given an order not to take any leave, and to present myself for work at weekends. Also management was unwilling to extend me any financial assistance with any loans. I had gone to Israel on the "Fly Now Pay later " Plan and the airways was pressing for payments. That meant that my salary would be garnished to pay for that trip. I had many items which had been bought on "hire purchase " terms and they had to be paid for.

All this time, two other events were taking place in my life. First my good friend, Ronald Fudu, wanted to get married, and married the Bahá'í way, and I was the chairman of the Local Assembly who had to see to this. This would not have been much of a problem if the other members in the community saw his urgency. Observing this, I had to take the stand of seeing that the wedding took place , and when the time came it did succeed. By then I had lost the confidence of even my wife in being on my side right through.

Secondly my love life was falling apart, for I was determined at the time to escape being home and go out as much as possible each night. Doing this during a time when I was supposed to translate a major Book of my religion was very hard. It meant that late each night , had to be spent with proofreading, and early mornings with mailing the work to Dr. Michael walker who was I Cape Town, so that it could be included in the book.

Doing this is not bad, but with a baby on the way too, it was hellish. Sleep was a commodity I seldom could enjoy. Late nights for any work at home, had to be the option , to avoid talking.

In order to show definitely that I had to leave, I had to show that I could find life elsewhere, but that was hard too. This then is the time, I was thought to be loose in behavior reminiscent of my early years, only the liquor was not there, but the late nights very present.

The strange part is that, by the time I had to face a divorce, I was alone. There was no girlfriend, and by the time the separation took place, there was not even food in the house. Financial straits forced repossession of some goods, and eating habits alone in the house became a disaster. A meal would be boiled powdered soup and bread.

I had fallen, at this point , to being suspect of a love affair with a person from overseas, and to stop that I had to look for a local love. As an act of desperation I took to seeking out a possible wife among the African girls I knew, but without much success.

The one success I did find was in the next town, when a friend introduced me to someone I had to talk to about religion. When that person accepted, It then talked marriage, a very unwise move. However I did marry the person and stopped all the talk of the possibilities I was supposed to have achieved. Thus it was that I found myself marrying with a forced situation of signing and affidavit of not forcing my wife to do anything she did not wish to do, at her request. Surprised as I was at the marriage office, I did draw the affidavit, because in the early life I was worked in the Tax Office for a month, before being fired as unsuitable, which I had expected. Having drawn up the affidavit I then presented it to the magistrate who knew very well that I had worked under him in the Tax Office. To him it was good fun, but he , however looked concerned, for African s never sign affidavits before marriage; this was new to him too. Done it was, and a Bahá'í marriage followed that very evening and performed according to stated rules of the Faith.

The rest of this story is history told in another book I wrote i.e. "This Side Up". Pieced together one finds what one author called "extraordinary and bizarre". But there it was. The result of the affidavit was that my wife found it very easy to do exactly as she pleased, even resigning from her religion without any discussion of such a case, and being able to stay away from home at a nursing hospital for more than three months without a word. Unfortunate as this might appear, it never helped to know afterwards when separation was a done deed, that my partner had a sickness she was dealing with of which she had not told me. One does not rest easy in the mind pondering that in the future.

'Adu'l-Baha has said:

> **You must in this instance (that is, service to humanity) sacrifice your lives, and in sacrificing your lives celebrate happiness and beatitude.**
> **(Abdu'l-Baha, Tablets of Abdu'l-Baha v1, p. 43)**

Strange events in the Air

In 1975 I was elected to the Bahá'í National Assembly and served until 1985. This meant traveling to Johannesburg once every month to attend weekend meetings and returning to home each Sunday night to prepare for regular work each Monday. On these visits one learned a lot about people who travel on airplanes.

Usually on the airplanes, Africans are accommodated at the back of the plane in those available seats. So that is where I would be. One night on the return to Port Elizabeth, there were two young fellows, probably of school going age, who were acting as stewards on the flight. They were quite friendly and easy to get along with. After serving on the flight they came to sit next to me and chat. I was a little puzzled, but we had a pleasant time. Then one of them got up and went to the front of the plane and came back with a half dozen pack of "Appletisers", drinks I often opted for on flights, and offered them to me. I took them and put them under the seat. The fellow then disappeared again and came back holding two brass pins displaying a Springbok. The fellow did not understand! How was I a Black man going to wear a pin with a spring-bok on it, the pride of the Nationalists , in New Brighton? I could not tell the person, to go away , could I? He did not understand that this could not be done and this was not a gift to give to an African! Not to offend, I took the gift and kept it stored in a drawer at home, never to wear it of course. I found I could not do otherwise. Perhaps his father would have known better!

On another occasion, I was again on my way back from the meeting sitting in the back of the airplane. A group of what I perceived to be tourists were bundled into the seats next to me. They were quite a jolly crowd, and explained that they were hockey players from Germany.

Sometime during the flight, , they produced candy and offered me a few pieces. However, on biting one of them I felt a kind of familiar burn. No, this was not candy, it was masked liquor! I kept my silence and waited. They were busily chatting and laughing when one of them asked if I wanted more. I simply said "No" I did not wish for more, and they all burst out laughing. Lucky I knew liquor when I tasted it, so saved myself from a drunk trip!

On another journey, I met a a family who came and sat next to me on the way to Johannesburg. This was at the height of rioting in the townships. I gathered that this family was composed of strangers to the country for they looked around a little oddly. After the while, the man engaged me in conver-sation and I perceived that his accent was American. I asked him from what part of America he was from and he said he was from Atlanta, Georgia. He pointed out that there was obviously many problems in the country at the time, and explained that in his town the chief of police and the mayor were Black. Very quietly, he asked if I could explain just what was taking place generally in the country. Even more quietly, I told him that, first of all, when he got off the plane later , I did not know him and he did not know me. We agreed that this was the truth. and it was! So we talked bended down on the seats. On getting to the airport of destination, Johannesburg, I asked him to leave and not wait. He hurriedly left and I then got up with some quiet dignity of one who knew very little. It worked. I was not followed by any Security Police, and I do not really know if he was, but he was with family, and could not be suspected of anything.

You travel, you learn! At university I had learned a lot about what was happening in the United States in the 60s and had read many magazines which were obtainable in South Africa in those days , examples being "Life Magazine" "Mc Calls ", "Ebony" and "Down Beat". But I had not quite got how serious the racial situation could be until I got into the country, the United States until then. It is very surprising in some ways because in most magazines it does not appear to be that serious at all. The only difficult part, at that time, was the dissemination of very graphic sexual magazines, which were illegal in the country at the time, and the resultant emulation of all perceived actions gleaned from such magazines, by people who had taboos about some issues. A real breakdown in behaviors ! But then, if one had an idea of some books that were legal and available , one would learn. Such books would be books like " Naked and the Dead" by Norman Mailer, which were graphic in descriptions. Of course, for a while, many were banned, but one could find channels

Reflecting on Brothers as Adults

Donald My Brother In Adult Life

It is curious that Donald Mthobeli became a doctor in his life, because Donald was , in his young years , neither very religious nor distinguished academically. But Donald was a great hunter. I know because I hunted with him. He grew up to have a very interesting career. We in my family never thought he would abide going far in school, as Donald in my family was known as a tradesman. He knew ways of making a living as a child, and he even devised the first means of our making funds for attending movies at the local theater.. Donald could be seen on a Saturday in the woods , with a small skin bag he mad de from some animal's hide, stalking meerkats , rabbits and birds. We knew him to be able to capture some birds live and bring them home. As a kind of breeder of birds, , Donald had a large cage in our backyard where a hoard of pigeons nested and were housed. The door to this cage was always open and they could come and go as they wished , but they always returned .

When Donald a was in junior high, he surprised me by getting into the country's team of young Blacks in rugby, as a wing. As one could tell, he was quite robust both in activity and in build. My mother always said he was more like my uncle Bruce, while I was more like my father.

Again, Donald went through junior high and passed with a first class certificate, another surprise. Because of that pass, he was offered a scholar-ship to study in the boarding college of Lovedale, a school of some prestige at the time.

During the first year of schooling at Lovedale, there was a students' strike and all students were sent home. Students were to be recalled as they applied individually back to school. Donald was called back by a principal of the school who took favor of him. He called him as a certain Mr. Weig. The man had a sort of Germanic background. It was at this point that Donald was made the Chief Prefect of the school. Robust as he was his duties involved keeping order in the school. The principal liked him so much that he advised him to go for a degree in Mathematics . For this reason, Donald came and saw me at Fort Hare University College, which stands across the river from Lovedale, to find out what I thought he should take up as a career. He had doubts about becoming a Mathematician even though he was offered a scholarship for that, by the principal. His other option was to become a doctor or what I had promised my mother and that of becoming a minister of religion,. I was to decide for him what to do since I was the big brother and was then at a university college.

I did not quite know what to say because I did not wish to decide on his future. I wanted him to do that for himself, because ,later if things failed, he would be sure to regret my decision. My advice then to him, was that, he should go back to his dormitory at the college and think carefully what he would like to do, and my part would be to support his decision whichever way he willed. In the main he wished to be in a position where he served people in his life. I asked him to concentrate on that.

After weeks he came back and told me he rather thought he would be better as a doctor, for either as a minister or a doctor he would still be serving people. I thought this a better decision, because Donald was always with animals and not books. Biology and Medicine would suit him better..

When he came for second advice as to how to go to a Medical College, I could think of only one: Natal University in Durban. However, not one of us had an address to the school.. So , mine was to tell him to address a letter, blindly, to the Registrar at the University of Natal, and for a town to just mail the letter to Durban. Somehow it would find itself to the university,… and it did!

After passing at the college, Donald proceeded to Natal University the next year. The year he registered I was refused admission at Fort Hare and so had to work.

That is when we parted company for a while. During the second year of his studies at university, Tumana, as he was sometimes called, ran into a financial problem. He did not have the funds to continue studies but could have opted for a loan from the university, if he had the funds to get on the train to reach Durban. I had only been able to assist him with his stay in Port Elizabeth by providing entertainment funds , but could not afford a ticket for him. However, for reasons of his own, he kept this need secret until later when he had a solution before informing me of his situation..

While checking on bookings in the city's train station, Donald found a stack of bank notes on the street. This amounted to over a hundred Rands and enabled him to buy a ticket and have a sum left over. Thus he continued his study in Medicine.

He found a college friend called Donald Bandile Lisa. I met Bandile later when he was schooling , and came looking for a school job at the hospital where I worked. Bandile was in the X-Ray department while I was at the Casualty Department, and I would occasionally see him at lunch in the lunch room. It is unfortunate that Bandile and I at the hospital, got interested in the same girl, whom I had to give up because one does not wish to compete with a younger brother's friend. It also unfortunate for his education, that Bandile did not continue in Medicine, but left university and joined the Black Peoples' Convention group, later working s a salesman for a commercial company. Bandile had then to travel for quite a while, and passed on in an accident between Port Elizabeth and East London, on a route he had used on many occasions in his job.

"Tumana", that is, Donald as his nickname was to his friends, passed and became a medical Doctor, but was not satisfied , for he wished to be a Surgeon. After a bad attempt at that, he then turned to Gynecology and passed there.

His schooling was somewhat troubled , because there was not enough cash for him to go on. So his younger brother , Wandile, who , after circumcision would not return to high school, but took up a successful job at the Ford Motor Company's Engine Plant, took over supporting him at college, while I tried to work out ways of getting out of the family to marry and have a life of my own. My problem was that I at this time I was separated from the family, because of not observing some customs, and joining a very foreign religion, which were efforts which offered no security for anyone in the house. Anyone siding with me at this time would not really know what I was up to, and neither was I too sure of that.

As shall be seen later, Wandile prospered in his job to the present day, retiring as a foreman at the plant, and winning awards for making engines. Wandile even after retirement, is still being occasionally recalled to work at the plant, and has a daughter qualified as a Computer expert, graduated at a local university in BS. Computer Science, who works in the company too. Wandile has now a business so f his own. He owns a shelter where he houses telephones rented by the public, and bought a neighboring house next to his , where he has exercises for those who wish them, especially ladies who want to do fitness classes , equipped with all kinds of exercise machinery. In the summer season he has enough machines and workers to cut lawns in all factories and schools around Port Elizabeth..

Donald worked for years in Durban, with an office near Merebank. It is strange that he used to hunt for *meerkats* ! However, he was buried in East London after a third marriage. His life became very difficult in Durban. Sometimes I blame myself, because Donald had many friends who were Indian ,and many, therefore who were Muslims, and I was a Bahá'í and visited him often. As all know there has been rigorous persecution of Bahá'ís in Iran and many Bahá'ís have perished in those acts of violence in that land. Donald did not know this as I never had a chance to explain to him, but once he said he had turned to the Buddhist Faith. The family buried him in East London as a Christian. One Friday night I visited Durban on the way to Inyoni in Kwa-Zulu where I was to help the followers of my faith. Tumana picked me up at the airport for I was departing on the Saturday morning for Inyoni. When I got to his house I was surprised to find a lot of his Indian friends , doctors at the hospital , King Edward VII, gathered for a party at his home.

I was invited to join in as all had a dinner at his home. I did not inquire in whose honor the dinner was.. However the long table was occupied by many visitors.

Donald tried very hard to please the family with his life, and that placed him a valley of divided attention, because he married twice , somehow because of that, before marrying a third time and throwing off that family responsibility. By that time, he had troubles of his own and soon passed on. Catering for family and siblings , while building a family of his own did not work so well, especially because, in the first marriage, he chose a lady the family liked in Port Elizabeth, while he resided in Durban, resulting in never living with his first wife before separation. The second marriage was then also challenged before it got off , though they both lived in Durban, where his surgery in Merebank , was. He however, conducted a thriving office in gynecology, writing several papers which were published. When he came into some difficulties he appealed for help. Because of the distances it was very hard for me to advise him much but I made the effort to be in touch with him. He had by then developed a drinking problem that he was trying to be rid of. In that difficult time, he managed to find study in the United States in Public Health, a course he took at Tulane University, successfully, before his change of residence to East London.

Also at this time he was estranged from my family for he had decided to concentrate more on his family instead of attempting to cater for all.. He was generous to a suicidal point, because he never wanted to look like he was leaving family behind. I, on the other hand, had taken the stand of striking out on my own, long ago, a choice my mother lamented.

Thus for years, instead of my brother as close family friend, I had my youngest sister, who I had nursed as a baby. I knew more of family through her, but my marrying also caused her some stress for she felt she was losing a much needed friend in her life ,and a good brother, for we shared experiences more. In fact I appeared to be more of the father to her then. I found her a good insider! One needs one in such cases because one is partly in, related, and partly out and on one's own. Family to Africans is a basic thing, for customs have to be performed. In my case I was omitted, because I was found to have strange notions which African did not take up.

It took me years to define a course of life, that took in all the customs in my family. Now I can actually explain customs and traditions with some logical thoughts included. Being on the Bahá'í Administration and dealing with a whole country helped much in defining a path of acceptance and understanding. Without that, chances are that I would have remained a stranger for many more years. The Faith accepts customs that do not break a Bahá'í law, and finds alternative behaviors for those that may look at breaking such laws, by finding ways of performing the same custom, in a method that is acceptable all around. Primal among those is avoidance of the drinking of liquor. The part of making liquor available is incorporated in the performance of many an African custom, but today one can be excused from partaking of the beverage but has to observe in some way the custom. As a parent to two boys I have had to go through that with both of them and they understood and so did the community. The three of us have learned to live by Bahá'í Law.

Wandile, my brother who now takes up performance of such customs recognized this and that he should inform me as elder brother whenever he has to observe any, something that works well for both of us and family.

The liaison with my brother, is because in my family, I stand the only one who knows family history, customs and situation best than anybody, having spent many hours with my father asking all the questions, where the rest of my family did not. My father was always conscious of that since my early days, perhaps because I look very much like him, and he had promised that the day I left home, he would also leave. Two years after my arrival in the United States, my father passed on. A year after that, my mother also did. I am only glad that when I left the country in 1987, they were the only two people who were in the house that I saw before boarding the 'plane. Both of them were too unwell to even come to the airport. I had managed to live temporarily with both of them for almost six months before departure from the land and both signed the consent to marry my present wife easily..

I pray that I am buried differently so that my Faith is honored. However, my Faith had been a divide between me and family for years. So after the passing of both parents and my moving first to Swaziland and the States, I was observed and seen very differently. For now I have to be consulted as big brother in all moves, and my Faith is accepted. This took a while and some doing! To have no family ties among Africans is trying, do believe that, for, somehow, one has no legitimate rights, and one is not informed of any activities in family, but hears from friends.. ..a very lonely stance... It begs for no sympathy, for one has to take life in hand and decide what to do with it, by themselves, and take full blame or credit for that life. It comes once, and there is no altering events, but acceptance of all in a responsible way.

Donald and I worked together on most issues and he was always understanding but could not do much to arrive at a situation where I could be accepted by family with all the differences and objections I had to normal African behavior. The one time we really disagreed was when I mentioned to family that I was transferring residence to the United States. To him this was the worst decision I could arrive at, given that at the time I was under treatment for a depression. He did all he could as a person to stop the departure, even co-opting a cousin I stayed with in East London to help, lest I needed a doctor to help, as he felt that such a decision could have come because of some sickness. For that reason I valued the help of my one cousin who was in East London at the time and supported the action of my leaving, I was taking, and that is Sipokazi Mampe.. We had long been good friends in decisions with that cousin and at that time she also had a friend in the United Kingdom she had wished to introduced me to so that I could speak to him as her big brother. That association alone helped me get along with my plan to leave until, while I was in her home, I received the call from my little sister, that I needed to go to Cape Town for a visa, as contact had been made with her. As a result I took off on an unplanned trip to Port Elizabeth to find methods by which I could reach Cape Town, as by then funds were very low.

It however gladdens me also to know that Tumana came to visit me in Ottawa , IL, while on his Public Health course, however his report back home had been that I was in abject poverty. To an extent he was right because only I was actually working at the time , and my wife was seeking work. Money was again a scarcity. It helped afterwards to know that while doing his course he had received very valuable help from a White lady who supervised his studies so that he got through, for he had difficulties even handling a snowy day . His way was to try a barefoot approach, after a night of a party, a thing which was fraught with disaster. At this time that he studied, it must be realized that he was having, not only marital problems , but was having difficulty with being accepted by the department of health in Ciskei as the only Gynecologist they had in Frere and Cecilia Makhiwane hospitals.

To understand these difficulties one has to know that my little brother was closely associated with the political movement on the ANC side, and this was not always placing him a in a very safe spot. Possibly, he and my father were the two members of that organization in my family. That being the case it sounded as if he was not in a good standing with persons in Ciskei, a homeland operating under the regime of the South African government. As I see it, he was in a bind, and could not leave it and the only way was to prove beyond doubt that he was the person for his post, regardless of how others felt.

He resolved to have a case of triplets delivered by himself singlehanded as proof of his prowess as a gynecologist. When that failed, Donald seems to have given up, for the surgery left him with no interest in going back to the hospital and in that very week, he had passed on. I can understand that, for my brother was a proud man about his work, and firm about his principles. That combination made it impossible for him after the event to face life. Even though he passed on well into the years of independence, certain events he related tell me that he was not quite in resonance with persons in the area, though he was in the organization that helped the liberation. That however, is just politics and I am not in that arena. This is about my brother and his sudden passing. He must have been in his late fifties when he did.

It worries me to an extent that he passed on in the very town I had visited every weekend in 1974 to teach the Faith, and in the very area near where some of my Bahá'í friends had to face execution. Here the spiritual mother of my first wife had taught many women who got onto the first a National Assembly of the Faith in the Ciskei., in 1985 , an event I attended. After that formation I even later went back in 1987, into the area from Swaziland to help teaching.

Rose Gates and I had worked there for years from 1973 to 1975 when I was elected to the National Assembly and she remained there until around 2005, if not slightly earlier. One would have to find the time of her passing in the United States to ascertain that. But by the time I returned from pilgrimage in 1985 she was still there even though not well. This time I am not working out statistics but telling a short part of a story. Why these events of execution in Ciskei occurred is very puzzling even from this distance.

When one works as a Bahá'í one meets many persons , high in financial status and low, and one gets along with all and is known as a Bahá'í. Being known as one makes it easier to get along with no undue expectations from others. Still my Faith is not militant, and as a moral and ethical standards it holds onto, forgiveness being a part of God's Plan. To know the occurrence in an area one knew so well does leave one with a feeling of guilt and responsibility. Could one have done anything to assist? Loss of the lives in the Faith is loss of teachers of the Faith, but we know God is able to take care of His own. We know that all these persons are now rejoicing for their share of teaching is done and is being done in their absence and by their absence. For none might want to forget the action. It charts the course of progress of the Faith in that area. For these persons passed on in the middle of a Black township where they had gone for a religious celebration with Blacks , a challenged community in Southern Africa at that time. I would someone had pondered on this and made a serious reflection on the impact before executing the action. For tears cannot bring these back nor can the action be retracted. I reflect that , at the time I waited for a visa, this could have happened had I failed to answer for myself in like words at any accuser. But my own reputation as teacher might have aided in arresting any such act, however, how many would know or honor what the Friends of God had gone through in teaching a Cause of Racial Unity, in that time and place.

Donald married for the first time in 1971 while still a medical student and among the boys was the first to take that step. I had thought and arranged a marriage in 1966, however that effort had failed to materialize. I was present at Donald's wedding n 1971n in the morning session and in the church as he took his vows, but had to work in the afternoon, reaching home past 10 P.M. that night. My mother had made a great effort of even inviting her employers to the wedding, for Donald was the favorite son with her.

My Last Visit To Donald's Home

The last Two Videos I watched at Donald's home
(Pictures scanned from VCR and CD covers by author)

Around 1983/84 I visited my younger brother Dr. Donald Mthobeli Mazibuko who had a practice near Merebank in Durban. The circumstance came n this fashion. I had attended a National Bahá'í Convention at Umgababa near Umkomaas which itself is next to Durban. and had travelled with my youngest son by train, because I had not really been with my son Luthando, since the time my wife took the children with her when we parted. I needed to know him better now that he was about to start school. At the end on the Convention, my brother who knew I was in the Durban at Umgababa where the Convention was held, turned up and requested that I spend time with him and family in Durban. I knew that train tickets would last a certain period, but had to return to work soon, but I agreed to accompany him home for a few days' vacation. Since it was still a Sunday night when the convention ended, we could have time to chat.

By Monday he wished me to stay a little longer and promised to provide transportation by way of a flight to Port Elizabeth for both of us, and so I stayed. On that Monday morning he informed me that he had to work but would soon be home . He still wished me to stay. To entice me he provided two movies that I should watch while he was away. VCRs were still a new thing then and tapes had to be rented. This was a novelty to me because at that time I had just consented to buy a television set which I had not had since televisions were introduced in early seventies.

It was well to watch the movies because then in South Africa it was the winter season and the movies featured scenes of winter elsewhere. They were a joy to watch.

Since that time, after his passing in 2003, I remember him by watching the two movies which I now have purchased as DVDs. At least one of them is in DVD format, but the other was now available in the United States as a VCR tape and not as a DVD and that was "Joshua".

After these few days at his home, he then flew us home. I remember this visit because it was the last time I spent with my brother in his home. The very last I saw him, was in the United States when he came to do his course in Public Health at Tulane University in the Southern States. That time, his course passed, he spent time with my family for about a week in Ottawa Illinois. However, even then, he abhorred my situation, for then it was not too financially bright, but my wife and I were surviving well enough. Of course this feeling he had also meant that he would not give a good report of my situation in my home away from South Africa when asked back home. I did not mind that, for I knew how my life centered, and that it never helps to fashion one's life after another without some logic, and that my destiny was my destiny and was not dependent on praise or others' opinions, for they have their lives to contend with. After a few years while we still resided in Ottawa, IL., we received the news that Donald had passed on while now residing in East London, Cape Province in his third marriage to a Zulu lady whom I never go to really know..

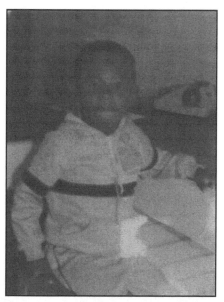

Luthando Mazibuko(Picture taken at Convention at Umgababa when we attended together)

Because I have no proper picture of my brother, and because of the sentimental feeling of having him somehow represented in his story I have found a picture of his youngest son, now engaged in Sociological employment in Johannesburg's busy Commissioner Street, and I post is here:

Onke Vala Mazibuko, Dr. Donald Mazibuko's youngest son. (from Google images)

One may wonder why he has such strange sounding names. Onke was named as "Vala", a clan-name among the Xhosa speaking, because of an old lady who was our neighbor. When Donald was unwell as a baby, and there was no doctor available to undertake treatment, MamVala who seemed to understand the sickness, was the only person who could be called upon to help in the absence of my father who was an herbalist, and she knew how. MamVala was not an educated woman but understood some things about health and treatment among Africans. Her home was outside of town in St. Albans, a rural setting known as Mduluswa among Africans, and was recommended for health ability and cures, and MamVala, would often leave town to visit that town. Vala graduated in a Master's Sociology and now works with Psychiatrists and Sociologists in Johannesburg. He looks pretty much like his father, so I guess his picture will do….

A hearse which carried Donald's body from his home

Donald's funeral

Donald was buried in East London and not in Port Elizabeth because that is where he passed on. His funeral in the Anglican Church was performed by two ministers of religion, one White and the second Black, and they alternated in performing the service.

I had been able to travel from the United States to attend and take pictures at the funeral. The church was full and many of his colleagues , who were medical doctors attended.

Family from Port Elizabeth and many of the Mlambo clan were present. His two sons by his first marriage were present, both Onke and Mandela could be seen mourning their father's death.

Reflecting on my brother's earlier experiences

I would not have written a word about my brother at this time, even the above if I had not come upon a message he sent me when he travelled abroad. His postcard to me read:

> **"Dear Rob,**
>
> **I'm now here in Sweden for a month from 08/04/96 to 10/05/96**
>
> **I was selected to attend a course on International Maternity Health Care. I will try to phone you later,**
>
> **Your dear brother,**
> **Tumana"**

Posted below is the card my brother sent:

Pictures of a postcard sent by Dr. Donald Mthobeli Mazibuko while he attended a seminar of gynecologists in Sweden, and Robert resided in the United States, years before his stepson married a Swedish wife. The area on the card is next to where Erik Anderson's (Gretchen's son) wife, Carolina Wallstrom works in Sweden.

(Donald had a habit of writing in block letters and enjoyed signing with his nickname, i.e. "Tumana", given him by mother)

The Monday morning after Donald attempted his last delivery operation of triplets at the hospital, he got off duty very disappointed in himself, only never to return to the hospital again. On the Thursday, following the surgery he succumbed to a headache which had him at home all week. It was found that he had a heart attack. This surgery was so important to him that he took his concern home and left this world.

My little sister Professor Eileen Mazibuko when asked to present a talk at the funeral, sung praises to her brother instead a of giving a talk., because her words were more of a poem than a talk, as I listened to her at the time. Her talk was in English, however, I was asked to give a reading from the Xhosa Bible, as the little article I had written for his funeral as an obituary, at the suggestion of the family, arrived in South Africa too late to be included in the proceedings of the funeral. However, I had brought bouquets of flowers and cards for family members in the United States, to be presented and that was done to satisfaction. Like the mourning for my two parents, mourning for Donald came much later at a time I reflected on being preceded by a brother.

Perhaps now is the time to tell a few jokes he told me about our situation, so that others know his thinking and his humor.

Quips by Donald, my brother

As we grew up in New Brighton, going to the movies was a good option for a pastime. Donald would attend with me. Once he attended alone and came back impressed by a movie called something like:" Seven Brides for Seven Brothers". I never knew if it was the singing, which he repeated from the movie or the setting of the movie that he loved so much. As we grew up to understand more about society and the ways of people, we went our separate ways. I remember finding a book in his room at the boarding school called " The Battle of England" and another " One Man Against Europe" and got the impression that my brother, though going for Medicine was interested in History.

Later when we were both married I met him at his home and by that time he had political attitudes which I understood for I had been to the hotbed of politics at Fort Hare University College for two years. These were some of the remarks that he made at the time:

" Do you remember when we went to cowboy movies in the old days?" and replied in the affirmative for I could. Then he said :" Do you remember the cowboy and Indian Movies". I still said:"Yes" not knowing which way the thing was going . He added " We cheered for the cowboys… what we were we thinking?'. I could see the point very clearly.

Another time we talked about the Bible. He said:' Moses was a Jew". I agreed ; then he asked" What color was he?". I had just been to Israel and seen some dark looking Jewish people, so I replied I that had no idea but He must have been dark.

Donald then quipped : " I have the strange idea that we are being robbed of our leader here!". I did not wish to tangle with that, so I did not reply. I believe in Moses and all the prophets for I am a Bahá'í.

The one and only time my brother really exposed himself to dangers he knew nothing about was only once and I could see that it told on him.

He had just fetched me from the airport in Durban, while I was a in the way to see Bahá'ís at Inyoni, Natal. I was to spend the night at his home and travel by bus in the morning.

It so happened that on that weekend my brother had invited some of his doctor friends and they were having a big dinner at his home. Naturally , he wanted to introduce his brother to the group, but in doing so he made a mistake. Most of the non-African population in Durban is Indian, and many of them are Muslims. I knew this from teaching the Faith in that area, but Donald had no idea of the sheer animosity existing among Muslims for Bahá'ís, and I had no way of cluing him in at that time. So, this was his introduction to the group of doctors at his home:' "Guys this is my brother who is Bahá'í. ", then he turned to me asked:" By the way, brother, what is the name of this Guru of your religion?" I had to come out and say: " Bahá'u'lláh" and I am certain that was a loss for my brother, on reflection it. After a while he was destitute because of also marital problems and had to be rehabilitated because he had started drinking hard because of all the problems he experienced.

I still feel this was also the result of the attitudes of his friends which he never understood the friction he placed himself in by speaking of the Bahá'í Faith to his friends. Had he asked he would have known how to account for his brother's religion and how to mention it! In a way ,I still blame myself for not having let him know what he was walking into by talking about the Faith to Muslims and about my activities in Durban and Cape Town, which the greater number of Muslims from Malay and Indian background knew more about. I feel that, from that moment, he was running against a hard tide, for his brother was involved and all in the house knew better than he did. I had been yelled earlier, at by some woman I did not even know for being in Durban and talking about my Faith, for she asserted that "Durban is not Cape Town where you had the run of the house!" for, Cape Town had a Bahá'í Center and Durban did not at the time. I knew just how violent this could become from Bahá'í History in Iran. Now that my brother is gone I can mention this, for, even my big sister never knew that in her hospital where I had worked , I was the only Bahá'í. To her this was some religion I adopted , when she was surrounded by parties who did not care much for such comments on the Faith. Small wonder then she found promotion hard until she studied more to attain a BSN.

I know that I had my problems where I worked for over ten years and was never accepted by most co-workers of Muslim background. Yet we all know that there is One God and One Next World we know about so far. Why we quibble about how we pray to Him still remains mysterious.

Donald's remaining family in 2020:
(L-R) Enthen Wandile, Eucinia Thobeka, Robert, Eileen Noxolo: Picture taken at
his funeral in East London.

Donald at the wedding counseling of his wife in East London(Acquired from No-
themba Mazibuko in 2020)

Years of Travel and Realization

The Truth Dawned

While I traveled with Lowell Johnson in 1969, and was able to meet Cassiem David of Cape Town, I came to understand many things about my religion which I did not before. My spiritual mother , in all fairness, when I was about sixteen, encouraged me to investigate all religions and not even shy away from visiting the mosque on Peel Street in Port Elizabeth. There was in my time a great move towards understanding Islam, especially after such victories by Abu Bakir Balewa the African athlete became known. Many wanted to know why he had a name of that kind, for, to many Islam was not that generally known at that time. After and during my travels, I did chance to stand outside a synagogue and a mosque just to get the feel of attending .I never entered a mosque until much later in Jerusalem when I entered the Mosque of Omar there because of its historical and religious associations with the sacrifice made by Abraham in the same area..later still I visited mosques in Istanbul and Edirne, Turkey.

From 1965 when I worked in a hospital situated in the Colored area, I could not understand why these differences between Muslims and Bahá'ís, but while travelling with Lowell who had pioneered for years among Muslims in Cape Town, the matter resolved itself, and I found my feet and knew just where I stood. Logical proofs, scientific evidenced had been valued in my life. I had learned to abandon African norms, and no one was going to cause me to adopt norms which were not logical, just because they sounded great. I had proofs of belief and nothing but some sense could change that. I stand anchored now that I know more about my world and its needs both, social , political, moral and spiritual attitudes, in a general way.

Today I stand willing give all in belief in of the truth, so that I can stand before my Creator and state what I logically have believed and followed all my life by following all evidence I am supplied with, and using the one thing God has given me to investigate reality, my own brain and spirit. There I would stand now!

"Increase my wonder and amazement at Thee, O God!"
(Baha'u'llah, Gleanings from the Writings of Ba-
ha'u'llah, p. 162)

Whoso seeketh Me, shall find Me. Whoso findeth Me, shall be drawn towards Me. Whoso draweth nigh unto Me, shall love Me. Whoso loveth Me, him shall I also love. He who is beloved of Me, him shall I slay. He who is slain by Me, I Myself shall be his ransom."

(The Dawn-Breakers, p. 72)

The earth is but one country, and mankind its citizens
(Baha'u'llah, Gleanings from the Writings of Baha'u'llah, p. 250)

A Reflection

It is a truism that cannot be escaped that beings are created as male and female by Whoever created them, and I write this in uppercase because whatever created us has to be greater and superior to us and must, by reason of having created beings, be conscious of the creation and be far superior to it. We cannot in anyway equate ourselves to Who made us. If we say it is nature, can we say we understand nature or that we are superior to nature or is nature just another creation. It is an endless thought for we exist, are conscious of our existence, but do not know the First Cause of our existence. If we knew we would really know what we are and why we are.

It is known that a bear is a bear and a cat a cat, and none of them seem to distinguish one cat as one thing or another except in procreation. Yet humans who are supposed to be superior to all animal life, perform this difference and attach to it invisible intrinsic qualities that cannot be detached from each sexual occurrence.

I am brought up by two beings, male and female , but none of that upbringing makes me two persons but is unified in me as one behavior. I am therefore a result of the upbringing of two beings, each contributing what they know to foster the safety of my knowledge of the planet and it's beings. Yet as a grown person, I am forced to relegate one group of mankind as being inferior. This ideology is in every culture I know, be it of the East or the West of the surface we call the Earth.

I challenge any human to prove that before the Deity the sin of woman is greater than that of man. Nowhere in the Holy Writ is it mentioned that women shall be punished less for sins performed on earth than men will be. As a matter of fact, I grew up knowing that angels do not possess a sex but are just generally known as angels.

We know and fully recognize that in the animal kingdom, sex is a mere convenience of functionality, but to humans it takes on a philosophy which is even studied in schools.

It is known that in some languages the pronoun of the Deity is male, but in most others it has no gender. It may be the norm that 'he who holds the gold makes the rules' but this is not true of who we exactly are, because all are confronted in the end with death, and none of that has sex, and no gold can buy us out of that final destiny, no matter how extensive and rich that gold may be. All are gathered under one dust.

The functionality of sexual existence is known and none can escape that, it remains the reality of our lives, but our philosophy thereof is a mere human construct, dependent mostly upon physical ability, and not spiritual strengths. Some men have been known to break down sooner than women in all societies. Very few men can undertake the tasks of nurturing that women can do without pay or remuneration of any kind, but simply out of compassion and feeling. This does not make females superior either, because there are very few women who can endure some physical tasks performed by men. This is also a reality, but each sex compensates for the other in a uniformity of functionality which should be recognized and acknowledged.

It is a reality of life that we come out of the womb, as males and females and not at our choosing of a particular sex , but as determined by nature. We do not know the plan of the universe just as we cannot say that the birth of a man or woman is entirely random or planned.

What we know of our civilizations extends to a mere couple of thousands of years. Yet the universe has existed with all it contains for longer than we care to know or can encompass. There is no way of knowing from present records to, what extent changes and chances of time have altered our philosophies or understandings about each sex .Yet in our times, which we regard as advanced far beyond what we know of past ages, women are regarded as being philosophically and otherwise inferior. This perception which is our own is unsupported by biological or zoological existence. .Doves fly as doves with no separation, and cats are cats, except when it comes to procreation, otherwise they exist in the environment as animals.

If anyone messes this planet up, be they male or female we shall all be in the danger of complete disappearance from existence. This may not occur or be manifest in all existence in creation, but let us really think again of what we are really doing and what we truly believe in as a species.

There have come many philosophies of existence on the planet with quite a number of followers. But we do not pause to think out just how many of those philosophies are based on a sure foundation of logic and reality rather than a hysterical behavior that is actuated either by supremacy or gain in some way that is not related to the reality of the matter.

In the past existence has to an extent been governed by physical strength, but our times dictate that the real strength lies in mental ability and spiritual resilience, and such forces are accessible to both sexes.

If we can have a choice to alter from one sex to another, this does not affect our souls and their responsibilities, but it becomes a choice we take on how we want to exist on the planet, and each choice has its natural consequences. If my child , at birth, were to have an option of being male a or female, that child would have to take on all the muscular and other options of that sex. But their soul would still be equally responsible for any moral or ethical infractions, bearing in mind that such infractions are the decision of the self and are not intrinsic qualities of the soul of that being.

This needs logical proofs and does not even mean one has to belong to any organization to decide upon. The occurrence of men and women is in every culture just as in the animal kingdom, of which man is partner, takes place naturally.

As an individual, I have grown up in a society where children are brought up mainly by female parents while the male parents provide the physical means of existence. It is therefore, to me, nauseating to know that some men regard themselves intrinsically to be nearer to God than women for the simple reason that nature made them to be men. Are not men and women born of woman? Who is to say how the probability was determined , if probability it is? If all my children are girls , I could not be said to be less a man in the plan of things, nor can a family who has no children be considered inferior whatever they may do or achieve. The determination of making a sex superior must be therefore bonded by chance. That means that chance determines whether I shall be superior or inferior. This cannot be just, and God is Justice Itself, and requires accounting for all sins , equally for all men and women. That means that we are all equally responsible to the Deity for all actions, be they committed by a male or a female.

It is not a hope to cause a rift between men and women but to cause a realization of equality of station between both sexes. I openly say that I shall be judged at death according to what I shall have done in my life. Just as any woman will be judged, in the simple way that my ancestor was judged according to the spiritual law of his day, and my progeny shall undergo same .If that is a crime, then I accept full responsibility, knowing full well that none can prove my guilt before the Lord, for none know Judgment at death and what it entails.

A Gift from Professor Brown

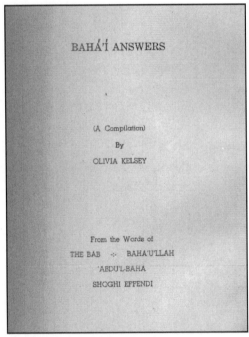

BAHÁ'Í ANSWERS

(A Compilation)

By

OLIVIA KELSEY

From the Words of

THE BAB ⋅∴ BAHA'U'LLAH

'ABDU'L-BAHA

SHOGHI EFFENDI

"The cover to the book "Bahá'í Answers" by Olivia Kelsey. Cover scanned from original by author

A gift from Professor Bishop Brown who resided in Durban as a Bahá'í pioneer from the United States. The book is inscribed as having been owned by Edyth Johnson whom I never met. The copy is still in author's possession from 1969. (L_R) Valera Allen, Dale Allen, William Masehla, Paddy Mazibuko, Bahiyyih Winckler, Ephens Senne, Bishop Brown

Now that mention has been made of my brother in Durban, it seems necessary that I mention some of the important people of my Faith that I met in that same city. For nearly seven years I communicated with Bishop Brown both as a pioneer and as the Treasurer of the Assembly without ever meeting him until 1969. Bishop and his wife Ruth were early pioneers in Durban. When I met them it was at their home in Congella, Durban, having been fetched from the train station by Lowell Johnson. This was my first visit to Durban and the first house In entered was Bishop's. Bishop was a good friend of Emeric and Rosemary Sala, and they often mentioned him in conversations with me in Port Elizabeth.

On my arrival at Bishop's home, he assisted by Beatrice Nkosi cooked a very satisfying large meal for Lowell and I. Lowell had come all the way from Johannesburg and I from Port Elizabeth, and both of us were to assist in the teaching work in Natal, especially in the Durban area. After the meal, Bishop brought Ruth Brown , his wife ,to feed her himself. I could see that Ruth had some health issues and needed full assistance. Bishop then assisted Ruth to say the "Remover of Difficulties" a task she was able to manage with some difficulty. I retain in my mind that picture of Bishop assisting Ruth so tenderly to recite a prayer.

When later I moved from Umlazi Township where I was assigned to stay with the Kubones' I stayed in Chesterville where it was a possible for Bishop to visit briefly. He would deliver all messages and mail addressed to me from his house to Chesterville every day.

At this time, Bishop's stepdaughter, Bahiyyih Ford(Winckler)had a curio store in downtown Durban on West Street. She collected African items of authentic nature and displayed them. She would make certain that each item was authentic by running a check through with the local Zulu population. As this visit was at the end of winter before any warmth made an appearance, Bahiyyih's present when I left Durban for the Transkei with Lowell, was a warm pair of socks and lots of encouragement.

On my return to Durban from Cape Town with again Lowell I found out that Ruth had passed on. The time of the passing of Ruth seemed to coincide with a time I spent a night in a ditch ,lost in the Transkei at night.

I have retained one letter written by Bishop on the occasion of my marriage to the first wife in 1973 and display on the next two pages to show how he cared:

P.O. Box 42, Congella, Durban, South Africa
Telephone 359790

Feb. 6 - 1973

Dear Robert,

I hope this letter finds you in good health and happy with your bride.

Thank you for putting me in the picture about your marriage. I knew it was to take place but did not know the date. I hope your mother is pleased with the action you have taken.

Mrs Ford will marry Dr W.G. Winckler on February 23rd It will be a quiet wedding in his flat with only family members present. Other plans had been made but it seemed wiser to change them during these uncertain times. Their address after Feb 23 will be P.O. Box 84, Northlands Johannesburg.

P.O. Box 42, Congella, Durban, South Africa

Telephone 359790

I am enclosing a money order for R.5.00 in recognition of your marriage. It is not much but it can be used in any way you want to use it.

I am pleased that you are planning to attend the Convention and I hope a strong NSA will be elected. We need more Africans on the national body.

Congratulations on your marriage and may you and your family live to serve Bahá'u'lláh for many years.

With Bahá'í greetings & best wishes,

Bishop.

It is a fact that after her marriage to Gottfried Winckler , Bahiyyih and her husband travelled to Port Elizabeth to congratulate me and my wife on our wedding. Gottfried was so interested in the Faith that he decided, at a very difficult time, to translate the Kitáb-i-Iqán, one of the major works of Bahá'u'lláh, into Afrikaans, to let the country really have a taste of what the Bahá'í Faith taught, for he knew Afrikaans and German while quite conversant in English. That Book together with the translation into Xhosa, which I had been requested to accomplish, is now available in South Africa.

Wandile, My Little brother The Car Mechanic

For reasons I do not know my brother as a soccer player was called "Aspro", and yet an Aspro is a pain killer in pharmaceuticals, as the active ingredient of the tablet is aspirin.. But then , that is his name in soccer circles. My little brother is a successful survivor, but he cared very little for a lot of education as a youngster. At high school age, he left school for work. This in itself assisted the family, because I had opted to support the family where I was needed, where he submitted his whole salary to be divided by the family. When he did get permanent employment , he struck a deal with my mother: One week , he would hold all his wages, the next he would submit all wages to his parents. This worked for him, but I wanted my independence and freedom to make choices. Granted, this does not leave one with a happy conscience when things go wrong, but I had opted out of family control on my first employment and, in my mind, there was no turning back. It was my decision and I saw fit to abide by it.

I got him his first job in the glass factory I worked in. He soon abandoned that and opted for a post at the Ford Motor Company which was arranged by one of our clan uncles. It is fact that, with that job Wandile earned more than I for many a year until I had a rise in a post as a Quality Controller in a tablet manufacturing company. However, still, his bonus for each year was higher than mine, yet I had a first year in university science.

Wandile met both Rosemary Sala and Lowell Johnson, my Bahá'í teachers, as did Donald also , but he never became a Bahá'í himself. Lowell met Donald in Durban and Wandile in Port Elizabeth. Wandile was and is still very appreciative of what I am, and even joined me in becoming a notable Jazz fan in the 60s. Wandile rose from a line worker at Ford to a supervisor on the assembly line to a foreman. Much earlier than I, he knew all about cars, however, as his eldest brother ,I had to financially assist him buy his first car, around 1977. In that endeavor of the purchase of a car, , the arrangement was that, I was to loan him a sum in the later part of the year and he would repay me before the end of December from the bonus. This arrangement worked but as big brother, I had to pressure him about repayment because that very following year I was preparing for a trip to Haifa to attend the International Bahá'í Convention, and for that I needed every available penny.

Before working at the Ford , or before looking for work at all, Wandile worked for a department store, as a part time employee ,at Woolworth's, while schooling. This was a weekend job. There is no way of finding out how he got the job except by asking him and I have never done that. At the weekend, Wandile who was good in sports at school, played for a township soccer team called the "White City". How it got its name is not known to me either. But I recall that White City in Johannesburg is in Soweto, near Mzimhlophe, an African name which means a 'white city" . You could hear them call out, during matches or in encouragement in the streets : " Up the city!", but his eldest brother never went along to see him play. This was his area and I did not interfere. The work at the Ford was more permanent than the weekend job and lasted all of the rest of his working life until he retired after over thirty years.. He knew much about Ford engines than most in the town, for by the time he retired he was a known foreman at the Ford Motor Company Engine Plant .

At some point in the 80s Trade Unions were permitted among Blacks in the country, but that came amidst much rioting in the streets. Anyone holding a foreman post was in jeopardy, as strikes occurred quite often, and the "downing of tools" was a call not to be avoided. This placed Wandile at a dangerous position as a worker. Even though he was a popular figure , he could not escape the fury of the day! Somehow he survived that period.

In his work he had won some prizes and been acknowledged as a good worker , but because of his choice of wife in marriage he was not much appreciated by family. I would go into that but that is family politics. According to clan rules his wife was too close to the family. However, that was not the reason for his unpopularity in the family, in my thinking. Somewhere along the line, he had adopted my policies in the home, and that was not going to be appreciated, for , at some stage I had been sent off by family to live outside family protection. This eventually happened to him and saddened me much. At this time, I happened to be his true resource on emotional problems.

Regardless of that, Wandile had made such progress as a supervisor that, he had a car assigned to him to use, and a brand new one at that, each year. From that position of advantage he was the one to take care of his older brother's needs, Donald, whenever he was on college vacation from Medical School. Donald found that his joy and advantage as a student. But then he soon graduated and that, in a way, left Wandile at loose ends. From then onwards, Donald was able to take care of a family needs. My thinking is that, handing over a job one loves can have its problems, because Wandile must have found this change frustrating and causing much anger.

His son after him also did not care much for education either and lived a different lifestyle from him, but his daughter followed family tradition and got educated such that today she holds a degree in Computer Science and is employed by Ford as his father was. At this point , Wandile enjoys retirement. I am glad to say that he trusted me enough to ask me to name his only son when he was born and I called him " Luzuko", a name that means " Glory", which was of course is more or less the same as "Splendor".

Left, Wandile Enthen Mazibuko at work at the Ford Motor Co. Engine Plant in Port Elizabeth demonstrating for a worker (gift from Wandile)

This year(2017) when I visited South Africa, I never lacked transportation to any place, because my little brother was there to take care of all that need. For that I am truly grateful and blessed to have him.

Wandile, my little brother, accepting an award at the Ford Engine Plant in Port Elizabeth. (gift from Wandile)

Luzuko Mazibuko, Wandile's eldest son who now assists him in his business

Friends: the past , the present

The Moorsheads' Michael Moorshead and his wife, Margie. Picture sent to author by Michael Moorshead his Head of Department at Lennon's in South Africa, now residing in the United States, as a retiree.

Michael and Marge , his wife are still in touch since the days I had to apply for a visa a to enter the United States, and their emotional support in those hard days of waiting all over South Africa had a value not to be measured mone-tarily. Today, each year Michael and I send each other reports of all events of the year as December closes in, for it was Mike who wrote to the Consul in Johannesburg, requesting that my papers be processed soonest. At that time he acted as an assistant manager in a pharmaceutical company in Virginia, ,in which he soon was Assistant President, in the States. That request to the Consul seemed to have worked wonders, for by the time I went to personally apply in Cape Town I was treated more like a gentleman and that eased much tension of the day, as those were pressured days of urgency. I had been temporarily housed by my parents and had no home of my own. His comradeship while I am in the States has been worth much more than can be explained in words. Yet all I really know about the man is that he is part of the generation of British Settlers who came to the Cape in the 1800s. Our comradeship seems to go beyond that.

To further assist my case, Michael wrote the Consul in Johannesburg and since I do not have the note which was used in this case, I have his notes that let me know of his action, and below I post them:

7/22/87

Dear Robert,

I enclose a copy of my letter to the US Consul General. Also is a copy of my reply to my last letter to you after you Nov. letter (the last I received). Good Luck!

Mike Woodhead

I wish you luck in your efforts to get here. If and when you do give me a call (work number is (201) 327 3100) and I'll see if I can help. Get Gretchen to call me anytime if she needs to discuss anything.
All the best

Mike Moorshead

(201) 767 1700

A note from Michael Moorshead to author

Ever since that period , Michael and Margie's family has grown to include grand children and marriages in our communication. He himself has retired and does find time to fish and relax:

Michael Moorshead with grandchild (gift from Michael Moorshead)

*Michael Moorshead at rest, during retirement. Fishing with grandchild
(gift from Michael Moorshead)*

Michael and Marge now live in Las Vegas .in retirement. Michael was the head of Tabletting Department at Lennon's Laboratories, one of the branches of South Africa Druggists. He soon came into a managerial position in the company, and hence moved to the United States where he became an acting or assistant president at Zenith Pharmaceuticals in New Jersey. Michael was instrumental in my obtaining an early hearing when I was applying for a visa in Johannesburg, and even wrote to the Consul general to expedite matters. Michael was instrumental in my receiving a substantial increment in salary when he was placed in the managerial position at Lennon's, the pharmaceutical company, where he had access to salaries, and promotions. We exchange information of life events by giving annual reports to each other, since I arrived in the United States., and this has worked out very well. Michael is in a curious situation of having been active in my life, in the two countries I have lived in during my life

The picture below was taken at graduation of the four workers after an examination in Pharmaceutical Production Technology, a study conducted by the Pharmaceutical Manufacturers of South Africa. Examinations were written at May Baker Pharmaceuticals in Port Elizabeth under Mr. Campton of May Baker

The group of Technicians who graduated from a course inn Pharmaceutical Production Technology. (Picture from a South African Druggists' magazine)
L-R Frank Plaatjies (Supervisor, Coating Dept) ; Jeffrey Watson, (Tablet Maker, Compression); Robert Mazibuko, (Quality Control Inspector, Coating, Compression, Strip Packing); Thaya Moodely (Technician, Granulation and Research and Development.) Picture appeared in the Pharmaceutical Newsletter of companies that included South African Druggists, Labethica, and Petersons, a family of SAD companies. Mr. Tony Karis was the then overall Managing Director of the companies. He later came to the company, Lennon's laboratories to congratulate the students himself, as he was centered at the head office in Johannesburg, South Africa at that time. Mr. Clive Stanton, Managing Director at Lennon's taking the position Karis occupied for many years there. (All but Thaya have now left Lennon's Laboratories)

Persi, Phoebe and Daya

Daya (Thaya) Moodley, Phoebe and Peter Persicaner in later years. Peter and Phoebe have now retired in the United States and keep very much in touch with me and family. (Picture sent by Peter Persicaner, who now resides in Florida, is past Head of Research and Development at Lennon's in Port Elizabeth.)

Persi was the last Pharmacist I saw at Lennon's where I worked for more than ten years, and who showed me around the company in order to bid farewell to all, for the last time. Persi is well traveled man, and mentored Daya to become a Pharmaceutical Technician. Thaya also received through him training in the United Kingdom in the same endeavor of Tablet making. Thaya went ahead in his younger years and married Jenny a woman of the Colored race group and lived with her for years with their two children , despite his father who disagreed with the decision. That way Daya is a champion of a good cause, for he is originally, as some Indians are, Hindu in religion. The most two remembered movies Daya watched and told me about are " The Sound of Music" and " Love Story". Unlike most of Indian friends, Daya is diverse in choices culturally, and did not strictly go by purely Indian culture music. That is one reason we became good company, for once he asked me to meet his family, a thing rare in those days. I did that, travelling on a Sunday morning to his home in Malabar, an Indian township in Port Elizabeth armed for comfort with an LP of "The Sound of Music" I had at the time..

This was a new experience for me in Port Elizabeth , and that is to visit the Indian township, even though I had stayed with the Noors for long periods in Durban. They were , however, Malay in origin. This is how separated in later years race groups were in my city. The mixing of groups in the South End of the city and in Korsten had long been discontinued by the creation of townships that honored the Group Areas Act that applied at that time. One could appreciated Thaya's bravery then.

It is fact that, though Persicaner is not Bahá'í, he edited two books I wrote about the Bahá'í Faith and those were : "Advancing Towards an Understanding" and "In Spite of All Barriers". We had often conversed about the faith in the past , and he had been to Haifa, and was aware that there is a Bahá'í Shrine on Mt. Carmel in that city in Israel.

This in itself is not surprising for Persi is well travelled man. Among all the Pharmacists I know, he is the only one who once worked in a clinic in New Brighton as a Pharmacist. It is even surprising that he can still tell me of that, for in the 50s many of the shopkeepers in that New Brighton area suffered some reverses during the riots at the time. It seems very true that anger makes one lose all reason , for thus was emotion without a measure of logic.

Persi had an appreciation of the world that I liked, and was the only person to challenge me to attempt to speak the French I was learning at the time.

Through knowing him I widened my scope of the view of the world . Persi therefore knows much of the world through international travel, and I would not doubt
it if he knew more languages than English that he could interact in. At the writing
of this book, he is off visiting friends and family in Europe with England and
Germany included. I await eagerly his arrival home with the news from afar.

An email from Peter Persicaner and words by author

Nov 24, 2012 at 5:09 PM

Dear Robert ,

**Thank you for sharing your news , as well as a selection
of your photographs.**

**I have always held you in high esteem , but now I stand
in awe of you and your accomplishments.**

**In your senior years you can look back with immense
pride at what you have achieved in your life ... and how
well you have adapted to the challenges that you have
faced.**

**You can sit back and reflect with pride on the journey
that you have travelled ... and when it is your turn to
leave , your children will have much to thank you for.**

**You are indeed a man in a million ... and I am delighted
to have you as a friend.**

**I send you and Gretchen my fondest regards.
Persi**

**A tribute to Robert Mazibuko on the occasion of completing to write a
second book,(*In Spite of All Barriers*) edited by Peter Persicaner, and
which was later published in Maryland, United States.
A note :a friend in the United States:**

Peter Persicaner was the head of Research and Development
at Lennon's Laboratories , Port Elizabeth, South Africa.,

where I worked in the Tabletting department for 13 years as a Quality Controller , qualifying later as a Pharmaceutical Production Technologist.. He had been previously a lecturer at Rhodes University in Grahamstown, South Africa. Persi is of the Jewish Faith and graduated with a Masters Degree in Pharmacy . He had lived before in the United Kingdom , before moving from there to South Africa. Later when he left Lennon's Persicaner worked for a pharmaceutical company in Australia. He is now retired and lives in Boca Raton, FL.

The Research and Development Department, at Lennon's was next to the Granulation Department which supplied tablet granules to the Tabletting area for compression into tablets. Persicaner arrived at Lennon's at the same time as the author in 1972, and worked there in later years after the author departed for the United States. At the departure of the author form South Africa, Persicaner invited him to go into the company, from which the author had already resigned , to bid farewell to management in the company.

Robert Mazibuko

ps
The head of Tabletting Department had been for years, Michael Moorshead, who now lives in retirement in Las Vegas. Mike who was a head in a pharmaceutical Company in New Jersey , called Zenith Pharmacies, when the author immigrated to the United States, took the trouble to write to the United States Consul General in Johannesburg, South Africa, to request permission for the author's documents to be processed as soon as the Consul could.

A picture of Michael Moorshead, and his wife , Marge is enclosed.

A picture of Peter Persicaner and his wife Phoebe, taken in London during a high school reunion in later years in 2017.

What the picture evokes

When this picture was seen by the author, it brought back good memories of work with a group of Africans at Lennon's, a pharmaceutical company in which Persicaner, known to most workers , as "Persi", worked. Such men as are now remembered had such names as Rooseveldt Tswanya, Amos Mhlawuli, Daniel Made, and dear "Fana", names which are hard to forget as workers at Granulation Department of Lennon's.

Such were the wonderful days at this company with Persi! As I crossed the street on the morning of my departure, I decided to visit another friend who was , an ex co-worker, and then owned a pharmaceutical establishment called "Ranbro Pharmacy" on Cottrell Street. For the first time in a long period I gave ground to some tears, as if losing an old friend, as I entered the store. The friend I visited who owned this company was Hilton Sin Hidge, and his wife Dolores . In private moments I had referred to Sin Hidge as " Sinny" with no trace of insult. He was a very nurturing man whose voice would soften when he heard a sad tale. On hearing that I had left the company and seeing me breakdown, he tried comforting the author, and he and his wife soon disappeared into the back of the shop. They came out looking almost shy as they presented me with two gifts for the parting. One was a key ring and the second a billfold both made of leather. I was humbled as I left because I had never thought they cared that much. I had visited the shop and cracked jokes with them quite often, but emotion of this kind was new. The realization came that I was leaving much that was precious in life behind, but it also made me vow never to disappoint these kind people by my behavior in the future, and encouraged me to show them that I could do this and succeed..

I kept the two presents for years until they fell apart when I was in the United States. Persi and Sin Hidge were and still are good friends to have in sad times and in happiness, with accent on the urgent moments, on the part of Persi. Thus are they remembered. At this point, with Persi, Mike Moorshead and I in retirement in the United States we have much to remember of the past though coming from diverse backgrounds.

Added Memory

One of the reasons that made Persi so easy to get along with was that he was diverse in his choice of friends and associates. One of the men he worked with in his department and with whom he still is in touch is Robert Cheong, whose picture is displayed below. He then took the trouble to send me a copy of a picture of the man which he has in his collection. Perhaps what actuated him to send also was the knowledge that my family with Gretchen has now a relationship in that part of the world he originates from, in that Gretchen's son, Erik Anderson. Erik has two lovely stepchildren from a previous marriage of his wife, Carolina Wallstrom, a Swede, and whom we all love them dearly as family. As Robert is originally Chinese and the children the same, this is very new on both sides of my family that we have the honor of that diversity, which is taught in our religion in the simple statement of "Unity in diversity". Further, as Erik, Gretchen's son, received some education in Fudan University in China, this seems to have been in the cards that it would someday occur and is now welcomed with joy. In this way we have in the family, managed to join four continents:: Africa, Europe, America and the Far East. With our religion added we are now related to The East, the Middle East and the West. As Bahá'ís we are proud of this and hold hands over it.

Robert Cheong who was assistant head of Granulation at Lennon's Laboratories, in his status as an immigrant in Canada at present.(Gift from Persicaner)

Robert Cheong, a Pharmacist at Lennon's was part of the supervisory staff at Galenical Manufacturing and the Tablet Granulation departments. He first supervised in Galenicals and was soon transferred to Tabletting where he headed Granulation together with another European fellow, John Kok. Kok , who was soon moved to the Tablet Compression Room while Persi, who had headed Granulation, became head of the Research and Development department .

The setup at Granulation was such that each man had his cubicle and a number of products to care for in making granules. Granulation prepared granules which were later compressed in the Tablet Compression Room into tablets. Each man had been trained to operate alone in each cubicle and needed no strict supervision except on pharmaceutical technical points. These men knew their work and were the highest number of African employees in manufacturing . They were also very capable of articulating their needs to the company when the need arose. Thus one had to tread with care in the department. Especially knowing that these were days of rioting and things could be uncertain. It was a good thing that Robert operated on a few words and lots of action. For he soon was left to head the department alone.

Robert had been a student at Rhode University where Peter Persicaner lectured in Pharmacy. Robert now resides in Canada. (As in Picture donated by Peter Persicaner). Larry Pow Chong was Head of Galenical Manufacturing at Lennon's who was assigned by the company to supervise the studies of Robert Mazibuko in his course of Pharmaceutical Production Technology at Lennon's. This course was offered by African Druggists and the South African Organization of Pharmaceutical Manufacturers. As it were , both Cheong and Pow Chong headed departments at Lennon's Laboratories in 1985 when I left the company, a company called "Aspen" today.

Larry Pow Chong compared to Cheong, was more articulate in speech and was best suited for his post at Galenicals, for there one had to speak up. I knew from experience for I worked in both departments before. I never worked directly with either Cheong or Larry but knew Larry through having to ask him some questions during my studies. My time at Galenicals had been before they both arrived in the company. Larry, when asked would have direct answers and no digression. Larry's cousin was a girl I had met as a Bahá'í. She had not been a Bahá'í but a contact I knew through friends. I had met friends of her's in Haifa in 1978 while attending an International Convention of my faith. The two friends I had met, had asked me to look her up in Port Elizabeth as she had been a student tin Journalism at the American University in Tai Wan. This story is told in the book: "This Side Up".

Robert Cheong whose picture I show here happens to be in Canada at this time and the picture was donated by Persicaner with whom he still is in contact.

Urgent Issues

Absence from home and rioting

In the seventies and the eighties, the years I was employed at Lennon's and in which time I was also a member of the National Assembly of South Africa, rioting had become a way of life in New Brighton, and "necklace executions" were known to a occur. One did not really concern one's self with that unless one was actually involved because taking such interest could get one into a difficulty, so to speak. One had to remember to stay unconcerned until involved. Bahá'ís are conscious that all this unrest is leading to a common end, and that was the unification of the planet into one homeland for a unified humankind. The Bahá'ís are more concerned with doing it peacefully, one person at a time, but accepting all consequences of performing that task, the world over. Getting concerned with anything else would then be detracting from the main purpose as stated. In the unification is involved also the improving the moral and ethical character of adherents to that Faith, for to build a society without a moral code would be a fallacy.

In 1975 I got on the National Assembly by election. There was just one other member of my age on the Assembly and that was Dr. Michael Walker, the Mathematician. We were both thirty three; he having been born in October and I in March of the same year.

There was a youth conference scheduled for the Cape Town area near September that year, a year before the huge killing of students in Soweto. Because of my age, the Assembly asked me to go to this conference as a representative of the Assembly and address the youth as such.

There was sort of lull in the rioting on this day, and the flight to Cape Town was not much a problem, nor was addressing the youth a problem. In fact that was the joy of the weekend, that I was being able to speak to all those youth in Cape Town, a town which Lowell and Edith Johnson had opened to the Faith as father and mother of that community.

On this trip, I had , again ,as in my last one in 1969 , to stay in the African township of Gugulethu, and travel to Lansdowne , a colored area , each day for the meeting.

On Saturday night I retired to Gugulethu after the meeting in the Colored area. The lady I stayed with was a mother of a neighbor, Lindiwe, and an old friend of my family in New Brighton where I grew up. That evening she invited me to listen to a radio show on as there was a boxing match in New Brighton, Port Elizabeth, very near to where I lived. I had no boxing connections in New Brighton and therefore had not learned of the match before leaving . Even if I had, it would not have mattered because such matches were not in my area of interest, unless there were a huge fight as was the case that was between "Big " John Tate and Kallie Koetze which I watched with zeal! In any case, there was a boxing match and we were watching it. Suddenly there was a commotion ,and folks were running all over the place…yes there was another riot. The radio station quickly turned the program off.

It was when I arrived on Sunday night in Port Elizabeth, that I was able to learn what had happened. The police had clashed with spectators and a killing ensued. Almost ten police vans were overturned and burned in the street near the Centenary Hall, where the fight had been staged. Of course, several people were arrested. It was no surprise then that very following year that I should receive a visit from the Special Brach and , was eventually called upon at my employment to attend a police questioning.

The Managing Director came to escort me to the police car from my department one morning , asking very quietly why the Special Branch should want to see me. My reply was simple" Probably because I am a Bahá'í. . He again asked why that would be a problem and I replied that the Bahá'i Faith taught unity of humankind, and he answered very quietly that he understood very clearly, and left me to continue to the questioning on my own.

*Representing the National Assembly at a youth conference in Cape Town in 1975 (I
am third from the right behind the sitting position) (a gift from a Bahá'í friend
now serving in Haifa, Israel)*

Managing Change in the region

On the first year I served on the National Assembly, I was requested to represent the National Spiritual Assembly of South Africa at a youth conference in
Cape Town as told above. It is poignant to point out that at exactly that time,
following the meeting, a condition of removal of Africans from Cross Roads
followed, thus triggering more violence in the country. However , following
that initial meeting, summer schools of the Bahá'ís were held in Cape Town
for years. I do not recall the very theme and subject of that first meeting which
was a youth conference, and , was followed in Port Elizabeth on the very weekend I was there by riots where police cars were left burned down the roads,
after an interruption of no less than a boxing match. That next morning I had
to pass those burned cars trying to reach work. Having been on such public
transportation at the time as the airways, it came as no surprise that in the next
year after a massacre in Soweto, that I was formally questioned by the Special
Branch. These were no easy times and survival was dicey. For accidents where
death was involved could occur, and regretted later. The hard part came also
as a division of interests, in the very next year 1976. That year I had my first
born child, and he was just a baby as I was questioned. However the reasons

for a drastic change in the behaviors of the friends came from the correct quarter , for it came from the Universal House of Justice on the Bahá'ís of the world. The statement from the House wished us to address the issue of adopting Bahá'í behaviors in all actions, and thus the friends were encouraged to attend summer school by the holding of those schools in December of each year. This may sound like a tiny move but it went a long way in developing the Faith in that land..

A Change of Stance
A Conference in Cape Town for youth

Among the races living in South Africa at the time, there was no basic tie linking many of them, especially considering the Afrikaners, the English speaking and the diversity of African cultures, except that they were all living in South Africa. A generalization of policy was then a hard thing to achieve even among the Bahá'ís. As it turned out, many of the friends were still in their original churches while hanging on to being Bahá'ís at that same time. It was at this time that the Universal House of Justice in one of its annual messages called on the friends to develop 'distinctive Bahá'í character' in all things they planned or did. Among the friends this meant a dramatic change to Bahá'í behavior.

South Africa being a Christian country in the main, had many Christian holidays one of them being at Christmas. At that time all companies closed down for at least two weeks while Christmas and the New Year were celebrated. It was an ideal time for families to travel or be together. The National Assembly of South Africa, decided that as this period was the ideal time, summer schools should be held then. First, it would find everybody at home, and secondly it would introduce the observance of Bahá'í Law despite the holiday season which would prevail at that time. This strategy would then find those who adhered to the Faith sincerely, much more readier to attend a Bahá'í summer school instead of the usual holiday festivities and thus be strengthened in their identity with the Faith..

Having agreed at a meeting on this, the Assembly put it into action by establishing the holding of summer schools in December spilling over into January. This worked wonders as it distinguished those who were true to the Cause of the Bahá'ís from those who doubted. From that time, Bahá'í summer schools were held in December. Of course it meant that the friends should be cautioned that they should try to wean themselves from all other past beliefs and adhere to Bahá'í Law.

In planning the summer schools I was given a slot to present a talk. My first talk was on the "World Order of Baha'u'llah", a talk that did not seem to go too well. Subsequently I was assigned talks on Bahá'í History which seemed to work better for some years. All these talks were delivered at the Bahá'í Center in Cape Town.

It was only natural that the Assembly should ask me to repeat some of the talks on Bahá'í History at summer schools in Mdantsane, one of which culminated in the joy of translating for a Hand of the Cause William Sears.

It was also during these visits to Cape Town, that I became acquainted with Sadri Farabi who was then a Persian student at Cape Town University's Economics Department where he studied for his Masters. It is my pride that the first color camera I owned was purchased at one of these summer schools from Sadri at a paltry sum.

Robert Mazibuko at Mnandi Beach near Cape Town, during a break at Summer School (Picture by Sadri Farabi in 1978)

Teaching Visits in Durban

As mentioned in the book of the title" In Spite of All Barriers" I visited Durban in 1969 with Lowell Johnson on a teaching project for the National Assembly of South Africa. Most of what I had to do then initially was to locate Bahá'ís who were on lists and document addresses for all of them. In doing this I had to walk all over Durban. So it was part of the journey to pass many famous buildings. One of these was the Mosque on Gray Street, which I learned later was the largest mosque in the Southern Hemisphere. I mention this because I was later to make many visits to this area, mainly to purchase recordings (LPs) of chanted verses from the Qur'an, out of interest.

It had been my intention when I stopped travelling with Lowell to learn all I could about several religions in South Africa at that time. This was the reason I had then purchased first a two copies on the Qur'an , one by Rodwell and another by Sales, for study. Also I found a copy of the Baghavad Gita, and a copy of a booklet containing prophecies by the Israelites which had not been included in the Bible, the *Apocrypha* . To add to that collection I had also found a Bahá'í book about Buddha. These were to help me become an effective Bahá'í teacher, for I had learned on that very trip that there were many more religions in South Africa than just Judaism and Christianity, the two which I had become accustomed to some time ago.

One of the things that encouraged me in this study was hearing chanted prayers both in Arabic and Persian. Up to that time I had only heard prayers and chants in local Africa languages, in English and Afrikaans. This was something very new to me and I intended finding out more about it, and just what was chanted in terms of what I knew to be Bahá'í. Call it curiosity, and I call it study. If I had to be a Bahá'í teacher as the case had changed into in a short time, and also if I wanted to translate Bahá'í Writings as I was doing, then I had to have an idea of the original text from the Manifestations and compare translations. To me this was mandatory .

To aid in the study of the Qur'an I found I had to hear how it was chanted. By the time I settled in Port Elizabeth, I knew not only the Noor family in Durban, who were Bahá'ís but also knew Casssiem Davids , a Bahá'í who had been a teacher at a mosque before joining the Faith in Cape Town,. In turn, Cassiem was taught more by Lowell and his wife , who of course, are the 'mother and father' of the Cape Town Bahá'í Community.

Through my Bahai friends, the Noors, in Durban, I purchased some recorded chants. One of these was the *Al Waqiyyiih*, or the "The Sura of the Terror" (Rodwell) or "The Sura of the Inevitable" which even today I sometimes visit in my studies, because, at an event at a conference in Badasht (Shoghi Effendi, p. 288) organized by early believers had seen the chanting of this Sura at the instruction of the Blessed Perfection. That chanting of that Sure, caused the early believers to understand that what they then had was not Islam, but a new faith . They went ahead and died for it in great numbers . For the time of uniting the planet had come! For God had spoken again!

At one stage, during a visit to Durban to attend a youth conference at the instruction of the National Assembly on which I served at that time, I asked to be guided to the area where I could buy chanted *suras* from the Qur'an. This I discovered was near the Grey Street Mosque. I never entered that mosque but did buy at the store near it. The one mosque outside whose door I stood at noon one day ,when the *Addhan* was being chanted was on Peel Street in Port Elizabeth.

At Peel Street, I stood outside the mosque until the noonday chant was over and did meet with the muezzin, who invited me to evening prayer. However I never turned up for that prayer. At that time I was by then keenly aware of the problem I would face in the mosque as a Bahá'í. Not attending saved me some trouble. I am certain of that. I had by that time, met Cassiem and knew of his sufferings in Cape Town when he joined the Bahá'í Faith, a suffering he found he could not alleviate by turning to anybody except God and the faithful. Had he not abandoned a public tailoring shop because of his allegiance to the Faith?.

Below is a picture of the Mosque on Gray Street, and a story of my visit to the nearby store to buy an LP follows. To state a fact, I had passed up and down this street many times early when I was looking up Bahá'ís in that city but never really noticed it until I was told it was there and apprised of its s importance. Maybe I was then more geared on finding my brethren , the Bahá'ís than looking up buildings. Nevertheless , I now recognize that it was there, and there all the time I was visiting Durban earlier..

A mosque in Durban's Gray Street, the largest mosque in the Southern Hemisphere. Robert passed it every day while he was in Durban as he left the railway station. Near here he purchased LPs of Qur'anic chanting by Addul Bassit. Most noteworthy chant bought were the Al Waqiyyih of Sura of the Inevitable and the Sura of Joseph (picture downloaded from Internet)

Community Life in Zwide
Two Women make a Difference

Grace Fudu with Xhosa decorative paints and dress (from personal collection)

Ivy Gcume conducting a children's class in Zwide, Port Elizabeth
(cropped from picture taken by author)

When I left the Bahá'í Community of Zwide in 1978, to reside in Kwa-Ford near New Brighton, I left a couple who had just married the Fudus, to occupy the house I had rented . I moved into a new scheme where buying property was easier. This was the KwaFord Scheme of housing. Ronald and Grace Fudu had been the first couple to marry under the Local Assembly of Zwide. On parting with the group in Zwide to move to KwaFord, Ivy and Mthembu or Tembu Gcume as he was sometimes called, got married under the same Local Assembly of Zwide.

Having become Bahá'ís the two women set out to improve their education. Grace left to study for a teaching certificate and a boarding school, while Ivy, having completed high school privately, left to complete a Bachelor of Arts degree at a local university. Today, both women are qualified teachers in the community.

Grace then educated her children who were born a year of two after my first born. Malibongwe the eldest of those children became an engineer had married a girl from California. Ivy who named her child just Bayan, after the first Book of the Bab, *The Bayan* , and she, Bayan, in turn married and became a Mrs. Hawkins , with a husband form the United Kingdom, who has relatives in the United States. This was phenomenal, for, when I met Ivy she worked shifts in a manufacturing company while Grace had just left schooling. Under the conditions of New Brighton, which I know only too well, this does not happen too often.

Both women are staunch Bahá'ís, in fact Ivy's picture was cropped from a picture where she was teaching a group of children before she left for school herself.

The story of mistaken identity

I was in Durban to attend a conference and had spent the night at the home of Ruwayda and Selwyn Henry, two young Bahá'ís. Ruwayda is a sister of Ludfi Noor now residing in Minnesota, a husband to one of the Skrenes' girls, i.e. Teresa Noor.

I had arrived on Friday night, and it was then Saturday morning. The meeting with the youth was scheduled for the afternoon. I then decided to go into the city to buy some LPs a I wanted. Ruwayda, wanted also to go into town for shopping. This was a help, because they knew the city, were known there as residents, they would find the store near the mosque easily.

Ruwayda, now residing in Australia, had with her a young child who needed carrying.

We got to the store, and Ruwayda wanted to take the child to the bathroom. So we asked the Indian shop owner for a toilet. Fortunately it was an Indian store so we could ask for that.

While Ruwayda was gone, the owner came over to me asked very quietly just where or what country we were from. Ruwayda is Malay and I am , an African, we had a baby with us .It seemed logical to ask this. I was least surprised because this kind of thing had happened to me many times in South Africa. Some of the Colored fellows even thought I was not even African!

I told the man I that I was from Port Elizabeth, and that the lady was from Durban. He shook his head in disbelief and left me standing there. When I told Ruwayda this on her return, she said even if I had said I was from South America he would have believed me, and we would have had lots of respect as visitors. In other words I had spoiled a good game , and lost a wonderful chance… That is my story of the store near the mosque…

Getting Established as a Bahá'í Family

Events that Led to International Convention

The faith having been introduced as a religion , left one then with the goal of how to live the letter of the Word of Bahá'u'lláh. It had by far been agreed by many that the laws of unity of the Faith were relevant to the cause of the Africans, but the question was which of the two was a priority, the cause of the Africans or the obedience of the laws for a New Age, for the sake of God and His command? In that question lies the whole participation in its fullest measure of Africans to the Cause of Bahá'u'lláh. The main being " How did the Faith answer the call for assistance from the Africans in their present predicament , considering the laws or rules of governmental powers, when the Faith proposed the idea of non-participation in political activity?"

To answer this urgent call then a path had to be found that guided all from a present lifestyle to a lifestyle that would both satisfy the need for relating to the rest of the world in meaningful ways ,a a life that would relate to ancestral belief ways that were not foreign to the African. Therein lay the whole issue of African participating in real ways to the activities of the Faith of Bahá'u'lláh.

To attend to this , there would have to be some thread leading from past behavior to a present behavior in a relevant way that associated both ways of behavior.

Belief in the Faith then had to start with a true belief in the Biblical issue and what that stood for, and try to reflect on African belief and how it was practiced in its pristine form that was not mitigated with present changes that obscured its meaning.

As the religion of Christ had been introduced by Whites who had somewhat failed to legitimize it to true Christian behavior by their desire to settle down in the land at all costs , even at the cost of limiting the true meaning of the religion of the Manifestation of Jesus. A true understanding had to be attained and related to present Bahá'i ways of behavior in legitimate ways.

Academically the Faith was acceptable and very much approved of, but to the rank and file , the unlettered African, it had not really taken root. This then was one of the very reasons some of us as Africans decided to translate the laws and the writ of the Faith into African languages, so that Africans had a fair chance of seeing what was being offered by the new faith and what its real demands were. It helped greatly to know that the religion was taught by pioneers who had no desire for land or any advantage, and it soon dawned in minds that the teaching was being really done for the sake of the religion itself and no other. This was not colonization.

Translating the works of the Faith into local languages having begun, now was the time to find a practical application. This was a hard thing to achieve in a country whose administration of a purely White dominant society did not believe at all in the oneness of the human race, and that notion being itself being a major thought of the new Faith.

It was the task of the pioneers and all South Africans who could perceive the spiritual meaning of the new teaching, to proliferate into the rest of African community. The obvious reason, of course, was to show the practical application of the rest of the laws proposed, so that the need for those laws, which could not be overtly taught, could be understood in behaviors.

In Port Elizabeth and the Cape Midlands, the Sala family had demonstrated the willingness to enter African homes as friends rather than as merely teachers. Many friendships had been created among the community, an action which laid a foundation for the acceptance of the Faith in the African community.

At the time of the coming of the Beers to Port Elizabeth, after Lowell Johnson had succeeded in making the authorities accept the possibilities of Bahá'ís holding meetings in public places owned by the government, the situation was ripe for further trials of activities for the Bahá'ís

Christine and Patrick Beer had functioned in the teaching of the Faith in Africa before, having taught in the Nigerian area, but they were not aware that the very person who was now teaching in this area, had been himself in the center of problems . These problems were cultural, social and ethical, and his non-acceptance of many norms was not going to be a help in any way. However through the act of the showing of slides and giving general talks on the laws of the Faith, he himself was more or less on the rise as a Bahá'i' teacher. Indeed there were some initial issues that needed to be attended to in the so called Bahá'í group that had been formed in the city's townships,.

First the Beers encouraged deepening classes, and not of the formal type, where one simply chooses a subject and talks. A more benign way of talking on general subjects had to be adopted, and a pointing at attending issues without mentioning the Faith undertaken, by providing logical solutions based on what was learned in the Faith. Secondly , they felt that clinging to habits in the way of behaviors was not acceptable. One had to be willing to drop the usual activity of a day, and attend to what was necessary for the Faith.

The other issue related to how Bahá'í Holy Day meetings were held. They felt that Africans had to be free to celebrate those days anyway they wished, if that did not break any law of the Faith. In that sense then, celebration of the those Days , did not have to be in the form of a Western style, but the style African wanted. This went far in normalizing Bahá'í behavior in the township. There was no foreignness about it and no real form about the holding of such meetings. The only form would be in the three parts of a Feast that had to be observed , and those were: the devotions, the consultation and the social parts. In this way Africans could see themselves actually being in the picture.

Because of these strategies , by the time the Beers decided to leave for the United Kingdom, there were functioning Assemblies in the townships, and the one I had lived in had decidedly performed two Bahá'í marriages.

Africans have a saying that if one wants a wound to heal, one has to make it bleed in order to avoid putrefying . In making the wound bleed one has to see all the dirt the wound holds and be able to deal with that equitably.

In associating with the community in that city, the Beers saw so much that they did not quite approve of , but this was a natural consequence of their having raised some issues which the Africans had among themselves and which they had always accepted. Now was a time to readjust and in readjusting those behaviors had to surface to be dealt with. In dealing with the Chinese culture , Patrick had once said that in Chinese the word "honor" was symbolized by a man standing next to a mouth. That indicated he who stands by his words. In adding to that, I shall add what I also learned about that culture .They say progress is a series of backward and forward movements. One has to go back to what they were for a while in order to see where one is in the present. My very mother would always say when working in the field or garden with her, one has to look back on what one has been doing in order to see how much progress has been done at that point.

Just before the Beers left that town, I had the experience of attending the first Bahá'í International Convention, and the only one I ever attended in person while I severed on the National Assembly of South Africa.

I had a chance to ask them the currency I should use while traveling. Though they were British, they did not mention the currency of their country, but felt that the German currency was on the rise at the time and that it would serve me better if I used that. I appreciated their honesty and true advice, however, I could not avail myself of that. One reason was because, at that time, I did not know that currency and my aim is not to use anything I had no previously tested on safe ground , before launching use in foreign ground. There I used the currency I had used to exchange with in the past and that was the United States Dollar. That did help because , almost the whole group I traveled with used that currency. It was not a general decision, but I found it to be so. The only other person I had discussed that with was the Secretary of the National Assembly who was planning the trip for the whole group from Southern Africa, which included Swaziland, Lesotho and even Zimbabwe.

It was through Christine and Patrick that on the trip to Convention I was to meet one of the members of the Universal House of Justice, whose talk they had attended while at university, and which resulted in their joining the Faith. That was Mr. Ian Sample. It drove me so giddy meeting him in Haifa, that I do not even remember any of the other persons he was with in his family, only a son called Nicholas.

Christine and Patrick Beer, with son, Simon and baby, David, pioneers in Port Elizabeth, from the United Kingdom. (from personal collection)

Mr Ian Sample, member of the Universal House of Justice from 1963, picture down-loaded from Bahá'í Gallery prior to 2007. Ian delivered a talk at Patrick and Christine's university which aided them to join the faith. Ian was met by author for the first time, in 1978, while he and the rest of the Universal House of Justice, left a meeting held at 'Abdu'l-Baha's House in Haifa, Israel, quite by accident as the author wandering through the streets during the International Convention of 1978. (from Google Images)

A View in Belief

The first view of Bahá'í life is, from the perspective of an African, important, especially when one has no comparisons is to match activities within one's life. This is the situation I found myself in at the very start of practicing Bahá'í life in a community of Africans within the areas assigned to Africans at the time . There were no comparisons or examples .One had to see how and when one could start a behavior from scratch . For an example given that Africans believed deeply in the existence of Ancestors and their presence in every aspect of life, how then does one begin to introduce to a very deep and fundamental extent the requirements of behaviors that the Faith needs one to attend to and internalize in one's life? The problem of the acceptance of past religions had been more or less a surface matter, because the ingrained belief in after life with the ancestors still persisted in many minds, even though to outward seeming they belonged to a Faith introduced in recent years. The whole issue of accepting those religions was a matter of survival and not an internalized belief. Our main task in the township was an internalizing worship as a necessity of life itself, and as the only way of placing one at a position of advantage in the afterlife.

The initial introduction of the faith in my area, had hit a good point with the youth , at most, but the youth were still dependent on parents for all subsistence, so that belief soon becomes 'one of those things children indulge in'. Somehow that had to be debunked before a proper introduction of the tenets of the Faith , and even before any energetic and honest obedience to such behaviors or laws that the faith taught for a new age, could be attained or ingrained in the new adherents.

Events After 1978

Congratulating ourselves as teachers from Mdantsane, in 1978 when Rose and I were delegates at the International Convention of the Faith, at the election of the Universal House of Justice, Rose and I posed from this picture next to the Shrine of the Báb on Mt Carmel. (taken by unknown friend on request)

Hand of the Cause William Sears in the Ciskei
Events after the Visit

Hand of the Cause William Sears giving a talk at a summer school in the Ciskei in 1983. Pictured with him is a translator from South Africa, Robert Mazibuko. The above picture was extracted from a video kindly recorded by Sirus Mahmudi, a Persian pioneer who was at the time Head of the Audio Visual Department at the University of Fort Hare, Alice, South Africa. Sirus was at the time residing at nearby Fort Beaufort , Cape Province. The Movie that resulted from this recording was coupled with an interview conducted by Lowell Johnson, then working himself as a Radio Announcer for the SABC and Springbok Radio of South Africa.

Mr. Sears was very tired from editing a book called "All Flags Flying" which was again illustrated by another American pioneer called Robert Reedy an artist and teacher. Because Mr. Sears was so tired he decided he would give a shorter talk than usual, because he arrived from the Transkei where his book was being edited and still was expected to say some words at this summer school. We were expectant, as we knew that the Hands of the Cause performed these tasks of teaching and protecting the Cause of Bahá'u'lláh so well. Mr. Sears gave a resounding talk on Prophecy and Progressive Revelation, one of the themes of the Bahá'í' Revelation, Today this talk has copies held in the Archives in the United States submitted by the author , and acknowledged with much thanks by the department of Archives through Lewis Walker, who works in that office..

The author felt honored, for this is the one and only talk that the he translated for a Hand of the Cause of God and he remains proud of it as a feat he was not aware he could one day achieve.

Later in 1985 a national community of Bahá'ís was established in the Ciskei where the talk had been given, and below is the picture of the eight members of the first National Assembly formed there.:

The Bahá'í National Spiritual Assembly of the Bahá'ís of Ciskei , formed in 1985.
The author is on front row with Fatteneh Scott, a pioneer)(from personal collection)
The Assembly members were mostly women who had been taught by Rose Gates ,
the pioneer in that region. The one lady who was not African on that Assembly was
Fatteneh Scott, a Persian pioneer, and the only man on that Assembly was Michael
Scott, an American, who taught Agriculture at the University of Fort Hare. He was
absent on business at this sitting. At the election Rose Gates and Robert represented
the National Assembly of South Arica.

Another Memory to Treasure from the Time

(a picture of Mr. Mitchell) (downloaded from Google Images)

During the international Convention of 1978, I was able to see some of the well-known Bahá'ís. One of them of great importance was Mr.. Glenford Mitchell, who was then the secretary of the National Assembly of the United States. I remember him more, because he honored the author by asking if he could make a video program of him while the author made the comments he had made during the consultation with the representatives of the Assembly of the USA and the Assembly of South Africa. As probably said before, the event of the video never occurred because the date set for it was on a Saturday and nothing is open in Israel on a Saturday! Mr. Mitchell later served on the Universal House of Justice, and later gave some advices to the author in 1985 while he was on pilgrimage, concerning the involvement of youth in political activities in South Africa that the author had mentioned. The advice was valuable as always.

A Departed Friend A brief statement on Michael Sears.

The best person who wrote about Michael was Lowell Johnson, but because he and Mike are fellow Americans in origin, some would not quite credit his praise of the man since he has such links with him. Let then an African Bahá'í testify of behalf of Mike. I was surprised when, while I was in the States in later years that I received a sad letter from Mike. It was a single sheet and written from a hotel address, where he poured his heart out. I had not been aware of any problems and indeed had not kept too much in touch with back home. Before I could respond he passed on.

Once I spoke to Mike on a very touchy question and before speaking to me he said:"Remember, between friends ,there is an area where a lie cannot be admitted". It was his popular statement to repeat words from one of the presidents of the United States when there was a question of taking or not taking action in a difficult situation. He would say" Friends, remember 'the buck stops here'!" In other words the buck cannot be passed on to anybody now , it has to be stopped as a bad one and we were the ones assigned to stop it.

On many occasions, as chairman of the Assembly, Michael faced the very hard job of selling a decision of the Assembly to the Friends, and asking them not to back down on principles of the Faith. Sometimes he would even sound violent in language when asserting the duty of the friends to promote unity and advance the cure of solving the problems of the world. He asserted always that the Friends as assisted by God, had this power, and that they should use it, for, it was the power of the sprit which had nothing to do with physical weapons , but was much more lethal for it was the tool God granted and given to humankind to use . It was that power which had caused the past religions to survive through many difficulties and should be visible today. Now God had given his injunction and it is love and unity for the whole human race. That was Mike and his testimony to the Friends. To disrespect such intentions would be a spiritual crime.

As Mike's testimony, I now post this poem which he gave to me to keep and peruse:

A poem by Michael Sears.

Marching Song Of The African Legions

Amidst thy shuffly footed crowd,
Stepping off the stairway waves,
Scuttling like a crab migration,
Sideways walking to our early graves,
Knowing that I'm moving with them,
Knowing that thy sea has left me,
Backward washing whence it came,
Stumbling down the black road winding,
Thirsting for thy confirmations,
Which, more than water, my soul craves,
I lift my eyes to Thee, O God, and pray,
Show me now before I die,
The place at the top of the long hill rising,
Where, in the shimmering heat of day,
This highway blends into the sky.

By Michael Sears - Johannesburg, South Africa

Another testimony of the love Michael Sears had for the people of Africa, as he taught the Faith, can be perceived in the song he composed on his guitar, which I remember off by heart as it was sung at many am meeting in Africa:

"Africa, Africa! Come let us sing
The song of the love and the glory of God
And quicken mankind with song that we sing
A song of the love and the glory of God
Rise up! Rise up sing
Tell the people of the Message we bring!
This is the Promised Day!
This is the Day of days!

Throw your woes and sorrows away!
Happy! Happy are we!
We are beholding God's victory
Africa! Africa! Come , let us sing, a song of the love and
the glory of God!"
(A song composed by Michael Sears and sung many time
in Africa.)

It is a very simple song, more invoking than singing.

At one meeting of the Bahá'í National Assembly we had in Johannesburg, Michael offered to say a prayer. Usually at a meeting, as chairman, he would often ask one of the friends on the Assembly to say a prayer before a vote is passed on a decision. This time he said one himself. It was not my initial intention to quote this but feel the need now , so bear with me I shall quote, for I remember it well. Mike was almost never present at the opening of the National Meetings in Johannesburg , but would arrive late. I once ventured to ask Lowell why this was so and began to understand why. Lowell's answer was that, to Mike meetings of the Assembly very serious because they were as if they were conducted before the Concourse on High and he himself found himself unworthy and wary of saying anything before that Concourse , and so tried very hard not to be present. I was once asked , just as the Assembly was convening for the meeting, to kindly go to his house and remind him that the meeting was on; devotion had been offered and we were waiting to consult on weighty subject on which he was very useful. He would then venture out. His wife , Ruth understood this and was very protective of Mike.

The prayer Michael Sears read at a meeting in Johannesburg with the members of the Bahá'í National Assembly present; the date is not known, but the memory is retained:

LIII

I know not, O my God, what the Fire is which Thou didst kindle in Thy land. Earth can never cloud its splendor, nor water quench its flame. All the peoples of the world are powerless to resist its force. Great is the blessedness of him that hath drawn nigh unto it, and heard its roaring.

Some, O my God, Thou didst, through Thy strengthening grace, enable to approach it, while others Thou didst keep back by reason of what their hands have wrought in Thy days. Whoso hath hasted towards it and attained unto it hath, in his eagerness to gaze on Thy beauty, yielded his life in Thy path, and ascended unto Thee, wholly detached from aught else except Thyself. I beseech Thee, O my Lord, by this Fire which blazeth and rageth in the world of creation, to rend asunder the veils that have hindered me from appearing before the throne of Thy majesty, and from standing at the door of Thy gate. Do Thou ordain for me, O my Lord, every good thing Thou didst send down in Thy Book, and suffer me not to be far removed from the shelter of Thy mercy.

Powerful art Thou to do what pleaseth Thee. Thou art, verily, the All-Powerful, the Most Generous.
(Prayers and Meditations by Baha'u'llah, p. 75)

Michael Sears and African beliefs

Many subjects come to the National Assembly table for consultation and action. The question on how to effectively teach Africans once came up when I was on the Assembly. In the course of discussion of African beliefs I mentioned that according to books I had read on the subject, there are two types of actions in that direction , outside of customs which themselves have reasons for being performed in the past in that land.

There is what is termed White magic, which is the use of herbs to cure sickness, the term white does not in that case refer to color but refers to being able to see where others perceive not. A white child is regarded as a child who feels what has to be done more than the rest of the family and manifests that feeling by odd behavior When this behavior is noticed, the parents get together with the child and ask what the child perceives in terms of feeling or life. The child may even fall sick, and depending on the sickness the parents can the decide what needs to be done with a custom .A remembrance of a past ancestor in the family and such decisions are then carried out and the child may become well, .If not, further investigation with the child must be undertaken.

Black Magic then becomes the use of herbs to kill life of a thing or a person one hates or despises etc. The feeling of Black magic is common in all cultures and therefore Black Magic is a human action performed to hurt. Many herbs can be used in that direction just there are many chemicals that do that in the Western World. The thing to do is to change the attitude of hate to an attitude of love and that is hard, just as hard as making an evil person think of doing good for anybody. This then did not have to do with anything invisible but with that which we all knew on the Assembly. Ask about herbs that are used for attraction: It was discovered that there are many such herbs which are used to attract in Western Culture, so nothing new was being dealt with here.

Mike then once asked if he and I could have an evening discussing this because he had books on the subject and had often wondered about it. We set a night before the Assembly meeting, when I would go to his house as a guest. Of course according to law of the country this was illegal , but it was arranged in a certain way with care, so that I would not to appear in public at his house, even though his neighbors understood that the American next door sometimes has Blacks for visitors.

I arrived on a Friday night, and got picked by Mike from the airport terminal in the city, from there to his .house.

We discussed book after book and question after question until we felt we had exhausted all the queries we had and could retire. In all Mike had an understanding of where I stood on the questions of witchcraft in Africa. For I have lived in rural Africa night after night , and rural Natal for weeks without ever coming across any Tokolosies, and I do not believe even in their existence. Were it so they would have been mentioned as concrete in the Holy Books and their being merely alluded to, just like many other things in Holy Scriptures, may be a symbolical representation, for us to learn to think. Even in chemistry there was a time they had to catch ants and animals to produce some useful chemicals for study, when they learned later to develop them synthetically in the laboratory .No fear, I know as an African that there are no Tokolosies in Africa. By now rural Africa would had shown me some. At one time, I even had love affairs in the rural area..But I care what I eat and what I rub on my skin, for there lies a lot of Organic Chemistry which could hurt or kill. I know that just as much as drinking acetone which an unobservant African once did instead of pure alcohol, and had his stomach torn off by the liquid. So there! It is only fair to look at cause and effect than look at unseen sources. I do believe that some things are still hidden and are only alive in what may be termed superstition, but a phenomenon that repeats itself in a certain and definite way can in no wise be a superstition but warrants investigation. Many things African have used, when fairly and honesty studied will come to be known as knowledge. This I mentioned to the Assembly.

The question of poverty in the rural area also came up as a matter of course. I explained that before a boy is circumcised he is not regarded as a person one can talk reason with , so is not expected to respond to known norms of behaviors. It is only after circumcision when he calls himself a man that he is expected to behave in any proper and respectable manner

> **Having created the world and all that liveth and moveth therein, He, through the direct operation of His unconstrained and sovereign Will, chose to confer upon man the unique distinction and capacity to know Him and to love Him — a capacity that must needs be regarded as the generating impulse and the primary purpose underlying the whole of creation**
> **(Baha'u'llah, Gleanings from the Writings of Baha'u'llah, p. 65)**

> **Fear thou God, besides Whom there is none other God but Him, the Sovereign Truth,**
> **(The Bab, Selections from the Writings of the Bab, p. 42)**

Invitation to a Prayer Meeting

In 1987 , while waiting for a visa to enter the United States , I lived for a while with my uncle in Soweto. It was during the worst part of rioting, but getting around was easy when one got used to knowing how. If I left home I had to make sure that I did in a way I knew well. Also I had to be sure that one person in the house knew where I would be going, and not just leave. My aunt was the most reliable person for that .

One day the Bahá'ís in Soweto invited me to a prayer meeting in an area known as 'White City' within Soweto. I was willing but realized I had to be very cautious what I did about that.

I was known by the friends to be able to memorize most prayers and many of them in English as the prayers I had memorized contained were mostly in that language. I was very much used therefore to saying those prayers from memory. Something , however was ringing warnings about this meeting. It was going to be in the early hours in what Bahá'ís recognize as Dawn Prayers, which are usually said before sunrise.

Of course , this would mean I would have to leave home in the early hours before light. I knew my way to the house I was invited to , so that was not the problem. The problem getting there in the darkness, in very dark unlighted Soweto, with the riots on. I was a stranger in the town , and strangers were not quite welcome, because there were those recruited from outside the country to help 'keep peace' in the townships. On that morning I took with me a paper on which I had written a prayer called the Tablet of Ahmad. I did not wish to say prayers in English at all, but in a different language altogether. One which was not spoken in Soweto to my knowledge at all. I shall explain this in the next paragraph.

At end of one summer school in Cape Town, I had spent time with a Persian friend, a son of Giti and Manucher Rauhani, of Transkei, who was attending the summer school. In discussion with him , I asked him if he knew the Tablet of Ahmad off by heart, as it was in Arabic originally , and not in Persian ,and I knew some Persians did not quite know that much Arabic. He answered that he knew the prayer. I then asked him to pronounce each sentence in the tablet so that I could write it down in a phonetic style that I could understand. I wished also that he gave me the meanings of each word. We sat down to this task and it took more than a day to do this. I kept that copy and travelled with it most time, because I did not know that much Arabic but knew some words, invocations and sentences in that language.

On the morning of the prayer meeting, therefore, I armed myself with that prayer. I had only used it once in Arabic, at a prayer meeting in Swaziland.

I found my way to the prayers without mishap. It was a quiet morning, but I knew chanting would wakeup many in the house if I started it. At the meeting there were a few African friends, and I am aware that in Johannesburg Sesotho is used a lot. I knew very little of that language too, and could sometimes distinguish it from Tswana, which was also common in the Transvaal area. I also knew that the Bahá'ís were used to chanting by the Persian friends at meetings.

I immediately saw my predicament. If I prayed in Xhosa , I would be identified to have a Cape Province accent; if I prayed in English I would be queried for a foreign accent and that was itself trouble at this particular time. From the point of view of anyone who was not Bahá'í and listening to the prayers, might I not be identified as one of the foreigners from the North who had been imported to keep peace? If that happened , what were my chances of survival? I had to say a prayer and was expected to , for I had been a member of the National Assembly, and all the Bahá'is knew that in Soweto. The prayer had to be sincere but had to relate to my hearers.

It was dark in the room lighted only with candles and a paraffin lamp and I could not see faces, and Soweto was not lit at all outside. Six in the morning in winter is not sunlight time. I had to think and think fast for my turn to pray around the room was coming up! I knew I had the Tablet of Ahmad in my bag and knew that prayer off by heart in English. I could not do that in English, not in Soweto and during the riots. I was left with one respectable option to test I would chant my prayer in Arabic and hope for the best among the Friends and be able to cause doubt of identity to outsiders. That is what I would do and again a hold on to hope. It was a critical moment, for recently I had heard of the parading of a group with an informers head displayed in public. If I were being challenged as a Bahá'í, that would be fine, but being challenged as an informer was not going to work and I would not submit to it. I could keep quiet when my turn came, but I had been invited by those who knew me as a Bahá'í and I had to say one with them, just like partaking of their meal. This was African.

When my turn came, I calmly took out the sheets of papers I had and started chanting. This being a long prayer chanting takes long to complete it. I chanted all of it. It was a surprise too. I was very right about the different languages used in Soweto, for the friends said prayers in Sesotho, and Setswana, and I was going to be left paying in English, a very dangerous thing indeed at that time. Chances are I would have disappeared in Soweto without a trace, but saying a foreign prayer had everybody surprised, for Jo'burgers pride themselves on diversity of language.

I seemed to have saved myself some trouble, for when I left I was more or less respected for the prayer. If that had been set up, it probably did not work. As I left n the morning light, I felt strange with people watching me as the fellow who had prayed in a language unknown to many. I knew Soweto to be the land of African languages, and someone must have heard chanting in North Africa sometime or other. I was shaky, and did not stay for coffee that was being prepared but got to the taxi and rode home. I had to explain my absence to my aunt , for she had given me directions of how to catch a taxi in the morning to the area of the prayer. My thinking is that when one is in Rome, one tries to speak Latin or something related to Rome in some way and not too foreign. Mine was Arabic as heard at the mosque, and learned from the Persians who were Bahá'í . I had succeeded in praying with my Bahá'í friends in the language of the original script of the Writings and was sure no Persian had been there yet!

Understanding a Health Condition

If someone asked me if I understood my own health condition , I would reply that I do indeed and if one asked me where it leads to , I would then say I have no idea. I have suffered what I realize to be a kind of depression, but, through it I have learned a lot more about human behavior than I would otherwise had done , had the condition not come. I soon realized that people relate whether they are conscious of it or not. It has nothing to do with deciding to relate. All aspects of life and beings are interconnected, in the same way that we breathe the same air and are not really conscious of it. That same air we breathe might be the breath from an animal or a plant for all we know, for they all subsist on the same air. People relate not just with sounds but with colors and very intricate methods . A man sings a song he heard during the war years and finds himself behaving in exactly the same way he did during the war, and may not even conscious of remembering. If one learns to track sounds and reactions, one can easily place a person in the correct context in his present state.

Life does not progress as a bland progression but in steps that are fast and slow, and during the fast stage, much happens that will determine the slow stage. What happens in the jumble of a cell will manifest itself in the condition of the organism. One has to do the best during the crisis without knowing why, but it soon steadies during the quiet season.

This kind of explanation may not make sense to one who has not experienced consciously the eddies of life but that should not worry one. We live life without knowing what life is. We are born, grow , and die without knowing the why of it. We have to be content to learn from the Great Beings Who come and go and leave us prescriptions of living, and be aware that the prescriptions is vital for a general survival. Many may pooh-pooh all that for they feel they know better, but who really knows what life is and why we are except the Great Beings? We are not forced to obey but have to meet our destiny someday. This should not be taken as a threat but an advice. While one lives in this life, one has to find all the avenues that may tell of a past or future events. That may not be part of what we call education but is an education one learns. For education is what is determined for us to learn and not all knowledge. As we go we add to what has to be known. As one may say: there is sickness and then there is sickness. One must tell the difference.

In the sense I describe above, I can say I understand something of what I am . It causes me no problems except in behaving as others may want to do, where I do not agree entirely with them. It occurs that when one has to deal with a serious matter one achieves a slant in the sense of humor, or loses the sense of wanting to laugh until a solution is achieved. When one is in that state, I wish not to interfere but let one find the avenue one wishes for. Life is unrelenting. What has to happen will happen one way or another, whether one agrees or not. We do not own this life, but live it and it has conditions of its own which are never defined except in the Holy Books. One has therefore to seek contentment with what is in one's life. When one delves in such contemplation , one may lose consciousness to the world and live a life that is not.

17. O SON OF MAN!

> **Be thou content with Me and seek no other helper. For none but Me can ever suffice thee.**
> **(Baha'u'llah, The Arabic Hidden Words)**

If health be the quest then one has to find solace in being content.

The Strategies of a silence

By the time I took up being an active member of my faith, the Bahá'í Faith, I had met many people in a number of fields .In interaction with those I met I had been verbal about many issues, however I knew very well that I would have to hold my silence were I under any official questioning. In retrospect, therefore, it served a good purpose than when I failed in a love affair I learned to hold my silence. Because had I been verbal under questioning by the police, much would have gone very wrong. What saved me was a sickness that had me rather more dumb than verbal. No one, at that time learned what my problem was , nor was there anyone able to hold converse with me whereby I would reveal my mind of what I knew. I was content to be described as a little off the mark for not opening up than to spill my guts under questioning. For I was aware at all times under police guard that I was more or less under arrest. Because I was not speaking, my condition by the doctor was referred to as being 'dumb'. This was an unrealized strategy because at that moment I was aware of one thing that I should not reveal anything that might place me in an unpleasant condition of being open at the wrong time and about the wrong issue. The very words I would use describing any situation would themselves be a revelation of thought. So the best strategy was to say nothing.

It amazes me how I got away with that but my whole character for a number of years to follow was governed by a silence and change of stance. I can only be grateful that I had also an embarrassing end to a love affair that I did not wish to speak of, that everything else I knew stayed hidden. As a minor undertaking ,it is also clear that the change in stance also helped me to change habits. Where I entered as a great smoker, I exited as a non smoker; where I had played music constantly , I was now silent except for a few favorites; where I had entered with no girlfriend , I was now in search for someone to marry ; where I had been strictly vegetarian, I could now partake of meat. This was the only way society of the time could accept one like myself and being what I was it no longer an act, for I was learning to be on my own with new friendships.

I was not outwardly aware that my whole life had changed but seemed different in many ways and that helped me make a good fresh start on everything.

My Doctor, C. Manga

After many years of being misdiagnosed, I found a new doctor who was to take charge of my Medical Aid account. After a short period of examination he determined that I was not at all seriously ill but should take something for depression at times. He then gave me a prescription for Diazepam 5 mg, a tablet also known as *Pax*, which in the United States is an equivalent of *Valium*. That then was the tablet I was taking on my way to the United States, the reason for carrying the above document, on the flight, which was required by law. This then was what I took in the first days of my arrival there . However , taking it was not a consistency but "as needed". Eventually I found I could then leave it off completely, until the time of the onset of a cancerous growth on my shoulder, when my behavior caused by the effect of the tumor was not quite consistent. After the surgery to remove the tumor, which occurred sometime in 1991, I had to take a tablet for depression again to satisfy also my wife's complaint that somewhat I was changing in behavior. That treatment continued until my arrival where I now live , at times being discontinued by doctors, until the present day where I have to take a tablet for sleeping times. All in all, between my arrival and 1991 I was off any treatment for depression, but would take non-prescription tablets for sleep because being acculturated was not easy. I now have a dose of a prescribed tablet at sleeping time.

Dr C. Manga schooled with my younger brother in Medicine, and was very helpful. Being himself Hindu where many doctors in the vicinity, were Islamic he helped me make a choice. Coupled with him I went to another Hindu doctor for dental problems and that was Dr Suriyakant Umley. This was an easy way to share news with fellows in the medical field without having to face religious challenges. Persecutions of Bahá'ís were known to occur especially with the world situation of the time of the 80s.

Thus when I left South Africa I had to carry Dr Manga's note in order to take tablets on the trip over to the United States. The note was a requirement of travel on airlines then. I had done that going to Israel twice in 1978 and 1985, so it was nothing new.

The added issue that required care was that, there was one non white Gynecologist in my town. The second Gynecologist I knew was my brother, however he lived in Durban. So to satisfy the conditions of my Medical Aid Plan at work, my wife had to find a Gynecologist, and the only one was a Muslim. I had known the doctor for some years as being a Muslim, for he had friends in Cape Town where many Bahá'ís lived. However, my wife, found him on her own and knew nothing about his religious affiliation. This situation necessitated that I play a low level in association but that my wife, Faith, was to deliver through the doctor for both children. In those days husbands were not required to be in the delivery room, and so my wife had to go alone and I would be informed by telephone after each birth. That worked fine for Dr Doodhat, the Gynecologist, was a fine gentleman himself and managed the treatment well. Dr Manga who was Hindu well appreciated my situation but kept his silence. As friend I had once said, it takes time to build trust and very little to topple it over ! These were hard days in my faith when it came to acceptance. To boot, my two children had Arabic middle names, Husayn and Jusuf, for in those days I was much in Bahá'í History and those two names occur prominently there. I had to give talks at summer schools on history and martyrdoms for some years every December in Cape Town. There amongst Bahá'is of Islamic background, it was necessary to know some of Islam.

My sister and a visit

At about this time , I found my little sister with a problem. She was doing a course in Economics and needed to visit a factory as part of her practical projects . I am not sure just what this did, but I allowed it. Going to the authorities at my employment and asking for assistance was no problem, but I am certain of one thing that, my taking her around the company was not viewed favorably, for no one I knew of had ever done that. However, I toured the company with my little sister having been granted time of absence from my work. It was not much of a problem for me at the time. All I had to do was stay with her and explain. Knowing that the company was so volatile at that time, I stand uncertain of what that did, but whatever it was, it did not assist my situation favorably, for after that problems intensified.

Work Issues

This specific story occurred just before I left South Africa, during a very difficult time at my work. It shall be dealt with then at his point.

At my employment we had a Workers' Committee , elected each year from among workers in each department, there being no allowable Trade Unions in the country. I was elected to this committee for two years, but on the third year which happened to be a time of great disturbances all around the country, there was a problem. The workers were not satisfied with the Workers' Committee and wanted a new way of communicating with the administration. In order to resolve this , the workers had to get together in a discussion on the issue. In order for that to happen there had to be a cessation of work for a while and a following discussion.

The authorities in the company agreed to a discussion by all African and Colored workers who wished to participate. This was rare and in a way magnanimous, for in some companies this might have called for the police to be present, but none of that happened.

The workers got together and rejected the Workers' Committee as being ineffective. Reasons for this were tabulated and it was agreed that a new deal had to be arrived at. I and all Quality Controllers were present at the meeting but had little to say as the main complaint was from the rest of the workers. However, since there very few of us who were versed in drafting such decisions, I and another Quality Controller, Russell Tisani, were requested to draft a document to be presented to the authorities. We were chosen because both of us had been to university and would know how to deal with that part of the matter. Russell was known to be in the Black Peoples Convention and I was known to be on the administration of the Bahá'í Faith.

When I got home that night, I sat down to make a draft in which Russelll assisted , for we were a couple of houses apart in residence. Having completed the task we set about presenting it the next morning to the assembled workers. It seemed that the deal would be accepted. Just when that seemed so, there came the announcement from the government that from that moment on Trade Unions would legal. That meant the dissolution of the deal and the coming of Shop Stewards.

I had my concerns about joining, therefore on one of our meetings of the administration of my faith, in Johannesburg, I presented my case with a request that it be clarified from the Writings whether I could or could not join a Trade Union. After much consultation, as the matter was on the agenda, it was decided that I should not join. First of all, all Trade Unions were in the struggle and were viewed as political in nature; secondly I was on the administration of the Faith and to join would give the green light for all Bahá'ís to join in the struggle. The principle of my faith stated that Bahá'ís shall not be involved in any political action. With that in mind, on my return to work, I decided to approach the administration and let them know that as head quality controller in my department , I was not joining a Trade Union. There were only two of us who would not join in the company. I was not certain of the other party's reasons, but he was an ex-teacher and would know. Of courses this placed me in jeopardy for I was just about the only one who was not joining, in the department. Given that I was in serious trouble with the Islamic society on the staff, and the fact that I was not in any political organization despite having been chosen to make a draft for the workers, this did not improve my situation.

With all those as problems I turned to prayer. Prayer resulted in pilgrimage

Additional Issues of the Times
Marriage and difficulties

After the divorce in 1979, I lived alone for awhile in what I considered a huge house. There were comments from other residents that I was living in the house alone, while there was a shortage of housing for married couples in the area. To add to this my electricity was often cut off for the least reasons. It was time to marry but who was I to marry? I had no current girlfriend!

At this point I realized I had to take care of both my children whom I had not seen for a while. I had no idea where they had moved to for they had. However, I felt that the maintenance I was paying for their upkeep, which through he government offices, was not enough, in fact was meager. I then approached a lawyer with a view to making representations to increase maintenance. I then had to appear in court again to determine this. The only reason that was embarrassing was that in court, where my ex wife was not even present, it was determined that she had complained, and therefore the court was being asked by her to raise the amount. I accepted all that so long there would be positive action. The amount was set by the court then and was to be subtracted from my wages before I received payment, and sent to the children.

I had gone to Haifa in 1978 through the "Fly Now Pay Later" scheme which was offered by the airways. It so happened that I missed a payment at this time. Therefore, my wages was then forthwith garnished by the government and they would then subtract a determined amount each month.

After the complaints about housing, I was pressured to leave the house I occupied and move to a smaller residence. This meant I had to appear before the Bantu Administration Board and make statements . I found an understanding Town Manager, who made me a suitable arrangement of rent payments for the house. It was noted that I was on the 'buying scheme', that I intended to buy the house. It was then not easy to make me leave. The administration was anxious to make residents move into the new houses at KwaFord, a new scheme.

Later still in the year, I found out that my children had been moved out of town to reside in the rural areas where my ex wife's parents lived. That started another train of difficult events. Finally, after months of arrangements, it was decided that I could have the children with me in town , each weekend I was not in meetings in Johannesburg for a weekend. That situation pertained until I left the country. It had been a hard uphill year, even when it is noted that I had to make certain I had the birth certificates of both children, in case their last names where changed while they were away in the rural setting. For it would have been desired that they have the last name of the persons looking after them then.

Having decided to find a partner, I eventually met a grill who was agreeable . This was through a friend in Garhamstown, Sadruddin Farabi,, who had a Bahá'í contact he wished me to speak to in the township of Joza. Sadri was a student doing a Masters' in Economics at Rhodes University. He happened to be the Bahá'í pioneer in Grahamstown and was wont to invite me to his digs so that I could assist in teaching in the town. The girl was a friend of the contact. After a short courtship, we married in the December of 1980. What followed is in the book by the same author, i.e. "This Side Up".

A Demand that could not be Acceded to

A further elucidation of the problem mentioned above is now offered for perusal as a statement of fact.

The workers at my employment knew about my being a Bahá'í and my having to go to Johannesburg for a weekend each month. They also knew that during the two years I was elected to the Workers' Committee, I had presented cases of the departments I represented to management. It then surprised them when I refused to join a Trade Union. I did that at the advice of the National Assembly of which I was a member, because , up that time there were no Trade Unions for Africans in the country.The first assistance Trade Unions could offer was in dealing with the political situation in the country generally. The issue then was that, the Bahá'í Faith in South Africa did not take part in political activity as it does not in the United States either. Having ideas and expressing them has nothing to do with voting for or being a member of a political party. That has to be clear. The agenda and principles of the Bahá'í Faith are not part and parcel of any political party. To be associated with an idea is not affiliation with a group. Viewing this, I had then refrained from joining a union, and there were about three of the workers who did not. This in a way was physically dangerous, but a Bahá'í would rather be in physical danger than spiritual danger, for disobedience to Bahá'í Law was risking just that. Even though this was not a happy situation it was tolerated by workers, as I was known to be involved, since I showed slide shows of international nature to teach the Faith, and was known to have friends from outside the country.

With that situation as it stood, it was a surprised when one year in June, I was approached and requested to dress in black in mourning for the deaths of students in Soweto in 1976. I immediately objected to the demand ,because, first of all Bahá'ís do not mourn death but look at it as a continuation of a journey towards God and perfection, and secondly , when there were deaths in my faith earlier I had not asked anyone to mourn but had taken the pain on my own as the one Bahá'í in the company , It then stood to reason that I would not be asked to mourn of over deaths occurring in other organizations, as mine did not mourn at all ,neither does it rejoice but prays for departed souls, that their journey be safe and they be accepted in mercy by the Creator.

This again was viewed as objectionable. I was then warned that if I did not show anything black on my clothing on that day of mourning, my house, ,property and me, would go up in flames that very night. I was willing to challenge that, because I had never been known in that town to run away from danger. I was at that very moment under the eye of the Special Branch, a fact many in the company knew very nor were many aware of the methods applied by that body in extracting information. That night I performed normal activities but expectant of a challenge sometime in the night. As this challenge occurred on a Friday that preceded a weekend with my children ,and I was living alone in the absence of my then wife, I went and got the children. At my home I had them watching a show of "Magnum PI" until bed time. That night, nothing happened. It did not escape me that there could have been more danger, as I had been previously warned by friends that , as the bus passed my home which was on the man route, questions would be voiced why my house was still there when others were burned down, and everybody knew I had what they described as : "White Friend" occasionally visiting the house. However, most of my friends knew very well who those friends were, what they stood for, and what they had already done for me and other Africans,. So it was impossible, in my thinking, for anyone to take legitimate violent action against me or my property. This may have seemed the major threat, and no , it was not. Not only was there the law of the country which I was viewed as having breached by associating with those who believed in the equality of races, there was also the persistent problem with the Islamic community which held my being Bahá'í as objectionable These issues did not just affect me at work but all the time. Many know that there was a stronghold of the Islamic faith in the next town, which had a township called "Kabah" an erroneous pronunciation of the name "Xaba" which itself the legitimate name for the township. The implications were obvious.

When one considered such events one comes to an understanding of a very short verse in the New Testament that " Jesus wept". To whom was one to turn for solace?

Stories of Courage and Sorrow

To demonstrate the tone and attitude of this part of the story, pictures will be pasted as a reminder of the time and the seriousness of the urgent message of the Cause of Bahá'u'lláh which is for no less but for the further survival of the human race. Having said that the author has to confess that , of these times and events, he can tell for a certainty what he actually knows and has experienced . In order for any useful presentation of any evidence to be given establishment of credibility is necessary. It is far better for one to tell a story of direct experience than hearsay. Sure knowledge can only thus be established. From facts justice can thus be determined. There is the sure and indisputable justice of God, who knows hearts and intentions. There is also an earthly justice which is determined by gathering facts or evidence from various sources in order to find the truth concerning any event or occurrence. In my thinking, there is no way of knowing the Truth or justice except through what Manifestations have taught to us as a means of peace and advancement and that it fairness and equity in making judgments on issues. We are given the minds to do that, and will be judged on how much we use those minds to find His Truth. Such judgment by us as beings has to be free of any bias. Otherwise it cannot be called justice at all.. With no just investigation, the truth will always remain hidden.

The Temple

The Bahá'í Temple in Kampala, Uganda, Africa.(Media.Bahai.org)

A recording of a talk by Borrah Kavelin with the title" Crisis at the World Center", given in the United States. This was an appeal to the believers in America, concerning the completion of the building of the Seat of the Universal House of Justice in Haifa's Mt. Carmel. In this talk these words were mentioned by that speaker as having been those of the Guardian of the Bahá'í Faith :" Joy and sorrow have joined together ". These were uttered because the completion of the temple in Africa coincided with the resuming of persecutions of the followers of that faith in Iran.

It had occurred again in the seventies that this persecution was taken up again by Iran. At this time, this event coincided with the building of the Seat mentioned above in Haifa. The building of the Seat had originally been given to the friends in Iran to finance, but the building was interrupted with the persecutions being repeated again. This had necessitated that Mr. Kavelin be dispatched to the Americas, to encourage the believers in that region to take up the financing of the building of the Seat from that point. Hence Mr. Kavelin was then in the United States.

By 1978, the building was observed by delegates to the International Convention when the dust from the Prison of the Bab was placed in a niche by the Hand of the Cause, Ruhiyyih Khanum. This solemn moment was also observed by the author who had been there as one of the delegates.

The Seat of the Universal House of Justice under construction in 1978 (The Bahá'í World, 1976-79, p. 311)

The Seat of the Universal House of Justice at the present time. (Bahai.Media.org)

The author was also fortunate to occupy a seat in the convention auditorium in 1978, not far from where Mr. Kavelin sat. It was with sorrow that he heard a few years later than Borrah Kavelin had also passed on, however , his joy was to have seen and been near him that one time. Because he had met Mr. Kavelin , he took joy in listening o the talk mentioned above i.e. " Crisis at the World Center" and hear just how earnestly he made his plea to he friends. As a result, he has copied this talk from a cassette given by an America pioneer in Swaziland, Carle Suebert to him, onto a CD for keep's sake.

A glimpse of a picture of the Bahá'í Temple in Africa was first seen by the author in a newsletter left by pioneers from the Canada in 1968, perhaps some five years after the temple was opened for worship., for that newsletter was from that exact time. One can easily look up the completion of the temple in the volumes of Bahá'í World. , but the comment by the Guardian was made before he passed on in 1957. In order to tell only what I know, I have refused to research the story of the temple, as it would make the story very artificial and not real. I get the feeling that when one is asked about this life later the answer should never begin with "They did.." but with "I did…"

The above explanation should serve as a preamble to the stories that follow. These stories are about events which occurred just at the time persecutions of Bahá'ís in Iran were resumed.

Death in Uganda

Contrary to expectation, even though I had been at university and expected to take interest in world affairs, it was not my habit to buy the newspaper each morning before work, but I would buy the evening paper, at times before getting home. The morning newspaper in my town was the "Eastern Province Herald". There was one gentleman who perused it each morning at my employment while sitting in the men's dining room as all waited to begin work, with a sipping of coffee supplied by the company each morning. For the sake of my friends who may know this gentleman, I shall put his name on , but do know that by now he has also passed on from this world. He was Richard Magaga, a well known man in the company and one no person could take him on in an argument about the goings-on in the country politically or not as he read the papers regularly.

Richard who knew I was a Bahá'í called me one morning and showed me news of the murder of a Bahá'í near a Bahá'í Temple in Uganda. This was Hand of the Cause . Enoch Olinga. I shall not tell of the details of this event because that would be more hearsay. I would rather wish that anyone interested would read that on their own or watch a movies called " Enoch Olinga", a DVD by Joyce Olinga of the United States whom I met a couple of times while working at the House of Worship in Wilmette, IL. earlier in the eighties on my arrival in that country.

Sad as this event was , I could only content myself with promising myself prayers on my arrival home.

Mr. Enoch Olinga, Hand of the Cause" and "Knight of Baha'u'llah"
(The Bahá'í World, Vol. XVIII p. 618)

The Ten Ladies of Iran

At about this same time, I arrived again at work when Richard showed me another article in the newspaper. This was a sad even t of the execution by hanging of ten Bahá'í women in Iran, for activities in the Bahá'í Faith.

For some reasons, two names of these women sat in my mind up to the time I went on pilgrimage in 1985. One was called " Shimin'" and the other who was then only sixteen in age was called" Mona" a teacher of Bahá'í children in her town.

It was during that pilgrimage that the Universal House of Justice had prepared for the Bahá'í Pilgrims to see the movie of the execution of the ten women ,only in part, in a that movie called " Mona's Story" and remembered by another Canadian Bahá'í in a song called " Mona With The Children" which he sings in the movie. The young man, who I know is no longer a young man is , Doug Cameron, for the movie was shown in Haifa in 1985 and the time of the writing of this story is in the 2000s..

For the first time, we saw instead of reading about the harsh treatment meted out to Bahá'ís in the jails of Iran, for simply crying out for the unity of humankind in all corners of the planet., a unity the Bahá'ís over the world are about today.

Mona Mahmudnizad, executed by hanging in Iran with nine other women for their beliefs in the Bahá'í Religion. She was sixteen and a Bahá'í Children's Teacher. (picture from Wikipedia.org)

On reading a booklet on Mona given to me and sent to South Africa by my then friend , and my present wife, Gretchen Misselt, and watching the movie she sent with it, I learned of two very good actions taken by Mona. One was that she wanted to be executed last so that she could pray for the others ; the second is that when her name was called, Mona danced to the execution rope!

Far better is it to die for a cause so noble as unity than to perish for one so ignoble as division.

An Attending Event in that Time

At the time of the execution of the ladies in Iran, it was then about nine years or so after the killing of students in Soweto.

On the Friday following that killing I was to attend a meeting of the National Assembly in Johannesburg. I had no other place to stay on arrival except at my uncle's home in Soweto. The challenging part about this was that, first of all. I would arrive in the aftermath of bad events and rioting was the main event now. Secondly, I would arrive in Johannesburg at night, well after ten PM and would have to find the train from the city to Soweto, arriving there perhaps after twelve midnight.. Thirdly, my uncle's home was not very near the station and I would have to cross the main bus route to get there, after leaving an unlighted railway station.

How all that came together that night after that rioting is another miracle, but that is told elsewhere in another book i.e. "Memories of Africa".

Taking Pilgrimage in 1985

Some Reasons for Pilgrimage

In order to make sense on why I took pilgrimage in 1985, when I lived alone in my house, one would perhaps have to know a little about a dream I had at that time. This is a dream that had me wondering whether all I had to do in that time was actually sufficient for the time, but it did not say what was to follow. Two years after the dream I found myself in the United States and having pioneered in Swaziland for a year.

There were three significant dreams I had at the time but one will be told now as it seems to relate to present events or state of mind:

A Strange Meeting

The third dream had perhaps more direction. I found myself near a doctor's office which had

a brass plaque with a name outside. Just then the office turned to become a lawyer's office. Still in the same dream. I found I was standing in a valley and saw men dressed in red coats and black pants, wearing woolen skin hats like sheep's skin ,down in the valley.. They were on horseback. With them was a man dressed in a long grey dirty coat, who was said to be a prisoner. On the far side of the valley was a hospital. The man in the coat was said to have come to die in the hospital , escorted by the horsemen. They entered the hospital, and soon some few nurses came out crying with the news that the man had ascended .One important part: Before the man entered the hospital I went near him, and he came close, kissed me on the face and said :" All things that need to be done have been done ".I was then left with that message by a man I had never seen or known.

From that moment I knew I was due for some change and it would be drastic, but did not know how that would occur .I lived in New Brighton, and rioting was at its height. My wife, who was on training as a nurse, had not been home from the hospital out of town, for months.

Late while at work one afternoon, I decided to take my pension fund money and go on pilgrimage . That was in 1985. I took pilgrimage at the beginning of July, 1985 and by December of that year I was living in Swaziland at a pioneering post

I shall not comment on this, but leave it at that. I am not quite certain why I think of this after this present pilgrimage of 2015, for that last one of 1985, was followed by huge changes in my life.

The Surprise on Pilgrimage of 1985

A gift of a book on the night of the beginning of the pilgrimage, from Robert Reedy, a Bahá'í pioneer from US in South Africa, and purchased from Hillbrow's all night' pharmacy in Johannesburg. (scanned from cover)

A Poinciana Tree that stood in the Gardens near the Shrine of the Báb near which marriage was discussed between the author and Gretchen his wife (the tree is no longer there) (Picture taken by author)

Event of a Meeting 1985

On the pilgrimage of 1985 when I met my wife, Gretchen Misselt, we were invited to listen to music and watch a video of the story of the ten girls who were martyred in Iran earlier. The video shown on that day had a performer , singing the song "Mona with The children". I was not puzzled at the movie but appreciated the singing of that song by Doug Cameron a Bahá'í from Canada.

When I pioneered in Swaziland after that pilgrimage in an attempt to find work and wait for the arrival of my then girlfriend, Gretchen, we watched this movie many times in Swaziland as Gretchen had given me the movie and I had brought it along to Swaziland..

When the copy I had was sent to me in South Africa by Gretchen, I was informed in my department at Lennon's Laboratories, that the Department of Excise wanted me to collect an item at their offices. That meant leaving work and getting into the company car all to claim a video from the government. The video came with a booklet containing the story of these ten martyrs and I treasured it while I travelled through Swaziland as a pioneer and a Bahá'í teacher in the villages. Taking, the risks of travel gave a sense of doing something for my Faith that was related to the music and story I had read about, heard and seen.

Below is a picture of Doug Cameron as he was dressed then in the movie I saw.

The Performance of the song Young man from Canada

Doug Cameron as seen in the short movie "Mona with the Children" in 1985 during Bahá'í Pilgrimage. (Picture from Internet). Doug Cameron (a picture from the Internet first seen in the short movie "Mona's Story" shown to pilgrims in 1985 in Haifa at the Bahá'í World Center in Israel . The story is about ten ladies executed in Iran for their beliefs in the Bahá'í Religion. It is being remembered in the song "Mona with the Children "for, Mona was a children classes' teacher. Doug is Canadian, but did visit the United States as attested by my wife, Gretchen, who worked at the Bahá'í Center at that time.

The performance and presentation of this song above sung by Doug Cameron, struck me as significant, and that feeling is now revived. This was performed by youth at a critical time in the history of the Faith, for , at this time, persecution of Bahá'ís in the land of the birth of the Faith was again a reality that was inescapable. However, it also brought home the fact that the Cause of the Bahá'ís was in the main, at its inception championed by youth, the Bab. Himself having been at the time in His twenties. In reflecting on this I now realize that even in my time, the first Local Assembly of Bahá'ís to be active in Port Elizabeth had been in an area composed of Bahá'ís in their twenties. Youth then have become a driving force in the Cause of Bahá'u'llah as they learn to handle, not only their lives, but those of Bahá'í Communities.

In my absence, when I moved from Zwide to New Brighton in Port Elizabeth, , these youthful friends of Zwide, performed one marriage of one among themselves and did it so well that we feel an applause to be in place. Patrick and Christine Beer, pioneers from the United Kingdom ,may feel reason to smile as they recall that this occurred during their watch, so to speak.

The actual event of the performance in Haifa, at the Bahá'í World Center highlighted not just the involvement of youth, but their involvement in the action of teaching children, for Mona was a teacher of children in Iran, at a very difficult time in that community, and she faced her martyrdom with a dance and a smile. Very exemplary indeed. May we find more of her everywhere…

Important Message

At the end of pilgrimage in Haifa, Gretchen was requested to proceed with the message of peace to the world to be presented to the Bahá'í National Assembly of the United States to act upon. This presentation was done by one of the members of the House, who had been a Secretary of the National Assembly of that country and, therefore, knew my wife as a worker in that National Center. This made her somewhat a bearer of good tidings!

A picture of Gretchen Misselt taken a year after her pilgrimage, while she visited Swaziland's Mbabane Bahá'í Center, during a Bahá'í Feast, in 1986. (taken by author)

Return from Pilgrimage

The Kind Managing Director

Clive Stanton , Managing Director at Lennon's Pharmaceuticals, Port Elizabeth in 1985. (Picture from a Lennon's pharmaceutical report magazine, from South African Druggists a copy forwarded to author by a Director)

At the onset of the riots, Clive once met me outside my department and asked a very direct question and it was:" Who do you regard as a South African?" and my answer was :" Anyone who loves South Africa as she ought to be loved". That satisfied Clive.

Having to write about Clive reminds me that I have to be precise and clear for he is a direct man who cares about security and safety. If he asked me today if I ever been dishonest period and I would say , yes inasmuch as no man is without some sin. But if he asked me, if I was guilty of any theft and found myself discovered , I would say no, but there was a case he would remember when I was accused of having escaped being searched, and I would say: that was a lie. I will however admit an omission that might have been seen as a misdemeanor. I once took an antibiotic and forgot to have it signed for , for the purpose of curing my wife who was in bed with a bad infection. He will remember the case of quality controllers accused of walking out of the company without being searched and I shall explain this entirely, so that also in my mind the situation may go to rest, and I hope someday he reads this. I was near the main entrance and the officer named de Lange was doing spot tests to search, and I walked out. He looked at first as if he wanted to stop me, but I knew him well and kept going towards him, whereupon he turned his attention to another person and I passed out of the gate. If I had remembered to ask a pharmacist to sign for the tablets , they would not be on my conscience today, because the next day it became an issue because a security officer's nephew was caught on that day with habit-forming drugs on him and was dismissed. The tablets I had were a course which my wife , who was a nurse, asked me to bring home to help, and they were for influenza . Yes, it is also true at the time that I was under treatment for depression and had to carry tablets with me. This is the reason I had to obtain a document from a pharmacist whenever travelling abroad so that I could carry the tablets with me when I travelled. I feel a relief that I have written that.

At Lennon's I worked for thirteen years in the Tablet Department, and obtained a certificate in Pharmaceutical Production Technology. Also , for two years I was elected to the Workers' Committee for the company and had to attend meetings with the director each month. It is also known that, when Trade Unions were allowable for Blacks, I could not join a Trade Union, because of my religion. We, on the National Assembly, had been warned not to, because of the principle that pertains to that religion, that members thereof should not take part in political activity, and Trade Unions , as such, were involved it what was known as the "struggle" at that time. I knew from my days at the University College of Fort Hare, what was involved in that , because there, I had attended all the student "mass meetings" and knew all those involved in sundry organizations. Because some of them knew that I was Bahá'í and they, in turn, respected that, without really knowing what being Bahá'í was , except that it was not wanted by the government because of its principle on uniting humankind into one family, I was never challenged on non - participation in political activity. I was at the" Fort" for two years and had no issues with that. If one knew what the "Fort" was in those days one would have an understanding of the student body. I never withheld myself from arguments but remained uncommitted when it came to political organizations. My religion stood for the oneness of the human race and for that, any sacrifice could be made.

It is to be noticed also that on leaving Lennon's in 1985, I was told there would be a farewell party organized by management for me and that I had to invite participants. I refused to invite the Analytical Laboratory staff, because, that department was sufficiently filled with those on Muslim background, and they had given me no end of criticism, and threats. In my way then, I was telling them to desist. Therefore, I spoke to Rooseveldt, the leading man in the Tablet Department that I was inviting Tabletting Compression and Granulating staff. Company Management ,would be included . I would also invite the Galenical Department where I had worked on my arrival in the company , with other friends I had in the company.

I gave no extensive speech in that party because I failed to see how it was going to be of any gain to explain my intention to the staff at the time. Many had failed to see how I could profit by moving out of South Africa to Mozambique where I had been assigned to work, because in those days , many were leaving that country for South Africa, for better prospects anyway. I did notice with keen interest that Company Management was aware that if I did not move out , I would soon be what they termed "Shishkabob". These were days when informers were being executed "Necklace Style" and it did not seem to take much for one to be termed that.

On the eve of the day of mourning for Soweto children, I had been approached to come to work garbed in black. I had refused to comply on principle, simply because, in the first place, Bahá'ís do not mourn for the departed, secondly, ten girls in Iran had been executed and before I could see the newspapers I was informed by workers that Bahá'ís in Iran ten Bahá'ís had died by execution. Later still, before I could even read the newspaper again, I was hurriedly informed by workers than an important Bahá'í had been killed in Uganda, and that was Mr.. Enoch Olinga, On both occasions I had not mourned, but privately prayed when I had a moment. At this time I was asked to mourn for a death that had occurred the previous year, hence my refusal to mourn then. I was promised that my house and property would burn that night. However, as evidenced by my presence at work the next day, that did not take place. I suspect the reason was that, I was the only Bahá'í who dared show slides of international racial content and teach the Faith openly in New Brighton for many years.

Since the departure of the Salas, who were my teachers in the Faith, we had been involved in forming Bahá'í Local Assemblies in three localities in the city of Port Elizabeth, and I was just about the only one who had, at that time, traveled to an International Convention of the Bahá'í Faith in Israel, from that town, and amidst the rioting and still survived. If at any time, in the course of those years, amidst the questioning by police through which I had to go, I had detracted into an informer, I would have burned years ago.

Also in the multiracial scene all had seen me outside the townships and in New Brighton arranging meetings with Whites and Blacks from many parts in South Africa, who had come into town. If all those invited had been government persons, why is it that they never approached the Influx Control offices which stood at the entrance of the New Brighton township, were themselves carrying entrance passes, and had at times been questioned by the Special Branch as this was known? If I were to run a manifesto, it would run on those lines, but as I am no politician. I talk explanations and not manifestos. None of these people I knew in the company had spent an hour of questioning by the Special Branch in their offices in the city. Did they know what that was like?

Besides and above all this, to a Bahá'í people who pass from this world continue to live in the worlds of God which are without number. We do not mourn for them but pray for them that they continue on the Eternal Journey to His Presence and to become whatever He has placed in them . Mourning would be of my own making and would deny that. Rather would I pray for each one's journey and think of my state as I would eventually have to leave this life and ponder on where I would be with development in relation to the journey I have to continue..

To show his good will and well-wishes, Clive Stanton the Managing Director, later made a me a present , when I wished to go to Cape Town to apply for a visa to enter the United States, of R300.00. I could then travel. The gift had been made because I had lived in Swaziland for two years without work and exhausted my resources surviving there, such that, by the time the interview in Cape Town with the US Consul came up I was without funds to travel, hence the appeal and the loan which Clive converted to a gift..

In another book, I have attached a letter from the Head Office f South African Druggists form Mr. Tony Karis wishing myself and wife well in the United States .I shall not reproduce that letter here. But trust that interested parties will, obtain the book in which it is and read that statement. In that book also I state my views as a South African, because while I am in the united States,. I am still registered as a citizen in that country too, because there I have relatives who have property and I happen to be the eldest brother who should be able to take charged of some issues in that country, should a mishap approach.

A Farewell note from the company

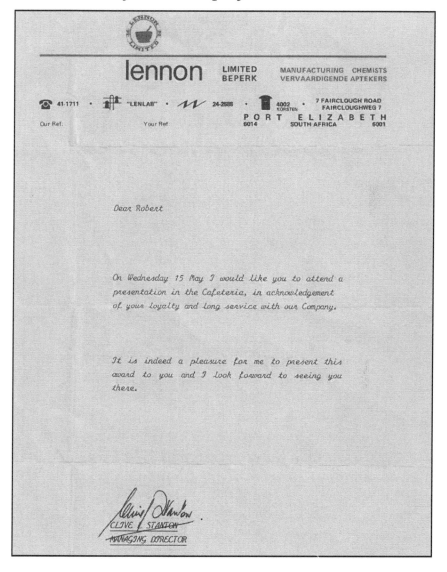

Clarification of Note:

Dear Robert,

On Wednesday 15 May I would like you to attend a presentation in the Cafeteria, in acknowledgement of your loyalty
and long service with our company.

It is indeed a pleasure for me to present this award to you
and I look forward to seeing you there.

MANAGING DIRECTOR

Leaving the Bahá'í National Center of South Africa

The feelings of joy and sorrow at having to resign from the Assembly seized
me and caused me to remember all the pleasant times we had had at the Center
during the meetings.

When I left the Bahá'í Center after resigning from the National Spiritual
Assembly in 1985, I had my last lunch with the Assembly members on the last
meeting. On that meeting I spent a moment with the Book-Sales Officer, Dr.
Robert Clarkson. He had made a date with me to have pictures taken at the
Center by which I would remember that building and the friends I served with
in South Africa, and on the Bahá'í Administration for ten years. Below is one of
the photos Robert took on that day. One would notice that I was garbed in what
appears as a suit. This was not really the dress code on the Assembly. At those
times of meetings, one was permitted to be dressed just decently and not formally, unless the Assembly had special business for that time, and the appointed
believer had something to do with that event, whatever it might have been. That
appointed believer would have to dress for that performance where necessary.

To me it was a poignant picture, because it followed the pilgrimage on
which I met my present wife, Gretchen. I remembered the details of that trip
to Haifa: I had been picked up at the airport from the midnight flight which
was the cheapest flight of the time , by Robert Reedy, who was reading a book
by Rollo May called "The Meaning of Anxiety"..

That time and the book were to prove my marker of the pilgrimage. I had
borrowed it and stayed awake all morning reading it I had spent the morning

and part of the afternoon at Robert Reedy's home , very excited about the trip and unable to sleep. Before departing for the airport, Robert Reedy asked if we could not have dinner with Robert Clarkson, at the café known as "Mike's Kitchen", where a Bahá'í friend worked as a waiter.

We had met with Dr Robert Clarkson at the restaurant and had the uneasy meal , for I was unable to eat either. It had always been a joke at the center that we had so many people going by the name of "Robert" and there we were all three Roberts !. After the meal Robert Reedy had asked if we could stop in Hillbrow, at a popular pharmacy which opened all night . There to my surprise Robert bought another copy of the Rollo May, which I had taken interest in, and asked me to have a copy of my own on the way to Haifa!

At this time also I recalled another experience with Dr. Clarkson. It was on the occasion the National Assembly had decided to have a first time conference in Port Elizabeth. Much preparation had been done for this, including booking a hall and requesting permission from the Bantu Administration Offices to have a permit for a number of White and Colored believers to enter the township to attend. An added problem was that most of the attendees would be from out of town.

On the day of the arrival of visitors, a Saturday, because my house was situated near the entrance of the township, I had been asked to stay home and direct Bahá'í visitors to the hall, which was some ways down my street.

Robert Clarkson had arrived and started at my home to ask for directions, for, as I said he was Book Sales Officer and had to be present. It happened that I was playing some music while waiting for visitors and my wife Nomabhadi N. Sishuta-Mazibuko was in the house. Fortunately, at that time, I was playing music by Billie Holiday from an LP which had been donated by Lowell Johnson to my collection, as such music was hard to get locally in Port Elizabeth. The song on was :"Billie's Blues" which had a preamble or introduction in some foreign language. Robert was interested in the music, and I asked him to identify the language that the introduction was on. It was German…

With all that said, the last time that I spoke to Robert Clarkson was when he took the picture below.

Some week ago while I resided in the United States, a common friend we had with Robert Clarkson informed that he had passed on the Eastern Coast of the States. It saddened me that we never met after that photograph appointment. Robert was a Physicist and lectured at Witwatersrand University, where I gather , he met his now present wife, Peta Clarkson.

When I first poke to him some years ago, he told me he had a problem. On enquiring I found out that he had a daughter from a first marriage, and she was living in the United States. The problem was that , his daughter was due to have a birthday party presently, and wanted a present from her father. Normally this would not be much of a problem, but the child was demanding that the father buy her a horse! Robert who lived in South Africa then was to get with it and get a horse for the daughter. He told me later that he had done so!

Robert Mazibuko at the last meeting with the National Assembly of South Africa prior to pioneering in Swaziland. Picture taken by appointment by Dr Robert Clarkson at the back of the Bahá'í Center on Rustenburg Road, Melville , Johannesburg.(Picture taken by Dr. Robert Clarkson, on request)

Bidding Farewell to South Africa:

As I prepared to head for my first pioneering post in Mozambique in 1985, I received some good encouragement from the friends. One of them anxious that I may have to learn a new language and that was Portuguese, decided to give me the books she had used in learning that language in the days she travelled in that country with her husband.

I had spent many weekends at the home of the Seepes' and now in the absence of Max, the husband, who had by now passed on, his wife May Seepe gave all he encouragement she could muster. To help me adjust she also gave me a grammar book in Portuguese which I still treasure from that time. There was a further conversational manual she also had that parted with at this time, however , with moving from place to place that manual is now no longer attainable. Below is a picture of the grammar as it was, with the first page containing May's encouragement:

(scanned from cover)

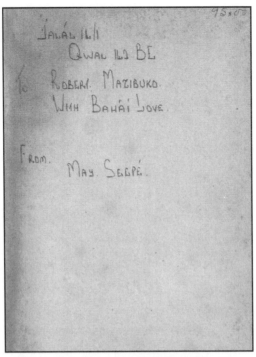

A Portuguese Grammar book from May Seepe

May Seepe of Johannesburg, South Africa (Heroes and heroines of the Ten Year Crusade in Southern Africa p. 246/47)

Because of this present , the Bahá'í month of *Qawl* (Speech) remains precious, for that is the time I left the country.

The story of my short stay in Mozambique and subsequent settling in Swaziland are told elsewhere. One could read the books "This Side Up" and "Memories of South Africa" by the same author.

A Two-Year Stay in Swaziland

On my return from pilgrimage, I found I had a situation which definitely required me to leave the country. My marital state had found an alteration and I had to arrange. As this story is told elsewhere, it shall not be repeated at this time except to point out that it was necessary for the author to move to neighboring Swaziland.

Rare Meeting

Until the period when I pioneered in Swaziland, I had not seen a pioneer form the Orient. But in my very life there is such a person. I met Yoshie Ragland when I attended meetings of the Faith in Swaziland. She is the brave lady who, having married an American went on to pioneer with him in Africa. Though this might not be of such note, to me who am from Africa and had not seen it, it is a marvel.

Her last note as I departed from Swaziland has been kept since those years. I have one picture of her and proud to display it. I was not the only pioneer from South Africa, but I was the first from my town and to see one from so far away and in such circumstance this had to make me pause. Yoshie is Japanese, a Bahá'í and an artist:

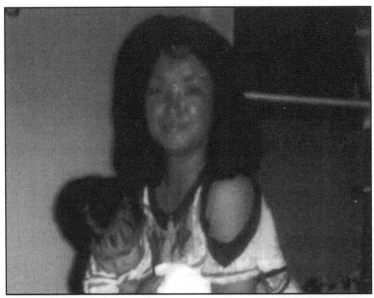

Yoshie Ragland and her son Ryo. (Picture taken by author in Swaziland)

Jan. 31, 1986

Dear Robert,

Thank you for your note and for showing photoes of Gretchen at work. It was very nice and encouraging for me to see someone weaving. I hope to see her and to talk more about her weaving. Please send my regards to her whenever you write or talk to her.

Love,
yoshie

(A farewell note from Yoshie Rgaland)
At the home of the Piggotts'

Crispin and Margaret Piggott

On the onset, let me state that had it not been for the Piggotts' my stay in Swaziland would have been a very short one. This was because, at the time I met Crispin at the Bahá'í Center in Mbabane I had been without a home in Swaziland. I had run out of ideas of where to go to wait for the visa to enter the United States in order to marry my girlfriend who was at the time residing near Chicago in Illinois. Crispin and Margaret took me in immediately I asked for a refuge. Of course I had met them while they resided in the Transkei earlier and knew that they originated from Canada.

When the Piggotts' went on vacation, at some stage, I was left to look after their house. They had two dogs, Axa and Zeus (which sounded like Greek names to me). The two dogs were shepherd dogs and where they came from , looked after live stock in the fields. I had met a fox terrier , a collie and a daschund, but out of dogs I knew these were very new to me. They had hairs that covered the face and one could just discern their eyes through the hairs. The looked just like two baboons but were very friendly. They had a puppy who went by the name of "Puppy" who once got lost and took a lot of finding.

While the Pigotts' were gone the dogs and I got along real fine. They followed me to every place I went in the town of Siteki. At that time, I happened to have a bank account in a Swazi bank and some funds at the standard bank which were in South Africa. I had had to sell my house and all furniture to move to Swaziland and still had funds there. My routine each month, was to go to the standard bank and transfer funds to Swaziland. Then I would withdraw funds and head for the post office. At the post office I had to purchase money orders in order to go home, place those in envelopes and send to my children in South Africa. This was a routine I had to keep and the dogs followed me on the rounds.

It was very fortunate that I had the dogs, because they were a comfort and a strategy at the bank and the post office. I got served first because everybody was frightened of the baboon-looking dogs!

In this way I managed to keep my sense of being a person with responsibilities .There was one thing which later bothered me. Margaret had been reading a book called " Clan of the Cave Bear" which she completed and left with me. In my life I have failed to make the pictures conjured by the book to attain a reality.

First of all I have studied Archeology for a year and completed two classes in Sociology, but cannot associate what I read in that book with a reality. It does not mean it does not have a meaning, but having read about the Ancient man in magazines and books I do not find it relating to anything like a reality in essence. In the fifties there were articles in the "Readers Digest" and the "Life Magazine" about ancient man with bones, pictures and drawings and somehow those do not tie up with the book, especially after seeing the movie made of the book.

My spiritual mother used to say when I read some books about early man:"Take it with a pinch of salt!". I do that because , most of the time after seeing bones and drawings by ancient man, I do not come up with the picture painted in the book I read. However, it makes good reading, since none of us really know ancient man and his ways for a certainty. I can excuse myself because of the things I have experienced as an African.

When I lived alone in South Africa with my wife away a living in the nurses rooms at the hospital, I watched a movie about "Jesus the Nazarene" and was appalled to note that Jesus was portrayed to be blond with blue eyes ! When my stepdaughter , who is blond, was in Israel, they found her to be a thing to be stared at because of her hair!

A fictitious story to be given credibility must have the ring of truth or be based on a real background. The bones found by Professor Leakey in the

Olduvai Gorge in Serengeti, accompanied by pictures taken and displayed of ancient man can be and are believable. This story is well known and was published in the fifties when the bones were discovered. Perhaps the knowledge of our past can make us wiser in our present, but it would not matter much if we made a mess of our lives in the present. Lessons are learned and the knowledge is stored by the human so the human does not make the same mistakes again or , at least, knows how to dispose of a situation should it occur another time.

Situations of Teaching Left Behind:

Robert Mazibuko and Reginald Vimbi on a teaching rip in the Ciskei in the early days. Reginald was serving on the National Teaching Committee of South Africa at the time and owned the only car we had amongst s in Port Elizabeth as a means of travel.

An Occurrence in the Ciskei: The Persian Lady who Dared

In 1987 while I waited for a visa to enter the United States in order to marry an American girl, I was requested by the National Assembly of South Africa to take a trip to Mdantsane and meet with Bahá'ís in that area as they had asked that I do sometime, through the Assembly of South Africa.

At some stage during this visit to Mdantsane, I was requested by the friends in Mdantsane to visit the Fort Hare area in Alice and work with Bahá'ís there. The man who was to guide me through the latter part of the visit was Riaz Razavi, who in later years was martyred at the Bahá'í Center in Mdantsane by unknown assailants with two other Persian pioneers.

In this area I witnessed an act I had not seen performed by any pioneer at that time. In Alice I found there was another visitor who had just arrived. She was also Persian and therefore resided with the Scotts family'. Michael and Fatteneh Scott were pioneers in Alice from the United States. Mike was a Horticulturist at Fort Hare University and Fatteneh , his Persian wife , also a pioneer. We were asked to take a trip to the rural area and visit some of the friends there, and the Persian girl came along.

I was introduced to this girl, or shall we say, lady, and learned that she was married in the United States and was a Professor of Architecture at a university in that country, but I was quite unprepared for her request. On speaking to her about Bahá'í life, she explained that she was brought up in New York, and for a long while did not take religion that seriously. It came of a sudden to her hat she was not doing the main thing in her life ,the reason for her creation. She was not living a Bahá'í life at all. As a result of this realization she had decided to take pilgrimage. From pilgrimage she sojourned in the Central African area , attending a wedding in one of the countries on that continent. From Central Africa, she had decided to visit South Africa, meeting there with Fatteneh and family. Her request: She wished to spend a week with the Bahá'ís in rural Africa, and chose Ciskei, and no less. She would have to live in a roundavel for all that week, a long time for one born outside that society, and I know from experience, for I was born and brought up in the ghetto of New Brighton, in a city..

She accepted these conditions, and as we left her there. I was worried she would have a difficult time. I had had to learn to take baths either in basins of in rivers while living in those areas: how was she going to do this, a professor from New York? Nevertheless we left her there.

On return after a week, behold then the Persian lady with a towel wrapped around her head and having a joyous time with African ladies all around her! I was astounded but kept my secret.

On asking the meaning of her name , she replied that it meant a beautiful dream one has in the morning as one rises. She certainly was one dream to me!

The Persians I had met until then liked their tea to be just so in taste, but not her! I then understood the stance of eating the sole of shoes at Fort Tabarsi when the Babís were under siege from government forces in the 1800s. , and could relate to the joyous death of the Seven Martyrs of Tehran who included the uncle of the Bab, whose wish was to be martyred first! Such women add astonishment to astonishment.

At this time I do even respect the Mother Teresas' of our time. Because I refuse to place this lady's picture, on this page, even had I one, for she left none, I shall not. but will consent to placing Mother Teresa's as an example of such sacrificial behavior in relating to others who are regarded as of low estate.

Picture of " Mother Teresa" downloaded from the Internet at the time of her passing

I am reminded, at this juncture of a saying from a poem which ran :

"Should the grace of the Holy Spirit once again deign to assist, Others will also do what Christ performed"
(Balyuzi , p. 35)

In such a vein I then make the confession that, I have from the time I learned more about nuns , often respected their effort, even though in my Faith they are commanded to come out of convents and cloisters like monks and perform good works for the sake of God. The reason for this respect is that these people have selflessly given up what men and women kill for, for the sake of their religion. That I respect! Many murders have resulted from love affairs or denial of rights by men and women for the conjugal aspects of marriage. They have given that up for life, on earth! Before the Creator they can claim to have given something up after testifying to belief. As sort of a fast for life…it becomes even more desirable to proclaim this when one witnesses some of the acts they sometimes are wont to perform for belief.

Many of us find it hard to fast even for a week! …let alone a month

If we do there is no end to complaints of discomfort!

A Powerful teacher in Hard Times
Rose Perkal Gates: Mother of Bahá'ís of Ciskei

If the services of Rose Gates are never remembered after her work in the Ciskei, then we have to consider that the women of Ciskei might not very even risen to proclaim in rural Ciskei the Cause of Bahá'u'lláh. To even think of forgetting her would be a distortion of the history of the faith in that part of the world. It is lamentable that her only relative felt so disappointed at her being neglected in the Ciskei after she suffered Alzheimer, but there is no need for sorrow on the part of the pioneering of Rose in Ciskei, for it was a great success. I would probably had never been even married had it not been her work in that country.

A little has been said about the times after her departure for the United States and a nursing home, but very little has even been touched upon concerning her marvelous strivings to establish the faith there , single handed . This is perhaps not surprising, because Rose Gates was the first Bahá'í to pioneer for the Bahá'í Faith in Alaska ,and was therefore named a Knight of Bahá'u'lláh for that effort. This latter achievement was only known after her passing and even then when it appeared in the Bahá'í News. Her story has appeared again in the book "Bahá'í World" but it is becoming that one of the persons she taught how to live and act like a Bahá'í should at some point , remember her.

Perhaps the reason she was forgotten was because her work was beclouded and eclipsed when three Persian pioneers were killed at the Bahá'í Center she had caused to exist in Ciskei. Tragic and unfair as this event might be, and yet accepted by the Bahá'ís as a course of accepted events in teaching the Cause, it must be remembered that , this first martyrdom in South Africa, came to pass in the very area Rose opened to the Faith as far back as 1970, when she first arrived there, culminating in the teaching of myriads of women , starting with those who attendee her at her firs stay in a hotel in the area.

So popular was Rose and respected by the Bahá'ís of that area, that African ladies would refer to her as "Auntie Rose", as a sign of respect in observation of the tradition of giving an elderly person some kind of title in that land.

She may lay in the dust today, but her pupils are very much alive and still teach the Cause she brought to them with such zeal and effort .

At the time of the Rose's arrival in East London, there was no small state of Ciskei, just dusty Mdantsane, and her first centers of teaching the faith were no less than at the building known as the XDC (Xhosa Development Corporation) Building. It was in the very midst of that , that Rose raised the flag of belief in Bahá'u'lláh. No authorities could stop her because her wisdom in all dealings prevented that. Even a member of the Special Branch of Police who had come to investigate one of her meetings held in the township, eventually declared his faith in Bahá'u'lláh. It might not have been for pure reasons but it is accepted that this man who was a terror from Port Elizabeth and had been transferred there on promotion, saw no danger in Rose as a Bahá'í teacher , yet we all know the international teachings of that Faith. The one good asset she had was a very disarming approach and very human outlook towards problems in that state, having, herself been brought up in the situation of a Jewish immigrant from Russia living initially in America's Los Angeles as a child.

Not only was Rose known in the township, therefore, but she was also known and respected by politicians who aspired to angle into the government and did in a later time. To mention all the women she taught who later served on Bahá'í committees would take time, suffice it to say, Rose served on the National Assembly of South Africa with her very African student, Joyce (Yoyo,) Dwashu, a sometime great travelling teacher from Ciskei, who became popular in the country in those days.

One wonders how Rose viewed her situation and history as an immigrant. It did not bother her much but was aware of it. However, her own selflessness in the situation is evinced by a remark she once made, on encountering the refusal of the Afrikaner to allow the teaching of the faith go unhindered . She was heard to remark" If they want at Aryan Prophet, they should know that Bahá'u'lláh was Persian and therefore Aryan!". She did not view that as offensive to herself. To her this was a consideration to be taken into effect and consideration by those who opposed the faith of racial grounds, because , after all , at the time it was taught only to Africans and Coloreds! Later she would say :" The first Persian believers were young people like you in Iran". This remark is in its way devoid of self and values of self., for Rose as I said, was born in Russia and lived as a child of immigrants in Los Angeles, a situation by any measure, not easy to even encompass for those who lived in those times or studied the history of that period.

Rose went on to serve on the first Bahá'í National Assembly of the Ciskei, thereby even having to resign from the Bahá'í National Assembly of South Africa, before her illness.

On my return from pilgrimage, in 1985, I informed her that I had found love in an American girl. She was so joyful and full of news herself. She said that I should not mention it to anybody, but that she was leaving for another country to pioneer. The next time I called her number in East London , there was no answer. I learned later that Rose had been diagnosed with the Alzheimer disease: Yes she did go pioneering! I doubt today if anyone knew of this plan, for she told me as her secret as it would have surprised many in South Africa that "Auntie Rose" was leaving after all her work! The latter was the last conversation with her.

A Glimpse on the Eastern Cape, South Africa

Between 1973 and 1975 when I was finally elected to the National Assembly of South Africa, Rose and I had a project in Mdantsane whereby I would travel to Mdantsane every Friday night, after work to teach with her. When she learned that I worked in pharmaceuticals , Rose saw another avenue of teaching the Faith in Port Elizabeth. She determined to speak to the Managing Director at my company about the possibility of making seaweed tablets with granules from a firm she knew in California. She, in fact, went out to Port Elizabeth to talk to the director and was cordially received , but according to her they reported that they had ceased making seaweed tablets because of certain complications. I knew they made this tablet some time ago , but was never told why we stopped. This was no figment of the mind, but real.

Even though Rose worked with Africans in teaching the Faith, she , faithful to the teaching of the faith of noninvolvement in political activity, stayed out of the political picture, though many people she knew served on the Ciskei government.

This of course did not mean that Rose kept away from rural Ciskei, no, she taught in that very area. To such an extent, that by the time the National Assembly of Ciskei, which had nine elected members on it who were of women , she being one of them, the membership of the Bahá'í Faith had stretched almost to all the villages in the Ciskei. As far as Keiskammahoek, and to the borders of the Transkei.

I remember clearly, once she asked me to be at the "Transkei Hotel" in Umtata on a Saturday to receive visitors from rural Transkei, who would attend a conference she organized there.I went there by bus on the Friday night , sleeping that Saturday night on a bed organized at the backroom of the hotel , in order to meet Rose and company who arrived en force on the Sunday. We had the conference, yes indeed! We may want to know how the persons in rural Ciskei learned so much about one man one vote: do ask Rose about the teaching of voting for an administration in the Faith and the participation of all the women in those communities!

There are myriads of pictures of Africans in the rural setting , but Rose does not appear in any of them, simply because she was the one taking all the pictures!

(L-R) Esther Nkonzo, Joyce Yoyo(Dwashu), Rose Gates, Mbulelo Nkonzo, Beauty Kato, Robert Mazibuko. A picture of Rose gates) in Mdantsane in the 70s. As I am in a suit, I would imagine that this was taken at the time of my wedding to Faith. The two ladies on the extreme left(L-R) are Esther Konzo and Joyce Dwashu, both very well-known teachers of the Bahá'í Faith in Mdantsnae, where Beauty Kato(next to me) and Faith Kato (my first wife)were the first to declare in East London. Jessie Dwashu(not in picture), mother to Joyce was first to declare in Mdantsane. This appears to be at Joyce's home in Mdantsane..

Joyce was the first African woman from the Ciskei to serve on both National Assemblies on South Africa and Ciskei ,and still continued to be a traveling teacher, for he Faith. She passed o in Cape Town, after Mike Walker and I visited her briefly in about 1998 or a little earlier. Rose was not the first pioneer to enter a township, but first to directly teach the Faith there, Rosemary Sala, of Port Elizabeth, had to enter and walk to schools and find contacts that way. Behind and obscured from the picture is Beauty Kato, Faith Kato's aunt and the first Bahá'í in East London. Beauty passed on as we , Faith and I, ended a relationship, an event that must have hurt her, for she loved unity. I had to stay home and mind Emeric, while Faith travelled to attend the funeral with Luthando as baby. As one could guess, this was no easy time for both of us.

So hard was the time that while attending an occasion in Mdantsane , Lowell seriously commented that if I did not shape up and eat well, I would not be long in this world. As this was the time of both my first travel overseas and the first time I went to Haifa to vote, there was much to digest on my side, not in terms of a trip, but in terms of purposes and settling down culturally after the visit.

Providence had it that when I departed from the country, I was forced to depart from my own city in broad daylight, so that none could accuse one of seeking asylum rather than immigrating for social reasons of a marital nature. When this time came , I looked back at the time to the 60s to the 80s between which time there were three pioneering families both from Canada and the United Kingdom and later even a family of one Persian and American believers had who had settled and had family in that town. It was time to let the story take its course where the faith was concerned and much of it would have to be with me being out of the way. Hence I say" Here I stand, I cannot do otherwise, God help me , Amen", just as Martin Luther of Germany once declared at the Inquisition of the Diet of Wurms! This is a quote from my teacher , Ian Sogoni, in his class on history of the Reformation, in the late fifties as being Luther's declaration..

Let no man pride himself that he loves his country but on that he loves mankind. I have made that pledge and endeavor to die holding onto it, at any cost. If then that be the danger ,please then hold me as dangerous for the pledge is , and was made as of old.

In another passage He hath proclaimed: It is not for him to pride himself who loveth his own country, but rather

for him who loveth the whole world. The earth is but one country, and mankind its citizens.

(Baha'u'llah, Gleanings from the Writings of Baha'u'llah, p. 250)

· I N   M E M O R I A M ·

Rose Perkal Gates was Knight of Bahá'u'lláh

Rose Perkal Gates, a Knight of Bahá'u'lláh for Kodiak Island, Alaska, also gave distinguished service as a pioneer to Switzerland and South Africa.

She passed to the Abhá Kingdom on February 2, 2001. She had lived for several years in a nursing home in Orange, California.

In a 1978 letter to the International Goals Committee, Gates wrote: "Actually my pioneering career began at the dedication of the Mother Temple in Wilmette in 1953, when in response to the call for pioneers I said, 'I would like to go pioneering but I would like to go to a warm place' and I ended up in Alaska!"

She resided in Alaska for nine years,

helped to form two Local Spiritual Assemblies, and served for two years on the National Spiritual Assembly of the Bahá'ís of Alaska.

From 1960 to 1966, Gates pioneered to Switzerland, where she helped to form the first Local Spiritual Assembly in Locarno.

On May 23, 1968, Gates arrived in Johannesburg, South Africa. She lived in East London, serving on the Area Teaching Committee, and in Cape Town, where every Sunday she would "pack lunch and refreshments ... drive 150 to 200 miles in a day ... singing, praying for the village we would be planning to visit."

She served as secretary of the Nation-

al Teaching Committee and was a member of the National Spiritual Assembly.

"In all my pioneering days," she wrote in 1976, "never has it been more clear to me that purity of motive is one of the most important attributes for a pioneer to have. Without words, Africans feel and know when you are sincere and respond accordingly."

In 1986, Gates left her pioneer post, in poor health and with failing eyesight, to join her family in California. In one of her numerous letters to the International Goals Committee, this devoted daughter of Bahá'u'lláh said, "I would like to shout this from the roof-tops all over the world: SERVE! SERVE! SERVE!" ◆

Above extracted from the " Bahá'í News" a Bahá'í newsletter.

Lowell's Influence on the young

It is fair to say that Lowell had a positive influence on those he met. Particularly is this true of the young people, many of whom he took under his wing and taught. Perhaps, one example is myself. I met Lowell when I was in my twenties and there was more than twenty years in the difference of our ages, but I never felt this, as his comradeship had no perception of age but aided one to understand more about life. It was easy to converse with him about the problems youth face and he would always offer very simple and accessible answers. I first perceived this of him on reaching Cape Town with him while we travelled together, from Durban via the Transkei, in the late 60s. When we reached cape Town, suddenly there was a very subtle change in him when he was with h friends. . No longer was he anxious about our trip, but he was found to be totally relaxed. In Cape Town he was "Lowell" or "Uncle Lowell" and everybody took off with him in conversation. As a result, up to that point in Cape Town., Lowell was known to the author as "Mr. Johnson" but seeing him in Cape Town with the friends and having heard him introduce himself to me by his first name, he changed altogether to "Lowell" without a doubt.

Lowell understood the problems that the young in that country went through and offered everyone a broader view of what one was experiencing by citing many examples of others he knew in the world in general and in his life .Not all stories of his life can be told as they would take up a great space. So, here are a few that are known to the author:

He once said that, in dealing with people one had to decide whether one was going to be the teacher or the student. But in my view Lowell could teach while he learned. For many African views might have been new to him but he caught on easily after reflection.

It is fitting therefore that before leaving the topic of my stay in that country I come to terms with telling a few stories of Lowell's contact with the youth of that time. A few examples are given hee.

Don Fouche and Lowell in an Effort

Don was the first of his race that I was associated with on religious terms. He and Lowell Johnson formed a coalition I admired. While they were both in Johannesburg, they opened a record shop they managed together. Though the effort did not last long, yet it was an indication to me than Don was making tremendous effort to associate with the Bahá'ís, given that Johannesburg was another stronghold of Afrikanerdom . Don went so far as to associate with a girl from the United States to the extent of marrying her and himself moving to the United States. For one of Afrikaner background to do both was a supreme effort on his part. Even when that did not work out for long yet , I found great approval for Don's effort in proving himself open minded in the issue. Don is from Mafikeng, and his father worked for the railways, an area dominated in the main by Afrikaners in South Africa at the time.

I have at present one letter from him which I have misplaced but can find the envelope with his hand writing on it, and will in time display it. This letter was written by Don I the days after Robert returned from a sixth month travel all over South Africa teaching the Faith with Lowell in 1969. Fortunately Robert has preserved the letter and has it displayed here.

Both the author and Don met Mr. Fatheazam, a member of the Universal House of Justice when he was in Johannesburg in 1970, and he promised to mention their names at prayer in the Shrines in Haifa, Israel.. Both h young people anticipated the day an looked forward to it as their special time, while they were in Johannesburg.

P.O. Box 11210
GHB
S.A.
8.3.70.

Dear Robert,

Things have been very unsettled here, but we left Salisbury and decided to come back to S.A. Ian S. was offered a very good work in Salisbury but I didn't want to go back to Rhodesia, it was a right move... [illegible] ... there from a spiritual point of view.

Dear Robert I was delighted to [illegible] that you wanted to hear from me from Jewell. I truly feel that things will... all of us will become better as the world's calamity becomes worse and worse because then we will see ourselves clearer and become more amazed by [illegible] grace.

The above letter is so sweet that I wish to share with others rewriting it:

"Dear Robert,

Things have been rough with me. I went back to Salisbury, and decided to come back to SA. There , I was offered very good work in Salisbury but did not want to go back to Rhodesia. It was a fight of conscience to stay here or there, from the spiritual point of view.

Robert, I was delighted to hear that you want to hear from me, from Lowell. I feel that things with all of us will become better as the world calamity becomes worse that we will see ourselves clearer and become immersed by Bahaá"u'lláh's grace.

Robert, I voiced your name in Rhodesia to the Friends there and told them of your devotion and sacrifice for the Cause, and that they must start to give themselves to God completely without constraints, that they will attain His bounty as well as His confirmation in His Cause.

Robert, truly I'm delighted in your personage and know that God will guide you to great activities in the world.

Be assured of my sincere wishes for your achievement whatever they may be.

Lovingly,
Don Fouche."

Petrus Madumo and Theophilus Nkonzo

After travelling with me for almost a year and finding this a probable way of introducing youth to the Faith, Lowell took a man from Soweto and travelled throughout South Africa with him. I had the pleasure of meeting the man when he came with Lowell to Port Elizabeth, as he spent a night and day in the home of a Bahá'í friend on my street in New Brighton.

When Rose had a group of Africans turning to the Faith in Mdantsane, Lowell saw another opportunity of travelling with another youth from Mdantsane. This time he turned to Theophilus Nkonzo, a son of Esther Nkonzo. Esther served both as a travelling teacher and a member of the first National Assembly in Ciskei.

With Theophilus again Lowell did the rounds in the country thereby finding opportunity to deepen Theophilus in the faith he had espoused . This was a grand way of teaching, for, as I said before, it had not happened then that cars would be bugged, and therefore it was a good way of introducing someone to the laws of the faith and the intents of the Bahá'í of uniting mankind, within the offensive environment of Apartheid.

The young man with a question

The one issue that still feels me with a sadness in that of a European man who asked me a question and had a tragic end. I tried to answer him but it probably did not help him. He was again a friend of Lowell's that I met on one of those evenings of arrival by night flight in Johannesburg. We instantly became friends on meeting in Lowell's apartment. Because we had started a Bahá'í community in my town involving a number of young people I was used to associating with the young and solving questions as Lowell did.

The man had a family who ran a business in town. He was in love with a very young person and wanted an opinion as to what to do in his case. I was just married and he felt I could answer him. His girlfriend was very young and he wanted to know from me whether to go ahead and marry her or not. This was because of her age. The marriage would have been possible in South Africa but he wished to inquire before plunging in. I answered him that: if he were sure that he loved the girl, and there was no doubt in his mind that he did love her, then he should go ahead and marry but weigh his chances of survival with her. I then added that if in his mind there was a doubt that he should and he was certain that the doubt would not leave then I felt it would be self-defeating to marry. I left it at that. I had no ideas he had any other troubles, for I had not known him that long and he had declared through Lowell.

I sadly heard later that he was no longer in this world and that he had had many more issues than that. I had based my opinion on my own issue, for I had married a girl I had met when I turned thirty and she was barely twenty yet. In fact she turned twenty one while I was with her. At the time of the advice, we had no children for it was the second year in the marriage.

It saddened me that whatever advice I gave him had not worked somehow. I wished I could have done more or, at least referred the matter to Lowell. The truth is I never thought this was in any way a serious problem that he could not get over.

The case of the Zoroastrian Man

I met most of the young people who became Bahá'ís in Johannesburg through Lowell, as most declared after being taught by him. These Lowell introduced on the night I would arrive in Johannesburg for meetings. There was one who caused much excitement with Lowell because he was Zoroastrian in background. Lowell introduced me to him. Krish dealered hs faiththrough Lowell and soon rose in service to become an elected meber of the National Assembly of South Africa and styed on for a number of years.

It proved to me that Lowell had a way with young people of all races in South Africa. After all he was the father of the great Bahá'í Community of Cape Town, the one community with the strongest Local Assembly in South Arica in the early days, all taught by Lowell and Edith his wife.

Lowell was indeed the friend of young people in South Africa!

Krish Naidoo (in dark jacket) at the African Regional Conference. (from PowerPoint)

Another Comment on the times
From the college to the township

This part of the story was never planned to be told, but it some way it insists on being told, mainly because the participants have kept faith with the author from a long distance of South Africa, and he felt proud to have known these gentlemen he tells of.

When I entered university in 1963, I was introduced to the English lecturer known as Johnny Melamo, who was from Springs in Johannesburg. He found among some things that my accent was strange , perhaps he had heard me sing a French song in a beginning of the year party at the women's hostel as a 'fresher". One other event which might have enhanced this perception was that at some stage there was the celebration of the Shakespeare Year on campus , and I was asked to read the part of the Duke in "The Merchant of Venice" and the part of Brutus in " Julius Caesar ,and the then English professor , Professor Greene ,had inquired where I was from with an accent of that kind. What he did not know was that I had coined an English accent in an attempt to learn to speak the language, and what came out when I did speak sounded foreign!

When I joined the Society of Music Fine Arts and Dramatics(SOMFAD), I found Mr. Melamo very much in that. The very year I joined the Dramatic Society I was asked to read the part of James in the "White Sheep of the family", a part which had been initially assigned to an Honors student in English. Somehow after reading the part I was asked to take it over.. This was very strange to many students because then I was a first year student in science, and not even in science, but in Agriculture.

The very next year, I was then elected chairman of the Dramatic Society, and commissioned to get some plays on stage, because at that time, no play had been staged for years. This was also because students had refused to participate in any social activities that involved the administration of the university as a protest against the changing of the university authority from Rhodes, University , which was English Speaking to UNISA(University of South Africa) which was Afrikaner dominated and very much under the government as part of the detested Bantu Education System.This was the atmosphere we were supposed to stage plays in.

The plays chosen for the year were one-act plays and three in number. One was " A Marriage is Rearranged" , the other two were " A Night at An

Inn" and "The Bishop's Candlesticks". I was then assigned the part of the "Toff" in the second play, a nickname which followed me for a year.

One of the actors in the play : " A marriage is Rearranged" was Stephen Gawe, who was an Honors Student in English. Briefly, though under protest from the student body, the plays were staged and several professors and students attended.

It is only unfortunate that after vigorously pushing for staging the plays and successfully having that done that , the administration would not accept my application to the college for the following year and refused years later to acknowledge my application for continuation of studies by not answering my correspondence..

Stephen belonged to a family whose head , a priest in the Anglican church, and was also involved in many social activities. In that way, as a member of that church for some years, I knew his father and some of his relatives. Stephen was an active man at college and very good at arguments . It was therefore and advantage to know him. I am not certain of what occurred after I left college, to him and any of my friends, but I did not hear of Stephen, until I met his brother, Mxolisi Gawe at the hospital I was employed in later years.

The one time I read in newspapers of Stephen was after I got to the United States, and independence was attained for Blacks in South Africa. I read in a newspaper that Stephen had become an Ambassador to Norway. Watching the South African newspapers revealed this. In later years this was confirmed by his brother, Mxolisai, who mentioned that he was , i.e. Stephen, retired, after the passing of his wife and a subsequent second marriage.

Friends on the Journey of Life

The Relation to Stephen Gawe

Having dealt with Stephen in I hope, an adequate a manner, as I can muster with the facts I have , I then come to Mxolisi Gawe, himself.. Most Mxolisi's friends know him as simply "Mxo". When I met him, because I considered him older than myself , I called him " O G" instead of "bro G" for Gawe". This was because I was refusing to give him a title according to African society. I have refused to do that for years because I did not see the point. Because of similar experiences , Mxolisi and I are now on first name terms, which works out very well.

On meeting Mxolisi at the hospital I saw that he wore green epaulettes, which indicated studies in Mental Health Care. But at that time he worked as a Male Nurse in a medical hospital.

Because of a problem with authorities at the hospital, where Male Nurses objected to not being accorded enough respect by authorities , who were in that profession, and most of them, of course mainly women, Mxolisi and several Male Nurses resigned ant d took up a other employment. Mxolisi took up a job at "Good Year Tyres" . Having studied is at nearby Technikon, Mxolisi became a Rubber Master at his job and was assigned to look after an office in Kingwilliamstown. Because his family lived in Port Elizabeth, he had to travel constantly by car back and forth between the two towns.

Though Stephen, his brother was not anything big in jazz music, Mxolisi was a great jazz fan and we met many times at jazz joints in town. However,

Mxolisi was a moderate in that area and kept a straight life, in comparison to many I knew in the 60s when jazz became a vogue in South Africa. This does not mean that jazz was not known there, but the kind known as " Avant Garde" or Progressive Jazz, was new.

There are a number of Jazz Artists , but I noticed that in the circles of nurses I joined, some artists were known more than others. Frequently one would hear music by Stanley Turrentine and Kenny Burrell, Les McCann, Miles Davis etc but not very much in those circles of Thelonius Monk who was popular together with John Coltrane, in my college. Seldom had I heard anything of Dave Brubeck either, even though at college he was very well known. But then , this was township jazz and different from "College Blues" where everything was acceptable..

Long Playing records were hard to obtain. One could not be very choosey about what one found at the record shop. Most of us bought from '"Michael's Records" on Grace Street in the city . Because of this scarcity, LPs turned up from different sources. The one that Mxolisi is remembered for by the author is one of Kenny Burrell where he plays the song "If I had You". Probably, this is the reason the author searched and found it on reaching the United States. It has a memory attached dating from old days in South Africa.

Mxolisi's Office in Port Elizabeth was near my employment, that is near Lennon's laboratories. So, occasionally I would see him during breaks. Regardless of that we were neighbors in the new section of New Brighton called " The Kwa-Ford Village" or Fordville..

On my second marriage, I found that my new wife did not quite like being in the house where I was with my first wife. I then had a deal with Mxolisi. He would move to my house and I to his. We were only one or two streets away, with him located on the main bus route. Because I was on the 'buying scheme' and he was on the 'renting scheme' he had to pay me the difference of what I had already paid in my original house. We had to do this legally, and so engaged a lawyer in the township. This was finally settled after some years, with many transfers from Mxolisi's bank to my account.

When I left the country, I had to search for friends' addresses and telephone numbers through the Internet, because after independence addresses changed drastically. In that way I found Mxolisi's.. On further investigation I found out Mxolisi was a Mayor of Uitenhage a town near Port Elizabeth. Before I could eve swallow that I learned that he was on a board at the Nelson Mandela University.

Between the telephone and emails Mxolisi informed me that he w as being made a "chief" of some village. Having told him off for suggesting that he had a title, he succumbed, I hope, by sending a picture of himself with some businessmen in Port Elizabeth.

Mxolisi Cumngce Gawe (ctr), with his friends at a ceremony in Port Elizabeth, South Africa with a grandson on his side (photo sent by Gawe)

This is the latest picture Mxolisi sent, but I would think it was taken some time ago, because as for now his health is not so good, but he functions very well. We have both aged and I am certain he would be shocked to see my recent picture which I have withheld from him! This is the same Mxolisi Gawe I met in Port Elizabeth about ten years ago and whose picture I displayed in an earlier book I wrote. To show his age, he is pictured with his grandson next to him.

Mxolisi Gawe in 2005, photo taken at my sister's home during a visit.
(picture taken by author)

Mxolisi Gawe (Front L) on a committee at Nelson Mandela Metropolitan Univer-
sity. Occasion undetermined (picture sent by Mxolisi via email)

Dorcas, A Family Friend

It has been reported in the past two days that a friend of my family is being buried in South Africa in a matter of hours from now, and today is December 2nd 2016. I need to bid her farewell because she was one of the most potent persons in encouraging education in life in my neighborhood. Her name was Dorcas Mokoneneane. She had a Mosotho last name , but she was not Mosotho and was actually Xhosa. Lacking much information about her beginnings , leaves me only with the fact that she was from the area known as Keiskammahoek of South Africa. If one once read a book about a man called ""Khwane" who was a chief in that area, then one would know that the particular man detested witchcraft ,and did much to rid his area of that practice. Dorcas never was known by a Xhosa name in my family, and my mother, lacking that called her simply " Dokase" which is more of a phonetic nature that a real name.

In order to speak of Dorcas , I would have to write a little about her husband , Sam Mokoneneane. Sam arrived in my lane as the man from the big city, Johannesburg, and for transportation used a motorcycle, riding it wearing a leather jacket. Later he changed all that to ordinary dress and a car we called 'the Zephyr". Sam worked for "Caltex' as salesman. In time he co-opted me into his exploits as salesman. I was told by him that for every can of Vaseline, produced by Caltex, that I sold I would receive a tickey from him. I was at that time about sixteen in age. Sam wanted to teach me driving at that age, but his method , he said, was to allow me to watch him drive and learn. A very hard process. So I never learned much from it. Sam was a friend of my family and when he passed on after my parents, he was buried next to their graves. This was because the graves of my parents were moved from a disreputable area to a more safer area and Sam was then buried there when his time came. Sam and I had great times, but it is about Dorcas I would like to write.

When I was seventeen Dorcas learned I loved music and so introduced me to the music of Glenn Miller and Patti Page. We had a record player in my home attached to the radio, and it was situated in the front room, next to a couch. This is where one would find me any day, listening to music or reading on the couch. This habit was not adored by my mother, but there was no way of getting me away from the couch. She yelled, she threatened but I stood my ground. Music was adorable to her, but it was perhaps hard to listen to rock at the time for adults.

Dorcas was a nurse and therefore , catered to some sicknesses in the area. I know that because, when I had a problem with what appeared to be piles, I received glycerin suppositories from her.

Day after day , Dorcas cautioned me to be very understanding of my mother as she was doing much by herself for her family. It was not long before they became close friends with my mother. Of course, this was hard for Sam, because Dorcas had now a protector, and Sam was not too kind a person to deal with. Besides , Sam had an eye for the opposite sex, and I happened to be the one who would be with him when he made some appointments. I could not mention that to Dorcas, so I had a double game to play.

When I left school, I worked part time as a salesman for "Sala and Co" because Emeric Sala, saw it as a possibility that I might become a good salesman, but it never worked. However, Dorcas was one of my good customers in buying soft goods .

When I grew up to about eighteen, Dorcas tried to introduce me to her sister who was in a boarding school, but I got along better with her in discussing anything than her sister, because , by that time I was eighteen, I had dispensed with young discussions and wanted more adult stuff. This of course, did not suit the sister either, so we parted as friends.

Dorcas was instrumental in trying to keep me in line as a young man, because she was wont to caution me much about staying in school and concentrating on a career.

The problem with Sam was a grim one for her, but she had my mother for an advisor. However, the strain was at last to great for her and they divorced.

Dorcas was Sister Tutor at the hospital in later lif. When she had to move from my neighborhood she, lived next to a friend I would visit. She would advise me to be very careful what I did about that because, as she said , my friend was older than my eldest sister. However, she never really objected.

I learned later after I moved to the United States that Dorcas had retired to the town of Kingwilliamstown, I tried to find her telephone number through her daughter but could never succeed. The one solace was that, when I went to bury my brother in East London, in 2004, her daughter offered to drive me to Port Elizabeth. This was the time when I was asked to give a talk at a high school graduation dinner in Port Elizabeth, I remember.. The talk was probably a mess , because I was still mourning my brother.

The reason I felt I should say anything about Dorcas in writing, is that up to the present day, I remember her kind face as she tried to warn me about many dangers in life, and cared so much that she followed my career even after she left my area. One does not easily forget such a friend. It probably is seldom that one writes about a friend on the day preceding the friends funeral, but that is all I can do for Dorcas, my friend and the friend of my family. This much I know that, my mother would want me to do so on her behalf.. Through both their pains , they held hands and carried on through hard times. It would be a crime to let this event pass without mentioning a word.

The Mokoneneanes' in my lane , had a friend in Fort Hare University who was of Tswana origin, a professor in Vernacular Languages, who would visit my area and stay with them every so often during the December vacations. Although the professor himself was not a popular person with students at college, still I found him much mo more approachable than any of the professors. While I was at college, I would some Saturday mornings go and crack jokes with him at his home, for he could be very funny. This was easy to do because in my second year he was my warden in housing. The strange thing is this that he never asked me about my neighbors, whom I knew he visited, for his caravan would be parked in front of their yard. I never queried that either. I was quite content to know what I knew without asking for too much. After all, he was a professor, and I could not question him much about his private life at college. That was separate.

It would waste a lot of time to tell more of Sam Mokoneane himself, but I knew him as a man who was associated with a lot of my high school teachers, who all socialized with him. I knew Sam more through his first two wives, for he was married thrice in my area. The first wife was great reader of comic books, and would loan me some of hers. After that I soon qualified into reading mysteries and that was not quite her area. I never knew much of that wife besides that, but the third was much younger than Sam and did not socialize much. So I avoided having to talk to her even though she trained in the hospital I worked in before qualifying as a sister. She of course was known to be able to keep Sam on a tight leash, perhaps that was very wise, and very goods for Sam! But, regardless, Sam was alienable person, and tried to acclimatize to Xhosa customs as a Mosotho, for there are differences. Sam never quit trying to attend Xhosa occasions, and was well known all around. The kids called him "Uncle".. He was so disgruntled when I left that he avoided giving me

ride to the airport as he had promised. I had, at the last moment, to get someone else to do that. Fortunately , I did not miss my airplane! For some reason
my leaving for Chicago, a bigger town than Johannesburg, kind of threatened
Sam for he was known as the guy from Johannesburg!

Now that I have written a little of Dorcas, perhaps it will be easier to
grieve over her departure. This is just a flash of memory and perhaps, no more.
But Dorcas would have wanted to know if I were happy where I am...

Nosidima Sishi, my good Friend and Neighbor The passing of Nosidima Sishi

When this lady passed on I was moved to send words to her funeral.

> *(sent to Dr. Sipho Sishi by email)*
>
> *To Sipho Sishi*
> *12/10/16 at 7:32 AM*
>
> *DEAR SIPO AND FAMILY,*
>
> *SO MY DEAR FRIEND HAS GONE AND I SOON WILL FOL-
> LOW. DIMZA, NOZIDIMA SISHI WAS A JEWEL AMONG
> WOMEN AND I COULD NOT EXPRESS EVEN A WORTHY
> TRIBUTE FOR HER. NO WOMAN SHE MET LEFT HER
> PRESENCE WITHOUT SOME KIND OF ADVICE ABOUT
> HER FUTURE. IN THAT SENSE DIMZA WAS A MOTHER
> AND CONSOLATION TO MANY WOMEN I HAVE KNOWN.*
>
> *AS I MISS HER I ALSO GLORY IN HER ACHIEVEMENTS
> BOTH AS A PERSON AND AS A WOMAN OF AFRICAN
> BACKGROUND.*
>
> *WE SHALL PLEAD THAT SHE BE ACCEPTED WITH JOY
> AT THE DOOR OF OUR GREAT HOME, THE DIVINE
> PRESENCE.*
>
> *MY WIFE AND I AND ALL OUR CHILDREN WOULD LIKE
> TO WISH HER FAMILY CONSOLATION AT THIS UN-
> HAPPY HOUR OF LOSS, BUT THEY ALSO REJOICE THAT
> DIMZA HAS ACHIEVED MANY A GOAL IN HER
> EARTHLY LIFE AND HAS BEEN A VERY HONORED*

*WOMAN IN HER LIFE. I GRIEVE THAT SHE, WHO WAS
MY COMPANION THROUGH SORROWS AND JOYS HAS
NOW LEFT US. BUT DO KNOW WE SHALL MEET AGAIN.*

*NO NEED TO DWELL UPON THAT , FOR WHERE SHE IS
WE KNOW SHE IS VERY HAPPY.
FROM HER FRIENDS,*

*ROBERT , GRETCHEN (NOMONDE), BONGA LUTHANDO
KAREN (NOMINCILI) MAZIBUKO CHICAGO, ILLINOIS,
WASHNINGTON ISLAND WISCONSIN, UNITED STATES*

An explanation

The above message was not sent in sorrow but in victory, for Dimza has
achieved much that was worthy of note in the education of many girls and
young men in my township in Port Elizabeth.

My first meeting with Nozidima was casual , because then I had just left
high school and was starting to work. My eventual task in the hospital in which
I was employed was to take care of the payments of Disability Grants for patients in long term treatment for Tuberculosis in that hospital. Nozidima as a
sister in the SANTA Settlement , which housed patients after the critical stages
of Tuberculosis to recover . Her task was to bring some of these patients to
the hospital for X Rays to monitor the treatment of those patients

I had not befriended her as a student because she was a number of classes
before me , though she schooled in the school I eventually attended , and lived
down the street from my house. Dimza , on the other hand , had noticed me
a number of months before I knew about her coming to the hospital, for kept
tabs on all the neighbors who schooled in her vicinity.

Even though this is a story belonging to the earlier days of my life, which
I have recounted elsewhere , yet it fitting at this point for two reasons :One of
those reasons is that I had been in contact with Dimza many times while I resided both in Illinois and in Wisconsin, both by mail and telephone, and at
the time of her passing I had known she was unwell.

Besides knowing Dimza that long, and also because she knew many
people I worked with , including the friendly Radiographer whom I knew as
Helen Tate, whose mother was a Bahá'í,. This last then was the second and
perhaps the most important reason. Dimza and I could talk, because all the

university students I schooled with knew her very well and had gained insights by visiting her.

An Apology

In an attempt to make my friend Mxolisi Gawe feel better about coming of old age and its aches and pains., I am placing some of our pictures as adults as a comparison of what we once were in youth.

To make this even real, I am posting one of my little sister, whom as a child I used to carry on my back and feed each time. Now she is grown and has become a professor in a university. Instead of feeling old and useless we should then feel proud in our achievements, should we not? In a sense I go beyond bounds and in a story of youth, include the present.

My sister , Eileen Noxolo Mazibuko accepting her PhD in Economics at Nelson Mandela Matropolitan University.(picture sent by Noxolo via email)

Robert and Gretchen with Ma'áni Mazibuko the baby, dressed as superman. At the home of Emeric and Karen, Evanston, IL.

While Gretchen and I try to look honorable graduating as grandparents, above in the picture, the same sister I cared for as a a baby now accepts pro-fessorship in Economics, a course I gave up and took up computers!

Thoughts and Musings

An Answer to a Question

Many people have asked me how I came to stay in the United States, and I just say that I know I came not as a refugee but to marry. I am an immigrant who saw a girl and wanted to marry her. I had intended living in Swaziland but found I had to go where she resided and that happened to be here in the United States. When I had difficulties with the Consul in Johannesburg I stated my case with him in this way :" I do not want to marry Gretchen the American girl; I do not want t to marry Gretchen the White girl, I want to marry Gretchen the girl I love". That put a stop to much I wanted desperately to avoid in the application for a visa to enter the country. Now I am here.

From the very onset of my love affair with the woman, I had problems . First of all I was the first African who as a Bahá'í came to the United States to marry a white girl and from South Africa. The one person I knew left South Africa to marry a white girl was a boxer called Jake Tuli, who left the country to live in the United Kingdom. The second person I knew had been Thozi Nomvete but he married in what then was free Transkei. The next Bahá'í to move in that direction was Ludfi Noor who married in South Africa after the Immorality Act was repealed. I moved to Swaziland, got engaged and moved to the United States to marry in 19887 November, having arrived a little before Halloween. You may call me the Halloween bridegroom…

Before I even arrived I got very upset , for just at the time when I negotiated coming over, my girlfriend lost her job at the Bahá'í Center in Evanston.

That astounded me! However, I was not aware of the employment situation at the Center, where my youngest son now works and has been for years. The funding of the Faith comes from Bahá'ís themselves and no amounts are accepted from non-Bahais unless they are told what their contribution will be utilized in, and usually that would be a Bahá'í and non-Baha' project, just a human social project. The contribution from Bahais is likened to the sheep of the sacrifice which is not touched except to make that sacrifice. Africans in South Africa would know this. So when one earns a lot at the Center ,usually they have to find employment elsewhere to earn more than the Center offers. That was the predicament with Gretchen. It would seem they were not even aware that she was to marry an African for the first time then. That meant she had to look for work at this poignant time in our lives. It took some years for me to come to understand that, but I had never been employed at a Bahá'í Center, nor did I know how that worked, even though I functioned on the National Assembly for years and had airfare to meetings paid for. I had been a travelling teacher in South Africa with only traveling and housing expenses paid, and had to leave after about nine months to find work.

Because on my arrival I had found this so hard to live with this that Gretchen had been dismissed just when we were to marry, I kept my peace but determined to find out the actual reasons someday.

On my arrival in the States I delivered a book to a Bahá'í working at the Center called, Yael Wurmfeld, as a gift from Lowell Johnson who was pioneering in South Africa. This was an introduction and of course, a way of letting the Center know that Lowell had a book ready . Yael then negotiated a guiding service post at the House of Worship for me.

I was willing to let this affair of the problem disappear, but an event brought it up again.

There had been a visitor ,a Persian who was serving at the World Center coming to the United States, and I had known of the man when he had come to visit the Assembly in Johannesburg earlier. So I wanted to meet him, because at the time of his visit in South Africa I could not see him as I lived in Port Elizabeth, some distance from the Transvaal. I then determined to meet him at the House of Worship. I had been warned in South Africa by American pioneers not to even expect to see members of the National Assembly as they are hardly ever seen by many believers for the largeness of the country, but are known to be in the United States' Bahá'í ' Center in Illinois.

I was lucky. Because, after the talk I went up to see the gentleman from Haifa and we talked. A man joined us and I soon found that he was the Secretary of the National Assembly. I had called him once from Swaziland to find out about Gretchen's employment but could not speak to him as he was away at that time, so was I told. Now was the chance!

When I had a moment with the Secretary I then broached the question why Gretchen had been dismissed thus making it so difficult for us to marry. He promised me a call and offered to drive me home. I refused that but held onto his promise made for day and a time.

It is unfortunate that on the day promised, Gretchen and her daughter had to leave for some distant destination, probably , as I remember to Gretchen's mother in Ottawa, IL. Thus I was going to be by myself to take the call from the Secretary. We had the call on that day and found it hard to come to terms with the fact that it could not be understood why I was upset. Now I find the Secretary could or should have easily explained this by telling me of the conditions of employment at the Center, and this would have been settled. Also I failed to realize the importance this that funds for the Faith came from contributions and that the Bahá'í Faith is not that kind of company that holds great funds, most of this was still part of the faith in God and His support of a plan He wants executed by the few we had. Thus the phone call still left an unsolved situation ,which at this time I have come to terms with in a more positive way , because understanding has come to the rescue. When one finds logic in life, the mind may then rest and find comfort to relate positively ,a condition I feel I have come to.

As it were it takes much time to achieve some understanding of anything and sometimes it takes even longer to try to verbalize feelings, but then that needs much patience while things resolve themselves. I take solace in that thinking.

What many people I knew did not quite understand was this: Here was a Black man ,from South Africa defending the job of a White woman from America , with thousands of Black people in America with no work! To that I revert to the same statement I made before, Gretchen is no white woman, just my wife or the girl I loved then. That stance may be dangerous to uphold but, give me a man who would not defend his wife, no matter she might be. I may be Black and have a Black brethren but I am also married for an eternal journey. When I go , there will be no Black or White bodies to take care of . I only try to get practice now in case I forget where I have to go like so many do forget and cling to the form we have on the planet. What if we met the fellows from Space? Will we allow ourselves to discriminate or be discriminated by them? We try now, and probably we can survive that. My thinking is that creation is not our making and we do not set the rules, we just exist, problems and all, and so that we can please Him. Mine was not to really set out to marry a white girl, but simply to go on pilgrimage and take a chance on finding a suitable wife, as my friend Rose Perkal-Gates had advised before I left home in 1985 to take pilgrimage.

> **Not everything that a man knoweth can be disclosed, nor can everything that he can disclose be regarded as timely, nor can every timely utterance be considered as suited to the capacity of those who hear it.**
> **(Baha'u'llah, Gleanings from the Writings of Baha'u'llah, p. 176)**

An Assertion that Avoids Denial

Rather than a question, the following is more of an assertion. With South Africa today having regarded itself as the so-called "Rainbow Nation", it is then an assertion that with the growth of certain integration, the Colored population will grow exponentially. That means that e future of the population in South Africa will have a greater component of Colored persons that it would of White persons. This is because there is a greater chance of a colored increase among the Coloreds than there will be among the Whites.

Having arrived at that assertion , the chances that this attitude will be taken up by the future world are very great. Today there is a great rate of accordance for marriage in the cross color and culture area than ever before. Acceptance of the oneness of the human race becomes a greater assertion than a prediction. The exponential growth of the gene pool will , of course bring about the possibility of a human being who will be more adjusted to the universes he well live in. It may even be possible that certain features of the human that were never seen will make themselves manifest in that future. This would not just be accident of nature but a natural occurrence which the human must expect and welcome, as there is, at this time, no method by which man can shut himself out from it. If we consider the situation of the Samaritans and Jesus' command, we will note that Samaritans were those Jews who mixed families with 'foreigners' and were not quite accepted as Jews. Hence the Parable we all know. We also know that those people were regarded as not being quite 'there' n their land , because intermarrying among themselves did not give that a chance of survival. This situation, might even pertain generally to the greater world, should any tribe of nation decide to intermarry within itself. This devastating phenomenon of weakness has been observed in nations where the royal family could only marry within itself. No people or nation would opt for itself to belong to such a group, that fails to adjust to existence, for hat would be an invitation of extinction for that group. We must bear this in mind.

At a safe time, which is our present the Bahá'í Religion has taught and fostered this principle of the oneness of the human race. It cannot be only because we must unite, but because doing so is an advantage , going forwards, whatever the destiny of the human on the planet might be, or have to be.

With that thought further encouraging them, Bahai's might well be in a powerful stance of teaching the integration of the human race, as the intended plan of creation. For their Faith , they maintain, is not just an outburst of principles of uniting the world but is well within the Plan of God for the human. Anyone trying to deny this, would be advised to look deeply at principles of science available today, concerning the existence and the plan of the human through the ages of its existence, and imagine, what man must have been like, when he emerged from water to take residence on land , and further to the present day, and wonder , if that is the end for that being. We know not whence we came, nor are we aware of where we go next. The question in my mind still stands, 'is the universe moving?'. The next is " Does the One Whom we call the Creator, have time to stop creating?" Or does he lose His title according to us, who live on a grain in the universe he has made ? Do we then actually claim to know more than whet science permits to know today? Is it the end of discovery in our day? And what is that day?

The earth is but one country, and mankind its citizens. (Baha'u'llah, Gleanings from the Writings of Baha'u'llah, p. 250)

It is not for him to pride himself who loveth his own country, but rather for him who loveth the whole world. The earth is but one country, and mankind its citizens. (Baha'u'llah, Gleanings from the Writings of Baha'u'llah, p. 250)

If we then deny all evidence to this effect, we might as well close all books on science and logic and live by some other unknown principle which shall, not, I repeat, shall not, be based on any logical conclusions. But will be based on a emotional perspective, which in itself is no direction related either to the cosmos or reality. If man lives outside a realty, how can he persist to maintain life or living on this planet, which is discovered in its principles and advantage, though logical laws. One man said that if a phenomenon occurs in the same way at the and same time within the same environment, it does require urgent investigation, lest we miss knowing it's laws.

Waiting in between

Return to Port Elizabeth after having been gone for two years was not easy. If it was not desperate it was bordering on being pathetic. Here I was back in town without a penny on my name; I had two children who expected much from their father; I had no and no home; I had only a bed at my parent's home and was forced to live from a traveling bag. Many thought that this would be the end. Given that I had health issues and no financial resources they could had been right in suspecting that.

I was somewhat between two governments. I had to wait for the Birth and Deaths Department to issue a birth certificate and had to wait for the United States Consulate to contact me again about my application for a visa. It was hard to find work because many knew I had opted to leave the country.

The real break came when I was in East London's Mdantsane location, when I learned from my little sister by telephone, that a call from Cape Town had been received and someone wanted me to set up an appointment at the United States Consulate there. I was not even aware that my case had been referred to Cape Town, even as I had not known that my case for the birth certificate was to be handled in Port Elizabeth, while I was in Johannesburg. It was as a bolt of lightning that I was summoned to Cape Town. However, how was that to happen without a penny coming in? Hence I resorted to measures that were at that time drastic by having to borrow, only to receive a gift from my past employer who sympathized with he situation and wanted to help.

I could only thank the Head Clerk at the Department of Deaths and Births for having been patient, even though he knew I was leaving the country. The fortunate part with him was that one morning when I visited the department, after having been visiting for three months, he told me that my certificate had been signed and was on the table in Pretoria. That to me just meant I had to persuade him to get it delivered, and that I did successfully and got the certificate the next day as he promised.

Leaving Africa

Nostalgia and Wonder

In 1985, having been on pilgrimage and met Gretchen, I moved to Swaziland to accommodate an impending visit to South Africa she had voiced. In doing so I had to sell all I had and move to a rented house in Manzini, Swaziland.

My stay in Swaziland was for about two years in which time Gretchen had come to visit and we had become engaged to marry. The idea of settling Swaziland after marriage was short lived for it was not too long after her return to the USA that she reported on the telephone and by mail that she had lost her job and could not travel because of further difficulties with the father of her children. The one solution on then , if we really wanted to marry was for me to travel to the USA and marry there. That in itself debunks that idea that I came to enjoy a better economy as has been suggested in some quarters after my arrival there. It is also to be noted that I flew out of Port Elizabeth , at midday, via Johannesburg and on to England. That also will do away with the thought that I escaped from my country or that there is something to hidden there in the background I have in that country. I dare say I have been quite transparent about my goings on in that country from an early age, for I wrote most of my activities in stories from those times in books that have been published. My aim therefore was to go and marry. Where I would settle after that was still a mystery until I got the first goal achieved. Hence I am still in the country today as a retired person.

Because of difficulties with travel documents for entry into the USA I had to return to Port Elizabeth, from Swaziland. Again because I stayed in Swaziland from 1985 to 1987 for the greater part with no employment, by the time I reached Port Elizabeth, I had exhausted my financial resources . That meant that I had to borrow. I could not legitimately go to a bank to borrow when there was no employment at hand. I the approached the one person I had once visited in the city and who I knew owned a business, and that was a certain Mr. Prussoff. He then accommodated me with enough cash to buy clothing, which I eventually used for travelling to the USA.

The note below came as a result of having repaid him the sums I borrowed. Prussoff was Jewish and an employer of my mother. Further, on Strand Street, in the city center, he had a paint business. I had once visited his home to show him slides of my visit to Haifa, Israel, and he had liked that so much we remained friends.

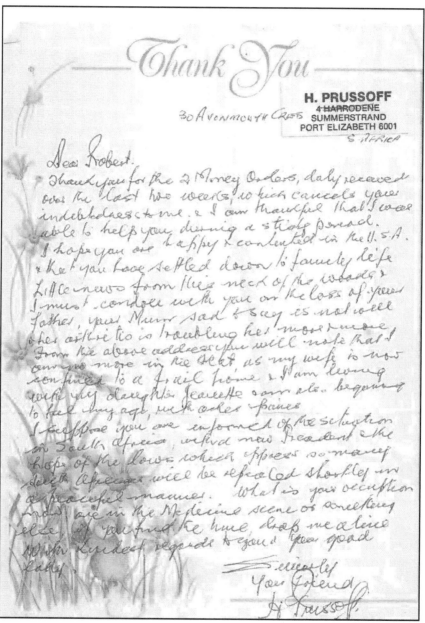

A note from H. Prussoff, Robert's mother's employer after repayment of a loan made after stay in Swaziland. Loan paid while in the United States.

The note above may not be legible but the words " Thank You" can be seen as well as the author's name, i.e. Prussoff. Prusoff was a businessman of

Jewish background who employed my mother, but wanted me not to mention that I had showed him my slides of Haifa, as that might have upset her, as an employee to know that her son had been there as a visitor. Prussoff, I wager, knew very well that I had manager at my work with whom we were good friends, called Israelstam, as well was a great friend, also Jewish called Michelle Bergman, a pharmacist at my company. Things worked out well in the difficult environment I was in as a a Bahá'í., and they from Israel, with full knowledge of what oppression meant. We all understood that and worked with it and round it pleasantly. My friend Persi would be very much aware of that as he once worked n New Brighton Clinic, as a Pharmacist. Shopping for goods at Midland Jewelers and Ellie Kolnick's was a good advantage too. We knew very well who we were !

As a friend I knew in the Faith once said:' We knew each other very well, and neither one is fooling the other!" The same man once said :'Between two friends there is an area where a lie cannot be admitted". Crucial years and delicate situations do that to one. One has to know who to trust and know that whatever they do does not break that trust. That is how it was in those days. You had to know where you stood and relation to the rest. To deviate could upset much one has diligently worked towards. Some situations can be irreversible. A step taken is a step taken.

The Despair of Moving Residence
Part of three pictures I carried with me while wandering from South Africa to Swaziland and back again and again
They were a part of a hope that somewhere I did have a home.

(sent to author by Gretchen while author in Swaziland)
Gretchen Misselt at the weaving loom

The dining room of Gretchen Misselt's home before we were wed...The second pic-
ture I carried with me from place to place in Africa (sent by Gretchen to author)

The third picture of the three I had with the above included, I no longer have, and it was that of the living-room. These I carried with me everywhere I went as I wandered around like the very homeless person, for at that time I had no firm residence. Meals and sleep were open to negotiation and wheeling and dealing. For an adult person with responsibilities of children this is no fun time! But it was done…

When I got home in New Brighton, to show the purposefulness of her son, my mother had some of these displayed on a window sill. I discouraged this very much and with all haste, for, such a move was fraught with danger during the riots. One would scarcely speak of having a white friend, much less a girlfriend.

Yet this seemed to stick with me all the way. The very last time I departed from New Brighton, Eghbal Ma'ani had to enter the township to take me to the airport. I boast that the time was midday. None can say I departed unknown, unseen. The air flight to Johannesburg was at about the midday hour.

Gretchen Misselt standing in the front garden of the House of Worship, near the time she met Robert Mazibuko. Gretchen was employed at the Bahá'í Center when they met

My last Word

Many people that I know have asked me where I stand with issues in the world as they are e today. I would ask them to study Bahá'í Principles, both Social and Moral, and find out the purposes of the Bahá'í Religion. If they understand this there would be no question as to where I stand, for I am standing identified with the purposes of that religion. At least I make the effort in my way…

Medication and me

Two years after leaving South Africa, I was out of work and looking for options, for I had already arranged to marry a lady who lived in the United States. Also I was in a new culture. By this time I had been asked by a medical practitioner to consider giving up taking some strong medication which was intended to treat an onset of a severe condition of nervous nature. The practitioner advised this because he saw no such indications as were meant for persons in that condition, Therefore from about 1982 to the time I left South Africa , I was not taking anything serious except for tension which I treated mostly with muscle relaxants. However , at this time of unemployment and being in a new culture I felt a need to have a tablet for a depressed condition. I then approached a doctor in Swaziland , who felt that I needed to be assessed to be in good health so that he knew what he hd to prescribe in view of my history of sickness. His idea then was to refer met o a local Psychiatrist to determine if all was in order. Hence I was referred to a a specialist in a clinic at the government hospital.

After a conversation with the doctor which I took to be her kind of interview she asked to get of all medications as I had taken before and take nothing else strong.

I followed orders and terminated all medications. By the time I reached the United States I was, therefore taking no prescribed tablets. Due to pressures of culture change both within a mixed culture marriage and establishment in a new culture I felt a need to return to some form of relaxing medication. Taking over the counter medications , I felt , was not wise. I then approached a doctor in Chicago, while schooling there in two colleges,. He would not give me any treatment as he was not sure exactly what he was treating.

My problem at this time was becoming very irritable. This led to my subsequently being admitted to hospital where they found that I had cancer on the shoulder. This report came after my wife had submitted that I was very hard to handle and irritable in the home. It was, however , a surprise to both of us. After due surgery, the doctor advised that I see a psychiatrist as there was a chance that at recovery, after a bone was removed from the shoulder, I would be hunchbacked. At recovery at the hospital then, after a week in intensive care, I had to be held for a week to determine how things would go. After the two week at which time I was now upset that I was there with no indication of why I was not released, the doctor admitted that he saw nothing wrong in behavior and physically, but because initially I was there because of a complaint from family, he felt I should take tablets for depression.

Thus it was that when I arrived on Washington Island I was taking what the doctor felt was very strong medication for depression and finally gave me a far less dosage to be taken at night only. Today , that is the situation. For the record I now include the report from he doctor in Swaziland, a doctor I thought had a foreign accent in English.

SWAZILAND GOVERNMENT

FROM Dr. Guinness. TO Dr. Monadjem.
MB BCh MRCPsych
Government Psychiatrist
Swaziland.

REF. NO. _____ DATE 4 · 3 · 87

Robert Mazibuko

This man reports a mental illness in 1968 when he was admitted to mental hospital in Port Elizabeth RSA for seven weeks. It sounds like schizophrenia. He was mute, felt that people knew what he was thinking before he said it [psychotic]. Ever since then he has been on Stelazine & Artane although he never had another psychotic illness and worked for 14 y as a pharmaceutical technician. He is out of work at present. He shows no sign of psychosis. I suggest tailing off the medication over 6 mths.
Stelazine 2 mg bd × 3/12
Stelazine 2 mg nocte × 3/12 then stop & observe.

Guinness.

Clarification of note from a Psychiatrist in Swaziland

Swaziland Government
From Dr_____
MB B Ch MRC Psych To Dr _____
Government Psychiatrist
Swaziland
Date 4.3.87

Robert Mazibuko

This man reports a mental illness in 1968 when he was admitted to mental hospital in Port Elizabeth RSA for seven weeks. It sounds like schizophrenia. He was mute , felt that people knew what he was thinking before he said it i.e. psychotic.

Ever since then he has been on Stelazine & Artane although he never had another psychotic illness and worked for 14 yrs as a pharmaceutical technician.

He is out of work at present. He shows no sign of psychosis.

I suggest tailing off the medication over 6 months

Stelazine 2 mg x bid 3/12
Stelazine 2 mg nocte x 3/12
Then stop &observe.

Stories Noted and Remembered
A Hand of the Cause in Port Elizabeth, South Africa.

We no longer have Hands of the Cause in the Faith, and their rare work is precious. It is then amazing that a Hand of the Cause should visit Port Elizabeth, which had then three Local Assemblies and only one functioning properly. This blessing came a bout through the instrumentality and efforts of Christine and Patrick Beer. Patrick and Christine had not only invited international travelling teachers to Port Elizabeth, but gave Port Elizabeth this station of having been visited by a Hand of the Cause. It is not surprising then that when the author went to the International Convention, that Patrick and Christine would ask him to carry a message of greetings to a member of the House of Justice, Mr. Ian Semple, who he was privileged to meet there and take pictures of him and his family, on that occasion.

For the friends to be able to meet with Mr. Featherstone, Hand of the Cause, Patrick and Christine arranged a space at the "Holiday Inn" , across town from the African townships, and at night. Of course, for this reason of travelling at night 'night passes" had to be arranged for Africans for the meeting at the Inn was going to be after work in the evening.

At the venue, even though we were a handful of African Bahá'ís, Mr. Featherstone addressed us as if we were any other regular meeting of the friends, with dignity and respect mixed with great concern for our spiritual growth. Port Elizabeth will always be grateful to the Beers' for having arranged this meeting, for they went to great lengths in preparing the ground and the assurance of safety of all the friends.

Port Elizabeth had not seen such a closeness to the Cause until then because all the Hands of the Cause who had visited South Africa had never had time enough to visit all the smaller towns, and so visits were limited to mostly Johannesburg. This is the reason such a visit is so momentous and does require applause and mention in any story about that town, especially now that the Cause no longer has these precious souls to protect and inspire the Friends as Stewards of the Cause of Baha'u'llah.

Hand of the Cause Collis Featherstone

A Fond memory

The events of this story occurred some years before the visit of the Hand of the Cause William Sears, to South Arica when he gave a talk at summer school(That talk is available as a video made by Sirus Mahmudi).... This is partly because during that talk he mentioned above a book called " All Flags Flying" . It then happens that in illustrator for the said book was an artist I knew as Robert Reedy. Robert and Mary Reedy both pioneered in South Africa from the United States. Much can be said of Robert but the little I know endeared me to the family.

Robert would sometimes volunteer to cook lunch for all nine member of the National Assembly and all committees when they all met at the Bahá'í Center in Johannesburg, for monthly sessions. On some occasions, he would during the cooking, ask me to suggest a dessert for the lunch, and invariably I would suggest a chocolate cake and he would bake one and serve it at lunch..

There is a statement Robert made in conversation which ,as years went by, began to mean more to the author. He had an old white colored and beat-up car he would drive over to the Center with family. I once commented that it needed changing as it seemed too old. Robert commented that it was not the outward bigness that mattered but the inner, a true statement. As we dealt in those days at the Center with spiritual matters the statement did not seem to have much of any depth in meaning. But as time went by the realization of its import came upon the author. The question of the outward that did not impact on the inward soon became an issue to be pondered upon. The realization that the outward has fooled many a person, became an item to consider in every choice the author had to make, and as he did the words of the artist , Robert Reedy came into his mind so much that he had to write about that.

Robert Reedy (from cover of book " All Flags Flying" by W. Sears)

Chocolate Cake (Google.com)

Deborah Dadgar(facebook)

On each occasion Robert came to the Bahá'í Center he was accompanied by Mary his wife and young Megan the redhead, their daughter. Megan may feel embarrassed by the fact that she had a baby blanket trailing behind her every time she came with her parents to the Center.

I do not have a picture of Mary, but have one of a lady I used to mistake her for, because they were both small persons in size. It would surprise some that I used to call Mary the 'school kid' because of her size and she took it in very good humor. Knowing how sensitive people can become about such characteristics has made understand just how saintly Mary was to allow herself to named thus when she was a mother of two!

I later met Debbie Dadgar when I pioneered in Swaziland also from the United States, and am indebted to her for all the assistance in getting established there, for she had a Sunday morning deepening class and a trip to the villages to follow each time. Such exploits leave one with warm memories of one's past and a courage in the present!

A story of a Prayer

I attended many meetings in the Transkei but once I learned, while in a meeting, how to chant a prayer in Arabic and succeed in doing so. At times of beginning any meeting, Bahá'ís usually start with a prayer. Once I was in a meeting and heard a Bahá'í from Persia chant a prayer known as the "Remover of Difficulties" which Bahá'ís say as a short prayer in times of difficulties. I had heard this prayer said many times in many languages in Africa and had heard it chanted in Arabic in Cape Town and elsewhere, but the style this gentleman adopted was so unusual a and impressive that I found I could not forget it, and in time learned to use it at meetings and privately.

As I wrote, this prayer begins with the words:"Is there any Remover of Difficulties save God…" which in the Arabic original text begins with" Halmin Mufarrijin qayr'ulláh…". The way this gentleman said it made it impossible to resist a refrain at the end of each sentence.

The gentleman who introduced himself as Yosefi , was an Audio Visual Specialist at a university and had recently arrived in my area. He was of dark complexion, darker than most Persians I had seen thus far.

One day, while I was attending a meeting in Johannesburg, we had to say prayers in the morning as a group. I chanted this prayer in Yosefi's style, and found the Persians in the room chanted the refrain. I quickly stopped because it scared me that I had stated something I knew very little about! But that built good friendships

Later I heard a very amusing story about Yosefi. During break at the university lunch room, Yosefi sat in a remote part of the room and was making little paper boats. One of the professors approached him and asked where he had learned to make beautiful paper boats.

Yosefi replied " In jail…"

The professor countered that as a gentleman Mr. Yosefi would have had a good reason for being in jail and Yosefi replied:" I had killed a man…"

Astounded the professor said :"As a gentleman you must have had a good reason for that , Mr. Yosefi !"

Yosefi looked at him seriously and said: " He was asking too many questions..!", at which point the professor let him alone..

Departure and Thoughts

On the day before my departure, my mother watched me keenly as I ironed and packed all clothing in bags. She had been aware of my going from the time I had left home for Swaziland and had even queried why the Consulate could not give me a visa on my word that I was her child instead of asking for my birth certificate.!However on the day I departed, she only gave me the caution that I knew what she had taught me and that it was time to go and show it. As it were she was unwell with arthritis on her feet, and in any case, to arouse any excitement at that time could have caused many a difficulty. This had to be done normally and quietly, as it was a riotous time anything could have happened , particularly when the populace knew I was leaving to marry a white girl in America.

On the other hand my father never said a word, and indeed, I never expected him to say anything as he was very unwell and in bed. I had paid my dues to him by giving him a bath once and he was almost happy about that though he complained that the bath was revenge since he had bathed me as a child!. At this time I simply went over to his room to tell him that I was now leaving finally.

Arrangements had been made between myself and a neighbor I had known since my school days, that he would take me to the airport. However, just before the time came, he was called away on some mission and asked me to wait for him. I knew him very well and that he would not expose himself unnecessarily and this was no moment to do that. Hence after some minutes after the time he said he would be home, I looked for alternatives.

Fortunately, there was a young man nearby who had just come home driving his car, for lunch. I then negotiated with him to give me a ride to the entrance of the township where I expected a Bahá'í friend to pick me up.

Having found agreement with the man we then set off to the entrance, and poignantly the entrance was near my ex-school teacher's house, G.T. Galo. There I waited a few minutes and Eghbal who is Persian came into the township against all danger and picked me up. By now Eghbal was used to my house and the township, but that did not mean he could not meet the danger of being challenged as a White person there at that specific time, for it was round noon and people were on lunch from around the Administration Offices nearby. It is to be noted that the Administrative Offices also contained the Office of Influx Control, next to a Police Station. Eghbal risked it because he had a permit to enter the township as an engineer employed by the Municipality..

It was Eghbal who saw me off at the airport as I left. It is only sad in a way that after I left he suffered a heart attack and passed on leaving two sons born in Port Elizabeth and a a wife, Sara Ma'ani who now is in the United States where she had pioneered from to go to in Africa.

Eghbal Ma'ani and Sara at Bahá'í Convention in Umgababa, near Durban, South Africa, with Sara is a child of one of the Bahá'ís.

Before the trip I had intimated to Eghbal just how destitute I was in terms of financial resources and he had, for the most part kept quiet. I knew he could not help much, for he and Sara had just undertaken a trip to the

United States and besides had a brand new baby at that time, but in a quiet way, he offered me a money order for R90.00 which I could convert at the airport before departure. That is all the cash I had on me as I boarded the airplane for the journey.

Further to that, either Eghbal or Sara had informed Lowell that I was on the way to the international airport, for on arrival there, I found him waiting in Johannesburg at that airport.

Lowell had by then written many biographies on many Bahá'ís but had informed me that he was writing a book of some of his thoughts as a teaching tool .I found out at the airport on departure that his book had actually been printed. He entrusted me with a copy which was to go the Pioneering Office at the Bahá'í National Center in the United States and specifically indicated that I was to give the book to the person at the head of that office, and that was Yael Wurmfeld.. This acted as my introduction on arrival in the United States. The copy of the book was duly handed over on my arrival, and added to my cheer of finding company where I was going to reside.

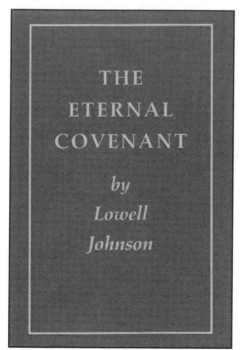

The picture of a copy of the book Lowell gave me at the airport to use an introduction to the Bahá'í Center in the United States.

To further show support in the pioneering effort I was undertaking, Lowell also sent me cassettes of readings from the Writings of the Faith, by himself. That way I would not forget where I came from, for his voice was always there to listen to whenever any doubts occurred. When he had turned ninety he sent an audio cassette of an interview by Peter Lotis, the Radio Announcer and his past coworker ,at the Radio Station. All these cassettes have been converted to CD format, by the author, for progeny and for himself.

Lowell at his apartment at Reynard Hall, in Hillbrow, Johannesburg. The apartment is identifiable by the picture behind him, possibly another Reg Turvey painting which I often saw there, and by the lamp on his right..

Comments

Thoughts on Division of Labor

While delivering a talk once in Cape Town, the question of duties of family members came up. My immediate response was that there are duties that women can best do much more capably than men. This comment resulted in my being stated as being discriminatory towards the sexes. I shall now attempt my stand because I still adhere to that.

As a child I was responsible for all duties in the home, but soon found that my sister could beat me at many home jobs. This did not matter because , to me at that time, there was no notion of her being a girl, just my sister. I did not classify her as anything except someone I could share with all my childhood growth nuances.

In my family one was debarred to see tasks as female or male tasks, so had to undertake any task given with full energy and willingness.

Having done this until my eighteenth year, I was then supposed to become a man through circumcision. For a start I did not see the point in being circumcised so as to be called a 'man'.. This attitude did not resonate well with both my father and my mother. It seemed so inconsistent to me.

Having arrived at a state where it was found necessary to prepare this occasion without much input for me, I had to acquiesce.

In the circumcision school I had to relearn many things that had to do with men and women. The first was that I saw my own blood being deliberately shed and heard the admonishment as I went through the change of bandages that I was bleeding so that I never found it necessary to belittle my sister for she bleeds monthly. Secondly I found I had to lose all interest in the opposite sex , for that would tend to disagree with the healing process. Thinking about them was out of the question. This had to be curbed. Thirdly I had to realize that I could not urinate standing up but had to squat. I was again reminded that my sister had to do this all her life.

It became not just a duty but a necessity to veil myself and hide from all women who happened to pass through the woods.

As a Bahá'í I had to process this all this in my mind, for I was to teach people that the Bahá'í Faith covered all those behaviors. This also meant that I had to deal with the Adam and Eve Theory. I soon found that, like so many things in the Bible, the story had symbolism in it. For, how could a snake talk and Adam be made from the dust of the Earth with God breathing down his tiny nose.? Surely logic here was no working! It took years to figure the thing out, but I managed to find allowances of thought in my Faith, for it is stated there that many a meaning is enshrined in the story and it needed unraveling. I shall not go into that at this stage but have done that elsewhere. The thing to note was that I was happy with the symbolism in the Bible and agreed entirely with it as a resource for spirituality, and it made sense logically.

In having to deal with this theme in public in Africa one had to have a strategy. I learned some tips from a man I spent time with unraveling this mystery. He was chairman of the Bahá'í National Assembly, a great spokesman and a good negotiator, and his name was Michael Sears. This is how he saw it:

In olden times in Africa men hunted and were built for long journeys into the wilderness for days looking for meat. Women stayed home and learned to survive by eating weeds and vegetables while the men hunted. Women learned to be much more adept at preparing vegetables than men did. As the animals disappeared in the woods, men would often turn up at home with meager gains from hunting, and not enough to satisfy family. Naturally they found they had to turn to the women for food. Not only that , women had learned to adapt easily to making mud houses better than men and had learned to weave all kinds of containers that the men needed, with grass. Therefore , the women were seen as assets. Now , when it came to marriage, the loss and the pinch was felt by the whole family. Therefore, for that loss was devised a way to recompense loss, by asking for whoever took a woman out of the family to replace her with something useable to the family. Thus came the custom of "lobola". A cow to milk for every woman the family loses , even though many of the skills were irreplaceable, this had to do..

To me this was logical. Even though I had never adhered to African customs that much I found the logic inescapable, and began to look for logic in other behaviors that Africans had. I have explained this elsewhere also and will not go into it again.

This was so satisfactory that I was able to go into the rural areas both in South Africa, Transkei and Swaziland and teach the Bahá'í Faith for years. The development in countries like South Africa where the women are beginning to take an active part in public life, do not at all surprise me then. This is an expected historical event in modern times.

Having said that, we find that in our illogical world proofs come nowhere when it comes to a belief, be that belief so superstitious. It is known in our world that several proofs tell us that evolution did occur. Secondly studying Biology we come to the certain truth that all parts in man are in woman. We study and pass this at school. Come time to go to church we now come up with the 'certainty' that woman is a rib of man! Our world accepts this and is reconciled with it…These are the beings who are now prepared to meet being from another planet. It matters not that all beings , be they male or female are born of a female, fertilized by a male, and that male born of woman!

This has given credence to students at one school declaring that" Let us study all this nonsense for better jobs!" Reality seems to stand between that which is proven and that which is believed to be true, all this taken up by beings who are the supreme intelligence of at least this planet who have vowed to find the truth about themselves. In the proof, the first premise is avoided as false; how far can we get and how long will it take to get to the truth? The one who said:"Love thy brother" was crucified, and the one who claimed that the earth was round died a sad death. Today we are asked to unite as a planet, the One declaring this spends life in jail. That is how very ,logical our world is, and we are expected to believe what we hear with heart and soul! So my friend at my college declares that :" Religion is a strong political forum!". I ask :where was politics in ancient times that it should govern our thinking today, and we have just found a definition we use so liberally on all things in creation, creation mind you? Which came first, politics or creation? Which should have precedence in our minds? That we are a creation of we are political tools? Tools for whom, and in whose country when there are no lines demarcating countries made by creation ? It boggles the mind that we all live a few years and yet want to hold time still, in a universe that does not seem to know we exist. Our assurances of continued existence seem to come from religion, for in mine it is declared that in another 1000 years we shall be renewed in religion, again and again *ad infinitum.* We might as well admit that we pray one God Who does not compete with Himself about His servants. Even if we imagine He could, how does the profit accrue, either way : to us to the Creator?

Society and Morals

For a society to subsist, it needs have a moral code as well as social norms. Somewhere in my mind it says that a social code is governed by its moral code. A breakdown in the moral code, may mean the end of a social order as has been seen by history. A moral code is not governed by a political attitude; it is basic to the human. A moral code determines relationships between one individual and another and enhances the subsistence of the political or social order .There are no two truths about what we are. A truth is a truth and remains one and the same throughout. It cannot diversify. It can be seen in its many facets but remains the same. There are no two truths about anything. It remains what it is. There is no reason to be gained by declaring: "my truth and your truth". A reality can only be one reality.

In the confusion of the ideologies I have heard in my life, I cling to the above as being true. For that reason, my concern in life has been the moral order as well as the meaning of the social order. I have avoided the bickering between two or more parities about the same truth which can be determined easily. In my way then , I am no politician. For in politics I would have to go by the group, and I do not quite agree with a mass agreement when the truth can be attained individually using my own mind and determination.

In every society thee are norms and these govern behavior. Where norms depart from reason I have no cause to openly adhere to them. I have lived in African and Western societies and do not see the point in behaving like a sheep by moving in the same direction as everybody. This is the reason I honor the law of my faith that belief must be in accord with reason and science.

Having stated my religion, I have to mention that, while investigating the truth, I have to be independent and not adhere to ideologies of a group ada-mantly. I then acknowledge that I cannot be a member of any political party but that does not mean that I do not think. I do that independently and make my decision about what I shall do independently, guided by my conscience and the law of my faith.

I have met the question of why I am not in politics before and my answerer remains the same that my religion prohibits that because it aims at uniting hu-mankind whether they are from the East or the West into one body called hu-mankind. In my judgment therefore, I cannot afford to be partial.

Because I was involved in my college with all parities it was regarded fair as calling me a "free thinker" but I am not a free thinker, but a Bahá'í. I am committed to the plan of the Bahá'ís of uniting the world into one entity. I shall be involved deeply in society so long as society does not wish me to take a political side but can find good in all.

> **Liberty must, in the end, lead to sedition, whose flames none can quench. Thus warneth you He Who is the Reckoner, the All-Knowing. Know ye that the embodi-ment of liberty and its symbol is the animal. 336 That which beseemeth man is submission unto such restraints as will protect him from his own ignorance, and guard him against the harm of the mischief-maker. Liberty**

causeth man to overstep the bounds of propriety, and to infringe on the dignity of his station. It debaseth him to the level of extreme depravity and wickedness.

(Baha'u'llah, Gleanings from the Writings of Baha'u'llah, p. 335)

O handmaid of the Lord! Speak thou no word of politics; thy task concerneth the life of the soul, for this verily leadeth to man's joy in the world of God. Except to speak well of them, make thou no mention of the earth's kings, and the worldly governments thereof. Rather, confine thine utterance to spreading the blissful tidings of the Kingdom of God, and demonstrating the influence of the Word of God, and the holiness of the Cause of God.

(Abdu'l-Baha, Selections from the Writings of Abdu'l-Baha, p. 92)

Fully aware of the repeated statements of 'Abdu'l-Bahá that universality is of God, Bahá'ís in every land are ready, nay anxious, to associate themselves by word and deed with any association of men which, after careful scrutiny, they feel satisfied is free from every tinge of partisanship and politics and is wholly devoted to the interests of all mankind

(Bahá'í National Assembly of U.K., Principles of Bahai Administration, p. 26)

It is clear from the above quoted statements that Bahá'u'lláh has shifted the focus for humankind , not to center on man as being a citizen of one land, but to that of humankind being citizens of one earth. This statement does open the vista for the human to view the universe as a vast fatherland, beginning with the earth being the home of man. Having done so with one statement, Bahá'ulláh does enlarge the estate of the human by pointing out that all creation if created for man to understand his Creator, and identifies man to be the image of the Deity in essence:

It is not for him to pride himself who loveth his own country, but rather for him who loveth the whole world. The earth is but one country, and mankind its citizens.

(Baha'u'llah, Gleanings from the Writings of Baha'u'llah, p. 250)

> All these names and attributes are applicable to him. Even as He hath said: "Man is My mystery, and I am his mystery." Manifold are the verses that have been repeatedly revealed 178 in all the Heavenly Books and the Holy Scriptures, expressive of this most subtle and lofty theme.
>
> (Baha'u'llah, Gleanings from the Writings of Baha'u'llah, p. 177)

This comes at a time when man is regarded as puny in comparison to the universe in which he dwells. This exalts man to height that may not have been understood before.

27. O SON OF DUST!

> All that is in heaven and earth I have ordained for thee, except the human heart, which I have made the habitation of My beauty and glory; yet thou didst give My home and dwelling to another than Me; and whenever the manifestation of My holiness sought His own abode, a stranger found He there, and, homeless, hastened unto the sanctuary of the Beloved. Notwithstanding I have concealed thy secret and desired not thy shame.
>
> (Baha'u'llah, The Persian Hidden Words)

To argue that man is merely earthbound would then be futile as these statements prove that he is far above having to limit himself to owning apart on a piece of clay called the earth.

The Problem that is No Problem

It is hard to discuss a problem one sees that everyone perceives as not being a problem. Harder again is it to introduce a subject that seems not to be related to present pressing matters, and yet one sees it as an impediment to progress. In such a state, broaching the subject becomes pain as a challenge.

To start with, one tries to consider the question of manhood without a bias, and one finds opposition for it suggests a bias. The one thing one can do then is to plunge in and forget the approval of the public in a quest of finding a truth.

We gave in to machismo and violence to prove strength in on manhood, and I learned it over years but at an initial point of initiation into manhood in Africa. Under very great pain in which I could not manifest in tears, for my face was in a cloak of clay, I learned what a man should be. First of all a man had to grunt in pain and not cry out in pain. A man has to hide his pain by saying " it is all right" quietly. In the course of initiation all thought of a sexual nature have to be abandoned otherwise healing takes longer. Thus meeting women compels a man in initiation to hide both his eyes and his body., for the consequences of sexual desire would set him back many days from healing the wound he nurses. He has to nurse the wound as a woman nurses a baby and remember that. He has not the strength to stand up and urinate but has the option of squatting like his sister. For the first time, he sees his own blood, shed even as his sister does each month. What to take from this is one thing and one thing only 'Never trivialize your woman's problems"! You learn that, you become a man, for you will heal faster. You appreciate consuming even food because for weeks you consume your food with no salt in it, and drink water only with clay in it. This is to help the healing process but also to teach you some appreciation and obedience to law. For, when these rules are broken, one finds that there are physical consequences to your healing. When these consequential physical results appear in you it is known that you did not obey the law and a man has to learn the law of the tribe and nation..

Today, in the Western World this attitude has to be achieved through killing one or two men, the more the better commendable. This proves manhood! The killing of my bother proves I am a man , and I should look forward to this treatment, while upholding a standard of " love thy neighbor as thou lovest thyself". King David was denied building the House of the Lord, for his 'hands were full of blood', and yet we know that he was in turn commanded by the Lord to kill in war. He had no option. If one sees an option then they might as well turn the Holy Books around to please society, where society owes its existence through that Book. Moses had to kill but commanded that one should not, because it was a command from the Lord to set the Law in place in a land where it did not exist. Today we preach love from the Christ and killing from Moses and call ourselves relevant. A book could be written on how we rose from individual to family, to tribe to nation, and how today we should be thinking planetary thoughts instead of tribal thoughts.

The mind shies away from mentioning all this for humanity today regards all this as irrelevant to issues, yet they are a concern. Many a mother has lamented away as the country calls for the assassination of sons through war. It repeats itself over again and we cry and never learn from it. A child finding aloes on the mother's breast learns to eat food. We learn to live and fight again. To be at peace in now considered weakness. Yet each time we use "shalom" and" peace be with you" and "salaam" one to the other. Relevance does not exist! Yet life is a small expanse of and averages eighty years and then we have to depart , leaving the mess behind us , gladly or not. Men of vision who advise otherwise, are considered freaks of nature.

There are countries still where lambara and duvali as well as many other celebrated days are recognized as valid. Take the land of my birth for an example, South Africa. There a divide as well a coerce is visible. Most African men go through the ordeal to become men, and in most cases it concerns the most painful part of the body where nerves congregate. Behold , this custom is available for Jews a, Muslims and Africans in the cultural setting. Look again, Hindus, Muslims , Africans were all concerned in that country with independence. What does that do, but cause a kind of brotherliness in the sector.

The religion of the Christ was extended to Jew and Gentile, and that itself should be noted. One cannot subtract these relationships easily. Throw into that being Bahá'í and you get quite a mixture. Where Muslims and Jew abhor eating pig, Bahai;s eat anything that is scientifically proven to be food. African abandoned being a society of polygamists but Muslims have this as law. Bahá'í's say that the journey through this world and the next , means negotiation by two who are married and growing together. Remnants of being polygamists remain in the African sector for this was in times gone by part and parcel of the culture. I cannot blame some of them in adhering to that , for Jews have adhered to Moses even at the revelation of the Christ, and Christians have stuck to love when nationhood calls; today we are stuck on nationhood when universality seems the way to go. These approaches and differences were meant so that God's creatures should meditate and think why these were and how to cause them to come together into a coalesced whole.. Without a togetherness on the planet we are open to many a danger. If the part cannot manifest the whole, then we remain very much separated. You cannot find a soup that separates its vegetables, nor can you find water if the oxygen does not combine with the hydrogen! What we seem to be intended to be is unknown to us but is valuable as a measure of security and well being of the human race. It is no case of ' the last man standing' will survive but it is a case of " we unite to survive" even as we formed civilizations to do the same. In shaving off parts of humanity you lose much of the original ingredients. We seem to want ourselves to determine the direction of the forces of the universe , and yet we seem to be less than a cart trying to pull the horse! Water manifests a rainbow for in water there are the colors of the rainbow, all it needs is the light to tell this. Any ingredient trying to maintain an independent existence in any union can cause many glitches in the union, for then bias and prejudice are easier to handle. We stand today with the realization that we are a combination of stuff yet we are determined to maintain a difference from the stuff we are. We know that these colors are disappearing in a blend and we are becoming something we do not even know, but we cling to the past in the hope that it will save our future, when all must in the end die and leave the planet, and not by choice, but design. We have to admit that with the forces of time and destiny , as they stand both passionately and otherwise we do not stand a chance, and a coalition as a merging has in the end to prevail to maintain life. We seem to be a jig-saw puzzle that will not come together for the pieces resist. No one ponders over the basic nature of the human and the diversity in color and structure...We take these to be intrinsic points of undeviating difference and call this wisdom and logic. We might ask why and why the human has to tested in faith before some acceptance..

With apartheid in place in South Africa, I listened to Hindu songs every Sunday morning, and had friends who played music from the Qu'ran for me, and yet I remained a Bahá'í. This was my way of relating. It gave me great pleasure to go a Jewish restaurant and order' tahina' a and falafels any day. That did not hurt nor change my innate philosophy, but enhanced it greatly. I can now appreciate Ravi Shankir without looking down upon Abd'ul Bassit and his chants of the Qu'ran. It does me no harm, for I know that the God we all worship is one God and United in Himself. To have given me the test of the present is His choice and desire for me to use the brain He gave me and my ancestors to come out of water and occupy land, a decision which must have been challenging for all he must have known was life in water! To step onto land must have been a taboo.

I fiercely protest that I have a right to think, as a being created to find it's God by thinking and worship once the thought is as established as the truth.

If it is founded on hearsay and no direct experience I cannot and do not wish to attach myself thereto. Thus being Bahá'í means living Bahá'í life as far as I possibly can. For to have a story that is beautiful in a book means nothing until the book is read and experienced.

The aforesaid should not be misconstrued in any way to mean that the author is not aware of the world as he lives in it and has for more than half a century. This is not the prattling of a child or the ignorant but a sharing with those who wish to justly investigate reality and come to some truths.

Unity to the exclusion of certain others has been the norm but does not suffice and has been a cause of much misery for decades. Here I speak as one matured through one world to live in a century where the destruction of war is till the impediment in uniting nations in a true consultative achievement, the goal of planetary existence, which was the initial goal of existence just as nations are formed from separate individuals..

We are aware that the universe is in darkness and all colors of all beings belong to that darkness, and were it not for suns we would not see nor exist. Were it not for the guidance of Wise Beings we would hardly know what to do with ourselves. Let no one man then have feelings of being exalted above other beings on this one single planet, for that would be a lie manifest as the dawning sun. It is true that politics of exclusion have been the rule of the day, but the ferment we leave each time lies under the peace we think we create, and will topple all , given time. Perhaps we do not care about that event since we shall not be in existence anyway, a very true idea of irresponsible living if living it be.

The purpose of the author is to lay a premise and let minds think on it ,and perhaps arrive a a just conclusion. In dismay the reality is the opposite. The darkness of our insides, nay, the darkness of our world, has deluded many minds that blue is the color of the universe , yet all it is, is an optical event which has nothing to do with the true reality of the matter. Because of our fears on non-existence we cling to any small detail that might justify our purpose, be it truth or not, so long as it will give a veneer of truth. That is what we have come to today. Gone is the investigation of reality but now the consolidation of position of supremacy becomes the norm for all. Yet the earth waits to place under a blanket all in the soil with all their perceived trappings, to boot.

Our children face the future and wonder just where we go and how they will live it. We call this all childish nonsense, yet they cry to no avail. We perceive that in all the bizarre actions of the day and do not wonder what the future holds, for soon the game for us will be over. How far shall we have developed then when we leave that life? To what avail will have been all our dear efforts to live a 'worthy' existence that can be emulated by progeny. Are we a lesson? Yes, of foolishness! Many animals live and die for progeny, we live for our miserable selves and call that wisdom.

The races of the world are in many colors and no one ever pauses to wonder why. Are we putting the jig-saw given together ? Can we see the picture of who we really are? If after all that we advance a plan to visit planets where we know not, what shall they call us ? We know to us they are nothing but aliens…and on whose planet? My employer in my country of origin ceased trying to call me dumb but would only limit himself to saying ' foolish' whenever I made a mistake. Where I am today, I am dumb whichever way one looks at it! That is called an advanced civilization and no less!

Let men find peace but before the peace let them come to terms with the diverse necessities of all races occupying the planet.

Finding Peace with the Self

This part is told here because of a consideration that the author has married three times and has never been able to fully give reasons for all changes in his life. He admits that when he married for the first time he had a good life just as he has now in his third marriage. Reasons for such a termination cannot be given only form the angle of one partner. Rather such reasons are better left alone.

The pain of leaving a union is never easy even to those who think they are capable of forgetting a past, for all experiences are engraved on one's conscience and may be reason for future untoward behavior. Again, the less said about the subject, the better.

Needles to say that, after such a termination one is left with many a scar which have to be allowed to heal. Healing them does very little to erase the memory. As T.S. Elliot writes in his book:"Murder in the Cathedral"..that time can 'sweeten' memory to such an extent that the events seem unreal as they fade into time.

The best advice that can be reaped here is that a union of that nature has to be approached seriously and not for play, for it involves two lives and makes them travel a journey that they cannot reverse.

I have a son who is not married and I pray that in some way I find for-giveness in him. I wish he would not hurry but consider deeply concerning the partner he will choose for his journey throughout the Worlds of God....

Rare stories by a pioneer

A Friend to a Fellow Pioneer

Sue Greer, a United States Pioneer in Africa

I met Sue Greer in the mid seventies when I went to Convention at Umgababa with my family. She looked like a very young girl in "North Stars "and jeans. Then it happened that in 1979 I wished to pioneer in the Transkei. Sue was the one requested to assist me look for work and show me around as by then the Transkei was a more or less an independent state in Southern South Africa. With her I visited many a company in search employment in Umtata where she lived. I was at that time housed by Bahá'ís at Owen street in Umtata while she resided at the "Savoy Hotel" in the same town.

She was the first young pioneer from the States that I felt free enough to mention many a subject and with whom I visited the villages in the Transkei, where we searched for the Bahá'í friends. Besides that , Sue was the first Bahá'í to want to share past life back home with fellow Bahá'í in the Transkei.

I could not find work in the Transkei and so had to return to Port Elizabeth. Later I was able to find a visa to enter the United States and marry a citizen in that country. While I looked for employment again, Sue was the first to offer financial assistance while I looked. She supplied this with a generous amount each month until I found an employer.

When I further communicated with her in the States, she then wrote short stories about her youth, and I felt , at the time ,that someday I would tell her story. This is the reason that at this point I share those stories with others, so they learn a cross-cultural friendship that does not pretend. Her stories are told by her in a simple but great style of friendship, and she has agreed that one day I would place them in an appropriate story. As I finish the time of being an administrator in the faith in Africa, I should tell hers , also a fellow administrator .When the Trankie formed its first National Assembly, Sue was elected the Secretary of that Assembly, until the time she returned to the United States. Sue Greer was a Physics teacher at St. John's Boys College in Umtata when I met her and like many scientists was troubled when there was a threatened nuclear fallout somewhere in the States at the time. We are at this point still in touch.

In the picture of the Bahá'í National Assembly of the Transkei, Sue Greer is on the extreme right on the back row. The one of the time she was actually dressed up for a picture.

Stories by Sue Greer

Long ago in the fifties, when the first pioneers arrived in South Africa, one of them from Canada made the prediction that in future pioneers would not only teach Africans but would enter in wedlock with some of them. This notion was communicated to the author by an American pioneer then pioneering in Swaziland. The time for that prediction to become real seems to be our time. For no less than three mixed families between Americans and South Africans have flowered in the last ten to twenty years.

Sue Greer shared her experiences with Africans as is evidenced by her stories in this book. Seldom in the past was this possible. The pioneers concentrated, for the greater part in passing the message of the Cause and refrained from mentioning personal experiences not related to belief. But now the relationship has become closer. In the closing pages of this booklet , Sue Greer shares her stories with the author and is now sharing them with the public. In a way, this makes her not just a teacher but a real person in my thinking. This is no standing on a pedestal to deliver teaching but actual relating in a personal way, a real necessity if one has to find out that the person is imparting what is real to the self to another person. Thus comes the reality of the seriousness of the message. For one gives what is seen as good for the self without asking for anything but belief in exchange. I am proud to admit that the person who made this initial prediction that I mentioned above, was my teacher, Emeric Sala, a pioneer from Canada..

"TOOTI"

Rúhíyyih Khánum has a parrot named Tooti. She lives in a cage, gets taken everywhere (just about), and can say a number of things, each in the voice of the person from whom it was learned. She says "Alláh-u-Abhá" three different ways: The right way (Persian, with the accent on the -há), the wrong way, and a very low, gruff, Persian way. The wrong way was picked up from an American and Rúhíyyih Khánum has never quite forgiven him for marring Tooti's pronunciation. "Alláh-u-Abhá" with the accent on the Ab-, rhyming with "cab".

Dear me, this parrot is something. In Swaziland we heard her say "Alláh-u-Abhá" the low, gruff way and then follow it with the most lewd laughter you ever heard. This went on throughout the only, Mbabane Local

Spiritual Assembly meeting we'd had since I'd been here when all nine members were present.

Violette said she used to try to get the parrot to say her name, but usually Tooti would say Rúhíyyih Khánum's name instead. Then, one day when Violette was coaxing Tooti to say 'Violette', Tooti came out with, "Rabbani African Safari"!

She also says "sweetheart" in Violette's voice. This gave Shidan Fathe-Aazam, our Board of Counsellors member, quite a scare one evening in a motel, as he was preparing for his beauty rest.... Add to these a few other terse sayings and a blood-curdling screech, dangling from the perch by one foot while flapping.

Tooti was the only advance warning I had that I was about the meet 'Amatu'l-Bahá Rúhíyyih Khánum, though at the time she really wasn't a proper warning, since I had not yet met her, and didn't know whose she was—another case in miniature of one of God's heralds needing perhaps its own herald? I had stopped by Mae McClinton's flat in Manzini, which is near Auxiliary Board Member Helen Wilks' flat, to ask Mae if she'd planned on bringing anyone to our youth conference which was coming up. I had with me Jeff Norman, an American youth staying in Swaziland to help the teaching work, Dr. M. Ahmadi, one of several new pioneers from Persia, and a Swazi youth, Elliot Hlatshwayo.

As we pulled up in front, I saw Counsellor Bahiyyih Ford's V.W. parked outside. I wasn't surprised because Rúhíyyih Khánum was expected the the next day or the next. I didn't consciously think about the possiblility of her having already arrived, and I didn't see the Land Rover which was parked in back, and it didn't enter my mind that the arrangement was for Rúhíyyih Khánum and Violette to stay at Mae's while Mae and Bahiyyih stayed down at Helen's. All this is the truth. However I may have suffered from a mental block. The mental block only made it more of a sudden shock to me than if I had been completely unprepared!

We found the door of the flat open, and a cage just outside the door with what looked to me like a gray little old woman wrapped in a shawl, sitting (rather than perching) inside, without moving or making a sound. How was I to know? I thought vaguely, "Where did Mae get this?"

I knocked briskly on the open door, and an unfamiliar voice said, "Just a mi-nute!"

I was trying to place this voice, not Mae's; Bahíyyih's?—not exactly, when up walked Violette.

I took a couple of gulps of air as I tried to pull myself together after having my mental block cracked.

Violette is a lovely person. She just smiled sweetly and greeted us. Rúhíyyih <u>Kh</u>ánum came strolling up looking formidable in a friendly way. She greeted us and asked who we were, and I made an attempt at introducing. Then she invited us in! Up until this time I'd been making the excuse that we had just stopped by to see Mae, and we'd just run along now, down to Helen's and we didn't mean to surprise them like this (ha!) and so on. She invited us in. Now, if I hadn't expected to meet Rúhíyyih <u>Kh</u>ánum that day, much less had I expected to be invited in. They had obviously just arrived and were unpacking. There was wreckage all over the place. This of course didn't need an explanation, but they explained that they had to be prepared for every climate and temperature, as well as a variety of occasions, each involving its own protocol, and after three years of travelling, they'd accumulated quite a pile, even though they always sent a lot "home" and gave a lot away.

With all this chit-chat my heart rate began to slow down a little. Violette put the kettle on. Rúhíyyih <u>Kh</u>ánum asked if we would like tea and I said I thought we should be going and Rúhíyyih <u>Kh</u>ánum said that Dr. Ahmadi wanted some tea. He hadn't said so in my hearing, but he certainly didn't deny it. So, we stayed.

The kettle took a long time to boil, bless it. We started talking about what kind of gas stove Mae had in her kitchen, whether the gas is under pressure, whether it comes out through a jet, whether this makes or would make it faster or not. The discussion was inconclusive.

Rúhíyyih <u>Kh</u>ánum speaks Persian (Farsi) beautifully. I suppose she speaks it well, too, but beautifully. Now and then she would turn to Dr. Ahmadi and say a few words to him in his native language. It was so melodious. Once she said, in English, that it was very good that he was here, in Swaziland. "Now stay. Don't get discouraged." She spoke to Elliot, and asked if he were a Swazi. When he replied that he was, she said, "Good".

Rúhíyyih <u>Kh</u>ánum asked me how long I had been in Swaziland, and whether I could speak Swazi yet: "You should really learn it." On sheer inspiration I said, "I'm learning it 'kangcani' (a little)." Heh-heh. The word 'kangcani' has the letter 'c' in it, a click sound. Of course it's true, I am learning the language a little, but I was glad to have a little proof.

Rúhíyyih Khánum said many things of interest, whether spiritual, informative or mundane, it was all interesting to me, but I can't remember much. I just remember her.

It was during that little informal tea party that I heard all about Tooti, and all her marvelous powers. We didn't hear anything out of her all during the time we were there, except an occasional exclamation when a motor vehicle went by. It was explained to us that Tooti was in the habit of mimicking the hooters of cars because of all her road travelling. The Rabbani African Safari often met with motorists who used their hooters whenever they encountered another vehicle, and often the Land Rover would sound off, too. In fact, you may be able to see a connection between Tooti's name and this little habit of hers.

"T O O T - T O O T ! !"

A Prize Chicken

My mother, Martha Lomax Greer, was formidable. She was extremely intelligent, an independent thinker. She was artistic, painted portraits and murals in oils. It is thanks to her that I came to appreciate classical music, and other music of high quality, such as Jellyroll Morton and Mahalia Jackson. She never tried to teach me to appreciate the arts, but I learned to value her views as they were expressed in long evening conversations with her friends who would come to visit. They drank wine and talked heatedly on any and all subjects. Any subject was treated earnestly, as long as it was not trivial. I don't remember my mother ever saying anything that wasn't sincere and worth hearing. She also tried her hand at writing stories, and her language usage was perfect. In addition to exposure to fine arts, thanks to my mother, I was introduced to literature and philosophy.

She was agnostic, not into religion at all, but I never heard her criticize or disrespect any religion—I remember her remarking about some matter that had come up, saying with a sense of irony, "It's like arguing with God. Even when you're right, you're wrong." I remember one time we were visited by some Jehovah's Witnesses. I didn't hear everything that was said, but, eventually, they said, with some disappointment and concern, "But ma'am, do you mean you don't even believe in God?" She answered, simply, "I don't know about that, but I guess I don't like Him very much." They left post haste. She appreciated people's religious background as part of their culture.

What she would not tolerate was any form of injustice.

I remember some stories and incidents relating to her sense of justice. She related how, as she was growing up in North Carolina, she had a nanny, of African American background, of course, named Emma, if I remember correctly. As she reached adolescence, one day Emma started addressing her as "Miss Marcy" instead of just "Marcy". She was surprised and asked why she was now being addressed with this title, "Miss". Emma replied something like, "Oh, Miss Marcy, you the craziest thing!" Like, this was something that should not have to be asked. However, from this point on she addressed Emma as "Miss Emma". I remember another incident in her later life she related to me. She habitually visited a local grocery store in San Jose, California, where she was used to seeing an African American woman at the cash register. One day, this person wasn't there. She enquired of the new clerk where the woman was. The clerk replied something like, "Oh, she doesn't work here anymore. She was, you know, taking advantage of her color." My mother straightaway replied to the clerk, "Oh, and we don't?" As I was growing up, I learned in no uncertain terms that race prejudice was deeply and morally wrong.

All this is in an effort to convey the immense respect I have always had for my mother. I never regarded her as playful, though she had a great sense of humor. I remember she told how, once, when my sister and I were little, we were all visiting with some other people. The kids were doing something that required reading. One of the kids interrupted the adults to ask "What does y-e-s spell?" and someone replied, of course, "It spells 'yes'!" A few minutes later, the child asked "What does Eee-y-e-s spell?" The adults looked at each other in perplexity, mumbling to each other, "There's no such word as eee-y-e-s." They asked the child to show them the word. "Eyes." Oh, well.

It was with some surprise that, when I was in my forties, my mother related to me a story from her own childhood. But first, a little background on her parents. Her father, Robert Lomax, I knew from earlier descriptions, though I have no memory of him myself, was honest to a fault, if such a thing is possible. It was inconceivable that he would ever cheat anyone. The townspeople all knew this. My grandmother, Mary Lomax, who was loved and known as "Mom" by everyone, was, while not dishonest, not very careful about keeping track of her check-writing. It was fairly commonplace for her to, unknowingly, write a check that wasn't covered by her account. The locals never complained or objected. They simply held the check and notified her husband of the shortage, which he would immediately attend to. Robert was also very stoic in his outlook. My mother once related a story about him. He owned a couple of duplexes in the town. One day, he had them inspected for pests. The inspector told him the bad news, that one of the buildings was badly infected with termites. Robert asked what the result would be if he did nothing about it. The inspector told him it would not be good. Gradually, the whole structure would weaken. Robert knew this, but, he asked just how long it would take. When the inspector replied, Robert just said, "Oh, well, I'll be gone by then." Now, back to my mother's tall tale.

One ho-hum day, a pickup truck went past the Lomax's house, and a crate fell off the back. The truck didn't stop, and was unknown to any of the locals. Robert collected the crate, which contained one chicken. He had not seen the license plate on the truck, and was sorely perplexed about what to do. He talked about it quite a bit. This was not his chicken, and he should return it to its owner. How to locate the owner… After mulling it over for a few days, he allowed "Mom" Lomax to use the chicken for a nice meal—she was quite used to killing her own chickens. My mother, in her early teens, saw an opportunity she could not pass up.

She went to a neighbor's house and shared her idea. The neighbor phoned her father, trying to mask his voice, and it went something like this—with my mom eves-dropping on her dad's end:

> **The neighbor:** "Hello. Is this Mr. Robert Lomax?"
> Robert, looking a bit puzzled, said, "Yes".
> **The neighbor:** Mr. Lomax, I'm Mr. Something-or-other from New York. I heard you have a chicken that fell off my truck. I'm so glad to hear that. Please hang on to her and I'll come collect her."
> **Robert:** Oh. Mr. Something-or-other…uh… Well, I tried really hard to find out who the chicken belonged to, but since you're from New York, nobody knew. There wasn't any way for me to track you down. We…uh…we ate the chicken yesterday evening. I guess I'll just have to reimburse you for the cost."
> **The neighbor:** What?! You ate her? Mr. Lomax, that was a prize breeding hen I had just acquired for a pretty penny! I'm going to have to come down there so we can settle this.

Mr. Lomax was very disturbed. He really couldn't afford to pay for a prize chicken, and he had tried, as he said, to find the owner. He didn't think he deserved to be in such a position. At the same time, he was a very honest man, and could not be easy with the idea that he had somehow taken advantage of this man's loss. My mother listened with great interest.

Mr. Lomax, not at all sure of what he should do, went over to the neighbor's house to seek his advice. The neighbor was working in his yard, bent over the flower bed. As Mr. Lomax related what had happened, the neighbor said nothing, just bent lower so Mr. Lomax wouldn't see his face. He was chuckling, but also very nervous, thinking it would not be good for him to expose his complicity. My mother was observing all this with utter delight. She said he mumbled about this for days, wondering when Mr. Something-or-other would turn up and demand payment.

So, I, in my forties, heard this tale from my respected mother. I was really amazed. This was a side of her I had really, really never seen. After a good laugh, I asked her, "What did he say when you finally told him what happened?" "Oh, I never told him!" she replied. So, I could only say, "You let the poor man go to his grave thinking the matter of the prize chicken was unresolved? Oh, dear!"

A Border Crossing

When I was in Transkei, in the early eighties, I had a friend, Thozamile Nomvete, who worked for the Ministry of Education. He needed to make a trip to Lesotho to visit their education department. He had some lab equipment to show them. I had not been to Lesotho for a long time, and offered to take him. I had a nice brown VW Beetle with super-sized wheels. It would take most of a day to get from Umtata to Maseru, Lesotho.

We reached the South African border at Queenstown, Transkei, at about noon. We stood in line, briefly, I showed my U.S. passport, and Thozi showed his papers. I felt a little uneasy, as I usually did when entering South Africa. (Transkei, which was an "independent homeland" of South Africa, did not live under apartheid. It was regarded as an independent country by South Africa, but was not recognized as such by any other country with the exception of, I believe, Italy.) Passing through the border, I briefly registered the fact that I was wearing a "Mankind is One" button on my jacket. I also recalled belatedly, that in South Africa, it was illegal for Thozi and me to travel together, with me driving and he in the front passenger seat. The border guards had not made any comment, so I dismissed it from my mind.

We stopped, briefly, at a roadside convenience store/café in some small town who's name I don't remember, just to pick up some snacks. I noticed many people looking at us, and realized they were taken aback by Thozi and me arriving at the same time. Maybe Thozi wasn't even supposed to go inside. It was like the deep south of the U.S. in, oh, the late sixties. It crossed my mind, that, all the sanctions the U.S. cooked up to pressure South Africa into doing away with apartheid could never be as effective as simply doing away with race prejudice in the U.S. As the writings say, "Let deeds, not words, be your adorning."

Eventually, at around four in the afternoon, we reached the South African border at Maseru. There was nobody else in line. I looked through the window, as saw an official who appeared to be entertaining himself by kicking a bottle cap against the wall—soccer is a favorite sport in the region. I thought, "Boy, these guys are bored."

Instead of simply passing us through to the Lesotho side, the officials decided to inspect my vehicle. Behind the back seat, they found a hand-made poster for some Bahá'í event, probably proclaiming the oneness of mankind, some other Bahá'í stuff, books and such, from an event that had happened long ago—whoever cleans out a car, anyway?— and a few boxes containing Thozi's lab equipment: Ehrlenmeyer flasks, funnels, distillation apparatus and such. The guards told us we would have to come inside for a moment. We were ushered into an empty interior waiting room. Thozi and I were having the same thoughts, but said nothing. We each took a seat on opposite sides of the room. We didn't speak to each other. I was thinking, they probably think we're making bombs or something. This could be bad. I was also thinking the Bahá'ís in South Africa would not be happy about our indiscretion, and I could end up getting booted out of Transkei. Also, if I was in this kind of trouble, what kind of trouble was Thozi in? That was scary. We sat for an hour or so, not saying anything, just waiting.

Finally, Thozi started reciting the Tablet of Ahmad from memory: "He is the King, the All-Knowing, the Wise! Lo, the Nightingale of Paradise singeth upon the twigs of the Tree of Eternity, with holy and sweet melodies...." He recited the whole thing, beautifully, and I was very moved.

At last, the guards came and got us and told us we were free to go. With much relief, but no comment, we proceeded to the Lesotho side of the border, which we found was closed for the evening. We sat on a bench and waited, and, at last, some Lesotho officials arrived and passed us through.

We supposed that the South Africans had spent some time doing background checks on us—or maybe they wanted to hear what we said to each other, and were disappointed when we didn't say anything in the waiting room—or, perhaps they were even more bored than I thought.

We arrived at the home of some Bahá'ís at around 5:30 or 6:00 P.M. There were some other friends there, and they said they had been concerned about our late arrival, and had said some prayers for our safety.

I drove home the next day by myself and had another adventure—nothing "official" about this one. I was passing over the Drakensburgs around sunset. It was raining and there was very heavy fog. These conditions have a way of distorting the whole outlook. I became worried that I might have made a wrong turn. This part of the trip was on a dirt road. In the fog, I clung to the left side of the road, just to see the edge and know what direction to take. At some point there was a rough exit from the road, and I unknowingly followed it. I found myself in a little camping area with tents and traffic buoys. It was a work site for some men who were doing work on the road. All I could do was turn around and head back. I met up with the road, and continued on my way, but I was a little worried about running out of petrol. The petrol stations had limited hours and I hadn't intended to wander all over the place! I wasn't even a hundred percent sure I was on the road I intended to be on. It seemed like it was taking forever. The fog does that. Anyway, no problem, I finally made it back to the tarmac and was back in Umtata by half-past-eight in the evening. I would have sworn it was at least midnight.

The Half-Life of Palmolive

I went to Cheyenne with Marge to help her prepare a house she owned for rental or sale. We took Ripley, my black-and tan dachshund, and a few supplies, like my kitchen broom and dustpan, an electric kettle, tea and mugs, some overnight stuff. Marge's dad, Bill was to meet us in Cheyenne, driving all the way up from Santa Fe, to lend his help. We reached Cheyenne at about 5:00 in the afternoon, and were a little worried because we were supposed to meet Bill there at about 4:00.

When we got there, we saw Bill's car, but he didn't have a key to the house, so we wondered where he was. It wasn't long before he ambled over from the neighbor's house, where he had been visiting while waiting for us. Bill was very sociable, and easily made friends with the neighbors whom he had never met. He seemed undisturbed by our late arrival, even though his journey was at least twice a long.

I hadn't met Bill, and I was interested to see what Marge's dad was like. Bill was in his 80's, very slight of build, and slim, very quiet of speech and unassuming, but interested in his surroundings. When he did say something, it was usually an understatement. He had also brought his German shepherd, so Ripley was very happy.

The outside of the house was quite a mess. The grass had not been cut and there were cinderblocks and bits and pieces of various nondescript items scattered about. The back yard was also full of detritus, including bits of lumber of all kinds.

The front door had some small glass panes at about eye-level. One of the panes was splintered, and had tape stuck over it. I had seen this house once before while Marge's daughter was living there, and knew it was an unholy mess inside. I wondered how Bill would react when he saw it.

We went inside. I recalled the general layout of the house. To the left was the kitchen. Ahead, and to the right was the living room. To the right of the living room was a bathroom and bedrooms. There was a hallway behind the far wall of the living room that connected the kitchen with the bedrooms. It also had a stairway down to a lower level. There was also a large family room on the far side of the kitchen, which had been converted from a garage.

As we entered, we stood transfixed and scanned around us. All but a few pieces of left-over furniture were gone. There were a straight back chair and a stool in the kitchen. The dishwasher was in the middle of the floor there. There was a bare twin-sized mattress on the floor of the living room. Every surface was coated with unidentifiable, crusted dirt. One wondered whether it was not a health hazard to spend time in this place. The living room wall facing the front door had been hand painted with a crude landscape mural.

I wondered what Marge's dad was thinking as he saw all this. He had provided the funds for Marge to buy this house a few years back. Bill stood in place and glanced around. Finally, he said, softly, "I'm steamed".

We immediately discovered another problem facing us. The power had been switched off because the dwellers had not paid the power bill. Fortunately, the power was restored without much difficulty. Bill had brought tools and equipment to work on the place, and we carried everything inside. Bill was going to camp out in the house. Luckily, we found box springs for the twin mattress in a room downstairs, and brought it up. Bill would use this setup to sleep on. Marge and I were planning to stay at a Motel 6. (This worked out really well. It was Superbowl weekend and the motel room had a pretty good TV. The three of us, Marge, Bill and I watched the game propped up in a row on one of the queen-sized beds—a nice bit of downtime.)

There was such an incredible amount of work to be done, we didn't sit down and make a plan—anyway, there were not enough seats for that! We just wanted to get as much done as we could in a weekend. Bill started in the kitchen. There was nothing right in the kitchen. The cupboards were missing shelves. There was a place for the dishwasher, but it didn't fit. The counters and the gas stove were crusted and layered with, what? Not just dirt. It was a strange and ominous cemented chemical-and-dirt mixture. The bottom drawer of the stove was missing—it was found later. Bill said little to nothing. He went about measuring, disappeared for a few minutes, returned, apparently from the back yard, with a few pieces of wood he had found, got out his power saw—yes, power saw. I was at first rather nervous seeing him wield this saw, with not even a work bench, just a small stool for support. Bill had a very slight tremor, and seeing him with that saw was a bit scary. I soon noticed, however, that when he took hold of the saw and the piece of wood, the tremor stopped, and he seemed to have little difficulty with it. He went about mending the cupboards and anything else he came across.

Meanwhile, we had a look at the general condition of the place. Hard to believe it had been occupied only a week or so ago. The heating vents in the floor were almost blocked with sticky masses of hair and dirt. In the family room, there was a ceiling fan, with something hanging off the blades. There was what appeared to be, perhaps, a smudge of peanut butter on the ceiling. The bathroom looked as if it would have to have all new plumbing. The sink and toilet were rust-stained and crusted with what was found everywhere. They were rather old anyway, and I didn't see how they could be cleaned up enough to not require replacement.

We all set about working on something—Bill, of course had been busy all this time in the kitchen. I don't know exactly what Marge was doing. I had a go at the stove and counters in the kitchen. I had never realized just how useful an Exacto knife could be. It was not possible to remove the grime from the counters with a sponge, or even S.O.S. It had to be scraped off. Later, to my amazement, Bill took an Exacto knife to the sink and toilet in the bathroom. He managed to scrape everything off, leaving them looking old, but clean and white, with no sign of what they had been like. Every couple of hours, Bill would go and lie down on the mattress and box springs in the living room, for about twenty minutes. Then, he would get up and go right back to work, as if this was the kind of thing he did every day for a living. Actually, he was in banking.

Our work was interrupted by having a bite to eat and retiring for the night. In the morning, Marge and I went back to the house, I got orders from everyone for something for breakfast from the MacDonalds which was only a couple of blocks away. When I drove up to the window at MacDonalds, I heard the order clerk speaking into his microphone with what sounded like a Cape Town, South African accent. I was breathless with excitement, and asked him where he was from. Yes!!! Cape Town! I was so excited I drove ahead after paying, and neglected to collect the food order at the next window! I circled around the parking lot and went back and retrieved it. No harm.

Marge and I spent some time in the family room, Marge feeding flammable trash into the fireplace. Her dad had suggested this as a way to dispose of some of the trash. I got up on a ladder and went about removing a big screw from the wall. I had a large Phillips screw driver in hand for this purpose. Unfortunately, I lost my balance and fell off the ladder. Luckily, I was only a couple of steps up, and fell squarely on my back—not on the screwdriver—and didn't suffer any harm, just a bit of a fright. Later, Marge had a mishap feeding the fire in the fireplace. Some burning cardboard fell out! She grabbed the first thing she could find, my broom, and shoved it back into the fireplace. The broom caught fire, but no major harm was done. I told Marge jokingly that she should have let it burn, the whole house, and she could have collected the insurance. She mentioned that to her dad. He didn't say anything, but he seemed to be considering the idea.

The last day we were there, Bill and Marge were downstairs, showing the house to some neighbors who thought they might be interested in buying it. I was upstairs, and noticed the dishwasher was running—Bill had got it working and fitted into its intended location. I noticed, though, that there were suds coming out around the edges of the door, quite a few suds. I called down-stairs to alert Bill and company. They came up, and opened the dishwasher. It was completely filled with foam, bee-bee sized bubbles in a huge mass. Bill looked chagrined. He said he hadn't found any dishwasher detergent, and had substituted regular Palmolive. He didn't think it would really matter. I looked at this mountain of bubbles, which were slowly popping, a few at a time. I said, "I wonder what the half-life of Palmolive is."

That's about all I recall from this wonderful experience. On a second trip, Nobuki, a friend of mine from work, and Marge and I painted the interior and did some more cleaning. The house got rented, and, eventually, it even sold—a happy ending.

Waiting for a Pass<ing>

My dad, Isaac G. Greer, Jr., was a great guy, very intelligent and empathetic. He came from an interesting background. His father was a highly respected person, a staunch and dedicated Baptist who grew up in the Blue Ridge Moun-tains, and settled in Chapel Hill, N. C. He recorded authentic folk songs for the Library of Congress, with my grandmother, Willie Spainhour accompa-nying him on a zither, or maybe it was a dulcimer.. He was involved with char-itable enterprises (founded an orphanage, I believe), had an honorary doctorate from a N.C. university, and, reportedly, at some stage was a gubernatorial can-didate in North Carolina. I have a set of very finely crafted wooden spoons carved by him that I am very proud of.

Dad made a career in the Air Force. (Thanks to the Air Force, we spent three years in England when I was a child and I started school in an English "public" school—what we would call a private school—named "Long Cren-don School" in Sheringham, Norfolk County.) After WWII ended, Dad had tried his hand in private industry, at the Broyhill furniture company in N.C., but, like me, he couldn't make it in the shark pond, as I like to put it, and reentered the Air Force for a career. After we returned from England, Dad was stationed in northern California, and that's where I grew up. My mom and dad didn't get along very well, although they didn't argue in front of Marcy, my sister (two years older), and me. Their backgrounds were so dif-ferent that I eventually had to consider the idea that the only way they ended up married was that they were never sober long enough to really get to know each other. (Of course, that was the end of World War II. Their generation survived by drinking.) Compared to some you hear about, they were the best parents ever.

Mom and Dad were divorced in 1963. I stayed with my mom in California, and found the Bahá'í faith that same year, and, what a year! Marcy got married a year later. (We all got something great except Mom.) Dad was in Duluth, Minnesota, where he was currently serving, and met and married my step-mother, Agnes. Her son, Charlie, eventually adopted "Greer" as his surname. Dad finally transferred to Colorado Springs, where he retired as the most senior noncommissioned officer they have, a senior chief master sergeant, or something. In other words, he was one of the people who ran the Air Force.

In June of 1998, I was working as a civil servant for NOAA, in Boulder, Colorado. I received a phone call telling me my dad, who had lung cancer at that time, was in very poor condition. (Dad had been a smoker up until about ten years prior. He smoked Camels. In the eighties, he tried to quit, using Nic-orette gum, but that didn't really work, and he went back to smoking heavily, this time cigars!) I took leave from my job and drove down to the Springs to see him in the hospital. I had just recently bought a used 1997 Toyota Corolla that was really not bad to drive on the freeway. At the hospital, they were get-ting ready to transfer Dad to an ambulance to drive him home. I followed, a bit disappointed that Dad couldn't see my new car. Marcy, my sister, also came from North Carolina, and Charlie and his wife Sandra came from Connecticut, where Charlie was a professor at Yale.

A hospital bed was set up for Dad in the family room. The home was a split-level, with kitchen and living room on the ground floor, a family room down a few stairs, and bedrooms and baths up a few stairs, over the family room. We discussed who would stay in which room. There were two spare bedrooms. The one I usually stayed in had just a twin bed. Agnes stayed in the master bedroom. Charlie and Sandy stayed in the other spare bedroom upstairs. Marcy volunteered to sleep on the sofa in the family room with Dad—she was the only one who had the guts to do that. Charlie's a fine per-son, mild mannered and well-spoken, and smart enough to be a professor of neurology at Yale University. He holds inside a considerable burden of stress. Sandy said he actually knocked a table lamp on the floor while having some kind of dream one night. He would have been a poor choice for the person to sleep on the sofa downstairs with Dad. There really were no other candidates.

We were there for a week or so, and some interesting things transpired. I got kind of creeped out one day, hearing a song playing through my head: "You gotta know when to hold 'em, know when to fold 'em .... You never count your money, when you're sitting at the table. There'll be time enough for counting when the dealing's done!" (Dad and Agnes often played poker at home with friends—a social occasion. Winnings were on the order of $5.) Later that day, I went down to see Dad. He was awake, and, though I hadn't said anything, he said to me "You'd better go ahead and start the game without me." His metaphor, not mine, but, gosh!

One morning, Marcy and I and Charlie and Sandy were in the kitchen looking for coffee or tea, and Marcy related a visit with Dad the previous night. She woke up in the middle of the night and got up to check on Dad. She walked over the the bed in the pitch dark, banged her leg on some protrusion on the bed, and said under her breath "Ouch!" To her surprise, Dad heard her and said "Ooooh, that must have hurt." Marcy noticed Dad's hospital bed was raised up at both ends! She said to him: "Dad, mmm, did you want to put your bed in that 'taco' formation?" He said, "Not really." She said, "OK, I'll fix it."

We cracked up when she told us this. All of us were starting to feel a bit strained, not knowing how long it would be. Not that we would want to speed things up, but, we were really in suspense, away from our homes and work, and waiting an indeterminate amount of time for Dad to go. A little comic relief was very welcome, indeed.

A few days later, it was late June, and getting pretty hot. Neighbors and friends had brought all kinds of snacks and treats for us, and they were in the refrigerator. The fridge was absolutely crammed full. If you opened it, you had to be careful or you might have a small avalanche on your hands. Then, ominously, the fridge started making a humming sound. We thought, this could be a real pain if the fridge quits now, in the middle of everything that's going on. Charlie called a technician to come and inspect the fridge.

Later, or maybe the next day, the Lutheran minister and his assistant came, to visit Dad and give him last rites. They were down in the family room, and the technician came to inspect the fridge. Agnes was downstairs with Dad and the minister. Meanwhile, the rest of us went into the kitchen to see what the story was with the fridge. The technician tooled around for awhile, and finally started to put his equipment back in his bag. We asked hime what he had found. He answered something like: "Well, it's not the compressor. It could go on like this for a couple of months, or it could just quit tomorrow. No way to tell." We all had the same look on our faces, puzzled and a little disturbed. I think everyone had the same thought, "This is the fridge we're talking about, right?"

After the technician left, the minister and his assistant, a robust and friendly woman, came up to the living room to visit. He offered the kind of sympathy and comfort you would expect. While he was speaking to Agnes, his assistant said to us, with a big smile: "Before I did this, I used to work at hospice. I saw a number of cases like your father's, and, really, some of them went on like that for weeks or months!"

We were thoughtful for a moment after she and the minister left. I was thinking maybe we should send for Kevorkian. Finally, Charlie said softly, "I know what to do. I can administer morphine. Whatever's necessary." It was amusing, and not so amusing.

I had never known about hospice, or I thought it was just another name for a nursing home. A light dawned. All my life, I had never seen anyone in America even admit there was such a thing as death. We were all supposed to live forever. In movies: "I thought I was going to die. Thank goodness you're all right. You're not going to die." One wondered how on earth Americans could ever deal with the complicated issues of the death of a loved one. Now it was clear. We have an organization that takes care of it, so we don't have to do much or think much about it: Hospice. Phew! What a relief! Okay, I know, that's an over-simplification.

That night, I stayed up late in my room and said 500 "Remover of Difficulties", the short Bahá'í prayer, not exactly intended for this purpose, but, for me this was a difficulty. "Is there any Remover of difficulties save God? Say: Praised be God! He is God! All are His servants and all abide by His bidding!" I don't remember if it was the next morning or a day or so later, I woke to learn that Dad was, apparently, breathing his last. We all gathered around his bed, and soon he stopped breathing. This was bad, but also good, and I'll leave it at that.

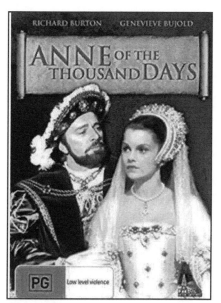

How Sue Greer found the Bahá'í Faith

The author concludes Sue's stories with how she found the Bahá'í Faith, a story she tells in her own words:

My Quest

When I was about fifteen years of age, I was a very serious person. I read and studied lots of things. I spent a whole summer reading Tolstoy's "War and Peace". I was a great admirer of Socrates and Beethoven. One question really puzzled me: Is there a God?

This seemed to be the most significant question. I was not brought up as a Christian, though as a child I had been to an Episcopal or Anglican church service a few times. My mother was agnostic, and an independent thinker. I never knew what my father thought. He was away at work most of the time. I never thought about asking my mother for an answer to my question. I would only get her opinion.

So, how could I find an answer to my question? Maybe I could ask God— if He existed—to give me a sign. Like, ask Him to make that cup fall off the table. No, I thought. If the cup fell off the table, I would come up with another reason why it happened. If it didn't fall off the table, it wouldn't prove anything.

Maybe I should try reading the Bible. I didn't really think it would help me. I knew it was very old, many people read it and believed it was from God, but many people didn't. It did not seem very promising as a real solution to my dilemma.

Finally, I asked God, if He existed, to help me find the answer. As a proof of my sincerity, I decided to read the Bible. I did this secretly, as I didn't want to have to explain this matter to my dear mother.

I read through the first few books of the Old Testament very carefully. Still, it read like any other book, to me. No answers.

One night, around 11:00 P.M., I went for a walk up the street where I lived. It was on Gustafson Court, in Novato, California. There was a street called Gertrude Lane running parallel to this street. I walked to the end of our street, turned left, and continued. It was a beautiful night. Our neighborhood was called "Walnut Park", and was quite open, surrounded by fields and trees. I should mention that I had never taken a walk like this before.

To my surprise, I met a neighbor from down the other end of Gustafson Court, a girl a few years older than me. She was walking home from visiting someone on Gertrude Lane. She told me that there was a family there who said that God had sent a new messenger to mankind. She mentioned the main principles of the Baha'i Faith, including the oneness of mankind, all the main religions came from one God, revealed progressively, the equality of men and women, the harmony of science and religion, and so forth.

I was quite exhilarated to learn about this. And, to make things easier, I had met the family she mentioned many years before, when we had first moved to Novato, and Walnut Park was a new neighborhood with few occupants. I must have been about eight years old. I remembered the woman, Phoebe Babo, because when we met her, it was in her yard that I stepped on a bee and got stung!

So, the next day, I walked over to the Babos' house and knocked on the door. I asked about this new religion, and I remember the first thing they gave me was a little booklet called "Communion with God". It had a few prayers. I also acquired a book called "Baha'u'llah and the New Era". I stayed up all night reading it.

I had my answer!

Considerations and Musings of Author

In considering my whole life as it stands today, I come to realize that the most important and crucial years of my life, were the times of the formulation, as I would term it, of my life principles, between the ages of fifteen and twenty five.

When I became a Bahá'í in 1962 I had much romanticism as to what life was, but soon one has to come to the realization of what one's life actually entails or involves. This is not dependent of praise or being known by others as one type of person or another, but an internal self realization which none can take from one, once that is established. No matter how much the world tries , once that state of that realization is reached life takes on a new meaning. From that point on, activities become only a manifestation of the thinking of the inner person, a state that has nothing to do with one's station in life, but has to do with what one is prepared to do to make manifest the feelings and decisions of one's conscience.

When I left home for college in 1963 my spiritual mother, Rosemary Sala, made the statement: " Go out and find yourself" for she realized that, with the kind of thinking prevalent in me and society at the time, she could not find me for myself, I had to do that on my own. The result of finding some of the norms of society gave me the impression that I was on my own, and that meant I would rebel against all norms, before I could relate logically to them. First I would have to find out how any change in my social or moral behavior impacted on society, and how I could integrate what society had into a reality, not for society, but for myself as a living being. It came to mind that without that realization I might has well stay outside of all norms and be more or less a deviant.

Given the norms Africans hold so dear, that stance of deviating from norm would mean being outside of society. That state of being outside I took up until it became a necessity to engage society in the real teaching of the Cause of Bahá'u'lláh. This did not come easily, and had to involve a n assessment of what I had in my life and what society among the Africans and the Whites in the country had. This was because, being outside of African norms had placed me in a queer position of being completely defenseless. That situation would not have to pertain for one aiming at raising a family, for family would require engaging the larger planes of society.

That integration , painful and confusing as it was in creating my own kind of person who believes in the wider range of ideas of internationalism, did not come easily. Having achieved that and having undergone much that was un-pleasant in doing that, it is unlikely I would then give in to a reversal of ideas as that would entail a complete idea of not being me at all. As it stands I now am committed to being a world citizen and not a citizen of any particular coun-try, and that state will pertain while I endeavor to find more devout adherents to the Cause of Bahá'u'lláh, for , in this life I see it as the only course worth even committing to death for. That is exactly where I stand today, knowing very well that this does not reflect on the story of my youth but rather the re-sultant issue thereof. That practically brings the reality of the story into life, for as I write I stand in my present and not the researcher in my past, though research needs pertain as I go forwards, for one's life necessitates a backward and forward movement as one reflects on deeds to see how some could have been accomplished to the best of lasting gain for the individual, and how les-sons gained could be a teaching for others endeavoring to take the same path..

Come the realization:

Whether one is a fool or a genius, one has to come to the conclusion that this life is progressive and cannot be delimited or controlled .Occurrences come to pass which escape explanation and yet become a reality. This being because they cannot be explained with the day's logic. If this world be a mere part of what is creation beyond the limits we see, how stupendous then must be the

Hand that actuates and gives it life? Might it not be that in time to come the inexplicable will find laws of use? Imagine us s beings rising from the state of crawling on the surface of the earth to that of ascending the air. How vast must be that which we know not of even ourselves?

> **The world is but a show, vain and empty, a mere nothing, bearing the semblance of reality. Set not your affections upon it. Break not the bond that uniteth you with your Creator, and be not of those that have erred and strayed from His ways. Verily I say, the world is like the vapor in a desert, which the thirsty dreameth to be water and striveth after it with all his might, until when he cometh unto it, he findeth it to be mere illusion. It may, moreover, be likened unto the lifeless image of the beloved whom the lover hath sought and found, in the end, after long search and to his utmost regret, to be such as cannot "fatten nor appease his hunger."**
> **(Gleanings from the Writings of Baha'u'llah, p. 328)**

Further Thoughts

It is the right and should be the occupation of every individual to retrace steps and ponder on past events to see where each could have acted differently to the positive achievement of any an endeavor. It is not a matter of forgiving the self, but a matter of taking life in hand and looking at the wrongs and rights committed. This to me to be a more responsible attitude. That having been accomplished one can feel pride of action or require forgiveness, as it is not wise to ask for justice when none knows what His justice entails. Often is it found that, on reflection, what was perceived as wrong can find justification as right logically. One has then to tell the difference between a misunderstanding and an outright wrong committed. If we were to forgive ourselves , then there would be no need for judgment, yet all the Holy Books do promise judgment at the end of the run of life.

Viewing this from a logical perspective, it would seem that suffering then in the afterlife, comes in when one realizes where one could have been, where one could have made progress while living, and at the point of death be unable to right the wrong, for the wrong may blind one to true enjoyment or deny one the same. Then one would entirely depend on His Mercy for any further progress towards attaining the completion of being His image in the true sense. However, this is merely a perspective which has nothing to do with the reality of the matter, but it does omit having to forgive ourselves for wrongs, for that is not in our hands. We can find the logic to deeds and find out whether we had another option we never took or considered at the time of the action. This is a human speaking to another human about an inevitable event called "passing on" and whatever he has to say may be rejected or investigated. Nevertheless there is one end for all humans: they have to pass on.

The Eternal Being, has given us the minds to find His Path. It seems that He has given this duty to us the humans, wherever they might be, and not the rest of creation which itself stands obedient to Him. We have minds and have to make decisions about belief or non-belief. Whichever way we choose we have to admit that there is always the reality of the truth in the whole issue. This does not mean that if we believe we shall have more sunshine in the phys-ical way. The sun will shine on all and perceiving it is our duty. But it means that we shall have to find the meaning of existence in order to progress to be whatever he has made us to eventually be. The diversity does not matter so much, as there are certain intrinsic values we all have equally or unequally if we behave the proper way or choose not to, in the view that we shall all attain, if we acted rightly to be one thing or another that represents His Virtues as the Being Whose vision each should emulate in obedience to His visible Image , the Manifestation of His Good and His Virtues in creation..It would seem that the physical embodies somewhat all that are the abilities of that which we call the soul, for does it not walk and talk in dreams or visions? All physical beings can attain to these why not then the soul which identifies with what we all can do or are? The endowments and virtues each has are His gifts to each, for if we are leaves, are all leaves the same and do they not partake of the same just the same way? We are, in fact , mixtures of our past and that mixture is all the same mixture, all features accentuated by time and circumstance to look different but are really the same. The soul stands transcendent to the body, governed only by obedience to the Great Being. The other physical parts, the vehicles to the inner, are all transient and disappear into the earth later. What will each have attained that will then remain?

We may find a necessity to dispute this and maintain that the physical is the manifestation of the Deity, and there we find a glitch. For, would He be heavy set or thin? Would He be blue eyed or green eyed , male or female ?Or would He be tall, as we presume, or short? In tongues would He peak Arabic or Hebrew? Is not language only sounds to manifest the invisible but visible thoughts of the mind. Which then is the sense , the word uttered or the Word meant? The essence of man is the essence of man .It becomes manifest in the visible. What then is sight, if we see with atoms? Are they perfect enough to see the Deity? It is spiritual crime to ascribe a body to the Deity when He created bodies out of dust, the dust He made ! If a man dare say the thoughts of man do not feature, let Him desist from living in house, owning telephone or listening to any television for those are devised by the science of man. Let us use minds and not follow like sheep mashed on a railway track because the follow the leader.

No outside clamor can achieve a truer realization of what we are or what we are supposed to achieve in life, outside an inner effort by each individual to understand the course we are to pursue. This makes us know that the individual is the basic brick of what we call society. Without the individual achieving a system of true values , none can aspire to any good in existence. All can be words, but all can be realization and action based on sure foundation as designed by the Great Ones Who have come from time to time and left a trail for us to follow. Were it not for Them all would be lost in the darkness of creation without true direction. Better then are people who follow such guidance through our lives and would give life as the Great Ones have done to give that guidance to generations yet unborn. For , guidance by words does not suffice but the life of an example can last generations as a teacher, as it stands as a beacon in the annals of history and existence. Life is no blind following but a coming to a realization and acting thereon. From that aspect it can take on a meaning it innately possesses even without our knowing it. We then partake of the bread of life and drink from the fountain of true guidance.

> **Even as the people have cried: "Verily we found our fathers with a faith, and verily, in their footsteps we follow."[1]**
>
> **[1 Qur'án 43:22.] (The Kitab-i-Iqan, p. 155)**

3. O SON OF MAN!

> **Veiled in My immemorial being and in the ancient eternity of My essence, I knew My love for thee; therefore I**

created thee, have engraved on thee Mine image and revealed to thee My beauty.

(The Arabic Hidden Words)

Always remembering that:
The essence of faith is fewness of words and abundance
of deeds; he whose words exceed his deeds, know verily
his death is better than his life.

(Tablets of Baha'u'llah, p. 156)

Even as the people have cried: "Verily we found our
fathers with a faith, and verily, in their footsteps we follow."[1]

[1 Qur'án 43:22.] (The Kitab-i-Iqan, p. 155)

The Price of Treatment: A Carry over

This part of the story belongs to the years after I left South Africa and is told
here because of a need to clarify facts .It concerns the price one has to pay for
treatment and for being one who believes in religion.

Of course, it is now known that when I moved and still carried on being
a Bahá'í. This story pertains partly to obligations of the obedience to law of
religion.

When we resided in Ottawa, IL, I had a bout of suffering from an anxiety.
This was at the end of the days I worked for a nursing home. My duties in the
nursing home sometimes took the obligation to work in the wing which had
many mental patients or patients who suffered from psychological diseases
.This work could not be avoided because I w as a Nurse Aid at that time. At
this time I had passed the examination for attending to Alzheimer patients but
I seldom worked in that wing, though I understood the concerns. I was at the
time taking a tablet for anxiety but no one knew that in the nursing home.

One might ask: What could have caused such anxiety at this time and to
make life difficult? The fact is that I had been editing a private file in a public
library out of town and I had accidentally left th file on the computer without
deleting it after saving it to disk. I was not at the time, ready for the world to
learn some details about me and about my friends who are mentioned in the
file. As I could not reach he library before closing time I wished somebody
would delete the file. I found there was no way I could communicate with the
library. Our telephone was out of order and the public phone at the store was

non functional. I was grateful to learn later that when they turned on all computers at the library all files on them were automatically be deleted. By the time I learned that I was in a hospital.

At some stage I ran out of tablets during working hours at the Nursing Home, and had to take one, and therefore, I approached the doctor on duty who was a psychiatrist for a dosage of the tablets. On his inquiry I told him a that I had an anxiety problem as a history. He then treated me more as a patient by reporting the matter to the nursing home. I was then restricted in duties for a while until subsequently I had to leave the work through dismissal.

The dismissal and the failure to find work soon had negative results. The anxiety worsened and I was forced to see a doctor again. I was then admitted for observation.

Now each Bahá'í has certain prayers he has to say each day. I could say some of these prayers off by heart but two are long and require genuflections while saying them. While in my room at the hospital I attempted to say the very long prayer. Unfortunately this happened to be the time the doctor sent a nurse to call be for a consultation. I could not stop the prayer and the genuflections even though I was not saying the words of the prayer overtly. The nurse called the doctor and he came himself and waited while I prayed. Later he left and when I was done called for me again.

I now am certain that the doctor thought I was deeply mentally troubled. The result was that instead of the one tablet I was taking daily, he gave me four. These tablets I learned later prohibited any sexual activity. I took them for years until I resided on the island on which I am now. This was a period of over ten years starting from around 1992 to 2007.

When I saw a doctor on the island, she dismissed all tablets except for one. And told me that I did not need so many.

This was not much of a problem because from the age of fifteen when I was growing up, I had abstained from sexual activity, even though it was very much available and something of a norm to be active, until the age of twenty when I was a circumcised man. Hence at circumcision I was named Solente, a name that had to do with the Christian lent, because I was never big in search of sexual activity until I had my two boys when I was married in 1973. All three time when I was married I had made a vow, and that was to stay with one wife and be active sexually with that wife. Though I am far from a saint, I have to some extent endeavored to hold onto that vow. In old age I am not sorry for, by that stance , I avoided much of experiences that could have been disastrous at an early age. The on person who could be considered saintly is my wife, Gretchen, for we have been together as a couple for thirty three years. This no brag but a statement of fact to prove that a marriage can be possible without it being overly sexual as a relationship between partners; a sharing of life's experiences.

The Attitude and Change

It is not mutual hatreds that will give us a relief but a change in attitudes towards ourselves and those we know. We have to redefine loving the neighbor to accepting that we are really one human race. Long existing hatreds have hindered us from becoming a brethren. To hate the evil one performs against another is relevant, but to hate one for the evil they perpetrate is wrong. This is because we are all prone to evil and in one way or another perform a hurtful action at some stage . Condemnation therefore has to be for the action and not any person. Loving one's neighbor has been limited to loving those near us but it should mean loving all of God's creatures. God is said to be the Most Merciful an also to be a Forgiver of sins. We should not take it upon ourselves to hold long living grudges when we know we have hurt someone at one time of another.

I say this knowing full well that I grew up under discrimination most of my life, but it is not the one that discriminates that I abhor but the discrimination itself. This is because overt discrimination is not the only discrimination that is in existence among us. There is always the danger of the hidden discrimination which can hide behind goodwill Those who perform that kind of hidden discrimination may even be the first to protest against overt and open discrimination, but that does mean theirs does not hurt for it does. It is far better to see overt discrimination and be able to openly fight it, than to have to deal with a hatred that is stored in the heart and presents itself as an act of good.

Many racial quarrels ensue not because the actions are open but because they are perceived and in the modern world nothing can be said openly about those hurts and affronts.

An individual attempt has to be made by each to purge actions of that are the making of bias; a bias for the self and a bias for those we say we love against those we care less about. This bias always manifests itself with a battle of words because we are too civilized to openly state that we are hurt and we see who the person who originates the hurt.

This again is no sermon but a mere observation of an occurrence no one ever mentions in our civilized world. This little actions even as the virus we fear have huge results in the hearts. We suffer them alone with being unable to confide in anyone, for they always remain hidden in the pleasantries of sweet conversation. One seemingly is surrounded by curses. One knows it and does not care who gets hurt. We live in our citadels of gold separated from accusation by the mannerisms of society. I would rather hear the curse again myself so that I can respond than perceive a curse in one's breath.

It is ar easier to explain myself when I know what wrong I might have mistakenly committed than to perceive it without uttering one word because I wish to be decent. It is easier to fight an evil one can see than having first to investigate it from facts and then fight it. This is because such investigation even if based on truth can be denied. Let us remember that the saying "sticks and stones may hurt me but words cannot" is not true, for words uttered against one can last a very long time, where a wound can be cured with a bandage.

For the tongue is a smouldering fire, and excess of speech a deadly poison. Material fire consumeth the body, whereas the fire of the tongue devoureth both heart and soul. The force of the former lasteth but for a time, whilst the effects of the latter endure a century.
(Baha'u'llah, The Kitab-i-Iqan, p. 192)

Epilogue

In view of the above, I am forced to ponder on where we in the world are today. We are in a state where we wish for democracy in all dealings. Yet there is no model of democracy anywhere. An atom is whole and integrated in itself and we are not in the form of the atom. For any ideology to take root it has to begin at the root stage. What are our families? Are they conducted the democratic way ? Or are we still rooted in old ways that have nothing to do with being democratic?

First of all, the rule in the home is set by the male person and that is more or less absolute rule from which we escaped in the world years ago. Yet day in and day out in the street and newspapers we yell that the world must be democratic in its view. For any virtue to be manifest in any society it must show itself in the individual. One cannot have a blanket peace until individual issues are taken care of. While there is disgruntlement in the individual, we can forget about peace in the social setting. Should we apply peace by law we would be opening the door to more revolution in the future whether we are there or not, and someone has to handle that. It seems therefore that the world cannot have democracy until the individual begins to think in a more democratic way when it comes to general affairs that affect the whole society. We definitely cannot afford to teach democracy in the street and not practice it in the home, for we would be fakes. If we want to be false copies of the human we define as intelligent then we might forget all our wonderful philosophies and live on . How do we then live on? What would be ideals? What would be the future in store for the human? The view is frightening!

In being fair in my statement even about myself I am urged by feelings of avoidance of being a fake even to myself. God forbid that I should confess my sin to man! But if I want to share the wisdom of experience with my fellowman then I shall and should set some truth about the self on paper. The irony of life in contained in this that, as old and wise men we deplore doings we were involved in as young and foolish men, but there seems no way of correcting the past, except by reflecting on the present and taking a vow to avoid all past action that is not based on both wisdom and logic in the future. For logic must be mitigated by wisdom, and thus a justice may pertain. It is all very well to say A , B, then C is punishment. But what if C will cause further problems in the future? Would not A and B find some other application as a C?

There are many things which we as nations wish we had not done in a certain way because their results have had future dangers for the whole. Can we learn from that? My example holds that a kid who suffers injustice and has a box of matches may well burn the house in anger, and later find recourse to ask parents for a place to sleep later. Which then shall it be for the world? Dealing with the effects of anger, or pursuing a course of general wise decisions that contain a victory for all?

Executing any action, but with wisdom, makes much more sense than pursuing a course of what we call logic and a justice that is devoid of all wisdom.

That is, in a word the matter. If the world is guilty might it then not suffer a punishment? If it feels logically and wisely justified what then does that matter, death or no death, for, a wise word if it be wise, will live on. It is a thought worthy of reflecting on that civilizations were established on the notion of surviving together. Democracy is no less such a strategy. If we wish to subvert the very ideology of surviving together then we can go ahead and destroy our world with our unwise decisions based on , not only supremacy but the very thought of the definite self destruction voiced by an angry person with a box of matches. Thus we stand poised into a future we wish would be for space exploration from a very tiny planet in a vast thing we call the universe which we hardly know. We enter in with sword in hand. It has planets that turn and form life peacefully without us, and we intend to introduce ourselves thus. Some imagine it is a game, based on what? With whom to win against or for? What prize do we expect? If it be a game, whose game is it? Can we attribute that to the Intelligent Mind that caused it to come into being with all the logic it has? The fool may think this be a perception of a fool, but would they kindly ponder what they themselves have in mind as the ultimate situation they desire for themselves ?For to say "I shall survive it" is far less than to say " we shall survive"! Instead of concentrating on the involvement of the self only, it would be far wiser to think of the involvement of the self to the betterment of the whole.

Let no man misconstrue the intent of words as above to have the intent of any political or other leverage, for ,my faith is entirely divorced from all political activity and should never be used as such, for that would be denigrating from the high position the Blessed Beauty states in His Writings and for which He spent the extent of His imprisonment in Akka, and never finding release from that imprisonment , all for the betterment of the manners of the Bahá'í Community and its dedication to the redemption of the fortunes of humankind.

> **Politics are occupied with the material things of life. Religious teachers should not invade the realm of politics; they should concern themselves with the spiritual education of the people; they should ever give good counsel to men, trying to serve God and human kind; they should endeavour to awaken spiritual aspiration, and strive to enlarge the understanding and knowledge of humanity, to improve morals, and to increase the love for justice.**
> **(Abdu'l-Baha, Paris Talks, p. 158)**

> **They that surround thee love thee for their own sakes, whereas this Youth loveth thee for thine own sake, and hath had no desire except to draw thee nigh unto the seat of grace, and to turn thee toward the right-hand of justice. Thy Lord beareth witness unto that which I declare.**
> **(Baha'u'llah, Epistle to the Son of the Wolf, p. 40)**

At my school in Fort Hare University College students were wont to say that politics is everything, and I disagree strongly, for I survived two years in that college, never having been involved in political activity .I am proud of that , for, working with the educated and uneducated in the city and the rural setting has given me that assurance, that it is not words that win the day but actions that determine one's commitment to a plan of redemption for humans,

Black , White or Colored, and I feel I am in that Plan. The principles of Bahá'u'lláh apply across the board. Anyone wishing to be a Bahá'í today must be bound by His word and not the word of man. The beginnings of the corruption of the Word is when man uses It for his gain and not for the gain of His Cause, as Thomas Becket once said that the Word has to be used : for the "honor of God". (Movie:"Becket")

Baha'u'llah says:

> This is the changeless Faith of God, eternal in the past, eternal in the future. Let him that seeketh, attain it; and as to him that hath refused to seek it — verily, God is Self-Sufficient, above any need of His creatures.
> (Baha'u'llah, Gleanings from the Writings of Baha'u'llah, p. 136)

> The beginning of magnanimity is when man expendeth his wealth on himself, on his family and on the poor among his brethren in his Faith.
> (Tablets of Baha'u'llah, p. 156)

Glossary

Addhan. A call prayer which is repeated several times a day in Islam.

Epididymis. A coiled structure acting as a connecting duct for sperms in the male. There are the caput (head) and the cauda (tail) parts of the coil.

Fatcakes. popular bread in South Africa, made of flour and baked dough over oil or fat.

Mealies. Samp or corn grains cooked.

Meerkat An animal the size of a rabbit found in South Africa

Minotaur. A half human half animal creature told of in Mythology.

Roundavel. A circular house built on mud bricks and a conical grass roof found in rural South Africa.

Shebeen An unregistered drinking private house where liquor was served at a price in olden South African townships.

Sura, A chapter in the Qur'an

Tickey . A coin in the English Monetary System about half a sixpence or three pennies.

Tokolosie: A dwarf with human and animal features that is believed to appear and disappear at will and is associated with witchcraft.

References

'Abdu'l-Bahá. *Paris Talks*. London, UK. Bahá'í Publishing Trust.

'Abdu'l-Baha. *The Promulgation of Universal Peace*. Wilmette, IL. Bahá'í Publishing Trust

Adib Taherzadeh. *Revelation of Bahá'u'lláh vol. 2.Oxford, UK. George Ronald.*

Austen, J.(1997) *Persuasion*. Dover Publications, Inc., Mineola: NY.

Báb, The: *Selections from the Writings of the Bab* Bahá'í World Center, Haifa, Israel.

Bahá'í National Assembly of UK. *Principles of Bahá'í Administration*. Bahá'í Publishing Trust

Bahá'u'lláh.(2018) *The Call of the Divine Beloved .Haifa*, Israel, World Center

Bahá'u'lláh. The Epistle to the Son of the Wolf. Wilmette, IL. Bahá'í Publishing Trust

Bahá'u'lláh. *Gems of Divine Guidance*. Haifa, Israel. Bahá'í World Center

Bahá'u'lláh (1971). *Hidden Words*. Wilmette, IL. Bahá'í Publishing Trust.

Bahá'u'lláh . *Ktab-i-Aqdas*. Wilmette,IL. Bahá'í Publishing Trust

Bahá'u'lláh. *The Seven Valleys and the Four Valleys*. Wilmette, IL. Bahá'í Publishing Trust.

Bahá'u'lláh .(1978) *Tablets of Bahá'u'lláh*. Haifa, Israel. Bahá'í World Center.

Balyuzi H.M. *The Bab*. George Ronald. Oxford. UK. 1973.

Drinkwater, J.(1919) *Abraham Lincoln*. Houghton Mifflin Company. New York :NY *Gettysburg Speech by Abraham Lincoln* retrieved 2016 from http://www.abrahamlincolnonline.org/lincoln/speeches/gettysburg.htm

Holy Bible *King James version*. Grand Rapids ,MI. Zondervan

Mona Retrieved 01/08/2017 from https://en.wikipedia.org/wiki/Mona_Mahmudnizhad

Enoch Olinga Retrieved 01/08/2017 from https://en.wikipedia.org/wiki/Enoch_Olinga

Frederick Gqola Picture Retrieved on December 29, 2017 from: https://www.google.com/search?tbm=isch&source=hp&biw=1280&bih=918&ei=v3tGWoDEDIrujwT3_7W4CQ&q=Frederick+Gqola&oq=Frederick+Gqola&gs_l=img.12...5382.16813.0.19768.21.10.0.11.2.0.187.1295.1j9.10.0....0...1ac.1.64.img..0.11.1227...0.0.jPkA-hvDm6g#imgrc=wEJdpcWh3F-FGM:

Fugard, Athol Picture Retrieved on December 27, 2017 from: https://www.google.com/search?tbm=isch&source=hp&biw=1280&bih=918&ei=J4NDWpLnIoLamwHcvY-IBw&q=athol+fugard&oq=fugard&gs_l=img.1.6.0l6j0i5i30k1l4.3349.5725.0.12142.6.6.0.0.0.0.174.874.0j6.6.0....0...1ac.1.64.img..0.6.871....0.Mk7F2uUeVMQ

Gettysburg Speech by Abraham Lincoln retrieved 2016 from http://www.abrahamlincolnonline.org/lincoln/speeches/gettysburg.htm

Sears, W.(1985) *All Flags Flying*. Johannesburg, South Africa, National Assembly of the Bahá'ís of South and West Africa.

Shoghi Effendi (1922-1932) *Bahá'í Administration* .Wilmette, IL. Bahá'í Publishing Trust

Shoghi Effendi *Gleanings form the Writings of Bahá'u'lláh*. Wilmette,IL. Bahá'í Publishing Trust

Shoghi Effendi. *Lights of Guidance*. New Delhi, India. Bahá'í Publishing Trust.

Universal House of Justice. *Compilation of Compilations* .Victoria, Australia .Bahá'í Publications

Universal House of Justice. *The Bahá'í World. Vol. XVII. 1976-1979.* Haifa, Israel.